Access to History for the IB Diploma

Rights and protest

Michael Scott-Baumann
Peter Clements

Access to History for the IB Diploma

Rights and protest

Michael Scott-Baumann
Peter Clements

HODDER
EDUCATION
AN HACHETTE UK COMPANY

Caution: several of the historical extracts and quotations in this book contain words that are vulgar and offensive.

The material in this title has been developed independently of the International Baccalaureate®, which in no way endorses it.

The Publishers would like to thank the following for permission to reproduce copyright material:

Photo credits: p11 Library of Congress, LC-DIG-ppmsca-03128; **p18** Library of Congress, LC-USZ62-128619; **p24** Bettman/ Corbis; **p29t,b** Images courtesy of the South Carolina Department of Archives and History; **p34** TopFoto/AP; **p45** Don Cravens/ The LIFE Images Collection/Getty Images; **p50** Bettmann/Corbis; **p53** The Ella Baker Center for Human Rights/Creative Commons Attribution 3.0 Unported licence; **p56** The Granger Collection/TopFoto; **p63** The Granger Collection/TopFoto; **p70** A 1963 Herblock Cartoon, © The Herb Lock Foundation; **p79** Hank Walker/The LIFE Picture Collection/Getty Images; **p86** *Student Voice;* **p93** Bettmann/Corbis; **p103** Topham/AP; **p119** https://commons.wikimedia.org/wiki/File:Murder_at_ Sharpeville_21_March_1960.jpg; **p129** Topham Picturepoint; **p130** Hulton-Deutsch Collection/Corbis; **p137** AP Photo/Dennis Lee Royle; **p161** Terrence Spencer/The LIFE Images Collection/Getty Images; **p163** Topham Picturepoint; **p173** J.H. Jackson; **p178** Africa Media Online/Mary Evans; **p179** Terrence Spencer/The LIFE Images Collection/Getty Images; **p182** Hulton Archive/ Getty Images; **p193** Sipa Press/REX Shutterstock; **p208** Hulton-Deutsch Collection/Corbis; **p210** AP/Press Association Images; **p223** Pat Oliphant/British Cartoon Archive; **p230** OFF/AFP/Getty Images; **p232** J.H. Jackson.

Acknowledgements are listed on page 258.

Every effort has been made to trace all copyright holders, but if any have been inadvertently overlooked the Publishers will be pleased to make the necessary arrangements at the first opportunity.

Although every effort has been made to ensure that website addresses are correct at time of going to press, Hodder Education cannot be held responsible for the content of any website mentioned in this book. It is sometimes possible to find a relocated web page by typing in the address of the home page for a website in the URL window of your browser.

Hachette UK's policy is to use papers that are natural, renewable and recyclable products and made from wood grown in sustainable forests. The logging and manufacturing processes are expected to conform to the environmental regulations of the country of origin.

Orders: please contact Bookpoint Ltd, 130 Milton Park, Abingdon, Oxon OX14 4SB. Telephone: +44 (0)1235 827720. Fax: +44 (0)1235 400454. Lines are open 9.00a.m.–5.00p.m., Monday to Saturday, with a 24-hour message answering service. Visit our website at www.hoddereducation.co.uk

© 2015 Michael Scott-Baumann, Peter Clements

First published in 2015 by
Hodder Education,
An Hachette UK Company
Carmelite House
50 Victoria Embankment
London EC4Y 0DZ

Impression number   10 9 8 7 6 5
Year   2019

Cover image © PhotoQuest/Getty Images
Illustrations by Gray Publishing
Typeset in 10/13pt Palatino and produced by Gray Publishing, Tunbridge Wells
Printed in Italy

A catalogue record for this title is available from the British Library

ISBN 978 1471839313

Contents

Dedication

Keith Randell (1943–2002)

The original *Access to History* series was conceived and developed by Keith, who created a series to 'cater for students as they are, not as we might wish them to be'. He leaves a living legacy of a series that for over 20 years has provided a trusted, stimulating and well-loved accompaniment to post-16 study. Our aim with these new editions for the IB is to continue to offer students the best possible support for their studies.

Introduction

This book has been written to support your study of Prescribed subject 4: Rights and protest for the IB History Diploma. This first chapter gives you an overview of:

★ the content you will study for Rights and protest

★ how you will be assessed for Paper I

★ the different features of this book and how these will aid your learning.

 What you will study

Prescribed subject 4 examines two significant movements in the quest for basic human rights in the mid-twentieth century. The two case studies, each drawn from a different region, highlight the struggles faced by black people as they sought equal rights. Case Study 1 focuses on the Civil Rights Movement in the United States from 1954 to 1965. In 1954, the Supreme Court decision *Brown* v. *Board of Education* marked a major legal victory for civil rights campaigners. A decade of struggle ensued until, in 1965, President Johnson signed the Voting Rights Act which finally ended the blatant disenfranchisement of millions of African-Americans. Case Study 2, which considers apartheid in South Africa from 1948 to 1964, covers roughly the same timespan but does not end on a hopeful note. In 1948, the National Party came to power and began a comprehensive programme to segregate South Africans on the basis of their races. Black Africans protested the succession of legal restrictions, without success. By 1964, the leadership of one of the major resistance groups, the African National Congress (ANC), had been jailed as a result of the Rivonia trial. What followed were some of the darkest days of apartheid before its eventual overturn in 1994.

You will study the intense struggles for racial equality in the following two case studies:

Case Study I: The Civil Rights Movement in the United States 1954–1965

	Chapter 1	Chapter 2	Chapter 3
Nature and characteristics of discrimination:			
• Racism and violence against African-Americans; the Ku Klux Klan; disenfranchisement	✓		

	Chapter 1	Chapter 2	Chapter 3
• Segregation and education; *Brown* v. *Board of Education* decision (1954); Little Rock (1957)	✓		
• Economic and social discrimination; legacy of the Jim Crow laws; impact on individuals	✓		
Protests and action:			
• Non-violent protests; Montgomery Bus Boycott (1955–6); Freedom Rides (1961); Freedom Summer (1964)		✓	✓
• Legislative changes; Civil Rights Act (1964); Voting Rights Act (1965)		✓	
The role and significance of key actors/groups:			
• Key actors: Martin Luther King Jr; Malcolm X; Lyndon B. Johnson			✓
• Key groups: National Association for the Advancement of Colored People (NAACP); Southern Christian Leadership Conference (SCLC) and Student Non-violent Coordinating Committee (SNCC); the Nation of Islam (Black Muslims)	✓	✓	✓

Case Study 2: Apartheid South Africa 1948–1964

	Chapter 4	Chapter 5	Chapter 6
Nature and characteristics of discrimination:			
• 'Petty apartheid' and 'grand apartheid' legislation	✓		
• Division and 'classification'; segregation of populations and amenities; creation of townships/forced removals; segregation of education; Bantustan system; impact on individuals	✓		
Protests and action:			
• Non-violent protests: bus boycotts; defiance campaign, Freedom Charter	✓	✓	
• Increasing violence: the Sharpeville massacre (1960) and the decision to adopt the armed struggle		✓	✓
• Official response: the Rivonia Trial (1963–4) and the imprisonment of the ANC Leadership			✓

	Chapter 4	Chapter 5	Chapter 6
The role and significance of key actors/groups:			
• Key individuals: Nelson Mandela; Albert Luthuli	✓	✓	✓
• Key groups: the African National Congress (ANC); the South African Communist Party (SACP) and the MK (Umkhonto we Sizwe – 'Spear of the Nation')	✓	✓	✓

 # How you will be assessed

The IB History Diploma can be studied at either Standard or Higher Level. It has three papers in total: Papers 1 and 2 for Standard Level and a further Paper 3 for Higher Level. It also has an internal assessment which all students must do.

- For Paper 1 you need to answer four source-based questions on a prescribed subject. This counts for 20 per cent of your overall marks at Higher Level, or 30 per cent of your overall marks at Standard Level.
- For Paper 2 you need to answer two essay questions on two different topics. This counts for 25 per cent of your overall marks at Higher Level, or 45 per cent of your overall marks at Standard Level.
- For Paper 3 you need to answer three essay questions on two or three sections. This counts for 35 per cent of your overall marks at Higher Level.

For the Internal Assessment you need to carry out a historical investigation. This counts for 20 per cent of your overall marks at Higher Level, or 25 per cent of your overall marks at Standard Level.

Prescribed subject 4: Rights and protest is assessed through Paper 1 and is the fourth of five prescribed subjects. Paper 1 will contain all five prescribed subjects and questions will be numbered 1–20. There are four sources and four questions for each prescribed subject. Sources are primary and secondary with most being in written form, although there is usually at least one visual source as well.

Questions for Prescribed subject 4: Rights and protest will be numbered as 13, 14, 15 and 16 in the Paper 1 booklet. The questions in this book follow the same numbering system. (There are no questions 1–12.)

Examination questions

The four questions on Paper 1 assess different skills and knowledge. You must answer all four and have one hour to do so. The question types are as follows:

Question 13: direct questions

Question 13 is worth 5 marks and has two parts, both of which test your reading comprehension abilities on two different sources. You need to answer both parts of the question by reviewing the source material and paraphrasing information from the sources. There is detailed guidance on how to answer question 13 on page 38. Examples of this type of question might be:

Example 1

a) What, according to Source A, was the importance of the Montgomery Bus Boycott?
b) What is the message conveyed by Source C?

Example 2

a) Why, according to Source B, did the National Party institute apartheid?
b) What is the message conveyed by Source D?

Question 14: value and limitations of a source

Question 14 is worth 4 marks and asks you to evaluate a source using the source's origin, purpose and the content you are presented with.

- The origin of a source is its author or creator. This might also include the date, publisher and type of delivery, which could be a book, speech, propaganda poster or diary entry.
- The purpose of the source explains what the author was trying to do, such as explaining the impact of an event or conveying a certain type of information.
- The content of the source can indicate many things, such as the point of view of the author, evidence of some historical event or its interpretation or, in the case of a cartoon or another visual source, the audience that the author wished to reach.

The values and limitations will vary according to each source. A value could be that the author of the source witnessed the event or is an acknowledged scholar. An example of a limitation could be that an author was involved in events and therefore may be less objective. You should try to explain at least two values and two limitations per source, although this may not always be possible. There is detailed guidance on how to answer question 14 on page 72. Examples of this type of question might be:

Example 1

With reference to its origin, purpose and content, analyse the value and limitations of Source A for historians studying the impact of *Brown v. Board of Education*.

Example 2

With reference to its origin, purpose and content, analyse the value and limitations of Source B for historians studying the ANC's decision to adopt armed struggle as a strategy in their resistance to apartheid.

Question 15: compare and contrast

Question 15 is worth 6 marks and asks you to compare and contrast two sources in terms of what information they convey to historians studying some aspect of this prescribed subject. Comparing means that you explain the similarities between the sources, while contrasting explains how they are different. You should aim to have at least three similarities and three differences. There is detailed guidance on how to answer question 15 on pages 149–51. Examples of this type of question might be:

Example 1
Compare and contrast what Sources A and D indicate about the aims of the Southern Christian Leadership Conference (SCLC).

Example 2
Compare and contrast what Sources B and C reveal about the living condition on the Bantustans.

Question 16: Essays integrating knowledge and sources

Question 16 is worth 9 marks and requires you to use the four sources in the examination and to integrate them into an essay that also contains your own knowledge. There is detailed guidance on how to answer question 16 on pages 197–201. Examples of this type of question might be:

Example 1
Using these sources and your own knowledge, discuss the extent to which you agree that legislative victories were more important than acts of civil disobedience in securing civil rights from 1954 to 1965.

Example 2
Using these sources and your own knowledge, explain why the African National Congress (ANC) and the South African Communist Party (SACP) were unsuccessful in dismantling apartheid from 1948 to 1964.

The appearance of the examination paper

Cover
The cover of the examination paper states the date of the examination and the length of time you have to complete it: one hour. Instructions are limited and simply state that you should not open it until told to do so and that all questions must be answered.

Sources
Once you are allowed to open your examination paper, you can turn to Prescribed subject 4: Rights and protest. There you will see four sources, each labelled with a letter. There is no particular order to the sources, so Source A could potentially be a map, a speech, a photograph or an extract from a book. Source A is no more or less important than Source B, or Source C or D. If you see square brackets, [ ], then this is an explanation or addition to the source

by the creators of the examination and not part of the original source. Sometimes sources are shortened and you will see an ellipsis, three full stops or periods (…), when this happens.

Questions

After the four sources, the four questions will appear. You need to answer all of them. It is better to answer the questions in order, as this will familiarize you with all the sources to be used in the final essay on question 16, but this is not required. Be sure to number your questions correctly. Do not use bullet points to answer questions, but instead write in full sentences when possible. The maximum number of marks that can be awarded for each question is shown in brackets after the question.

 # About this book

Coverage of course content

This book addresses the key areas listed in the IB History Guide for Prescribed subject 4: Rights and protest. The chapters in each case study start with an introduction outlining the key questions they address. They are then divided into a series of sections and topics covering the course content. Throughout the chapters you will find the following features to aid your study of the course content.

Key and leading questions

Each section heading in the chapter has a related key question which gives a focus to your reading and understanding of the section. These are also listed in the chapter introduction. You should be able to answer the questions after completing the relevant section.

Topics within the sections have leading questions which are designed to help you focus on the key points within a topic and give you more practice in answering questions.

Key terms

Key terms are the important terms you need to know to gain an understanding of the period. These are emboldened in the text the first time they appear in the book and are defined in the margin. They also appear in the glossary at the end of the book.

Sources

Each chapter contains several sources. These sources indicate the title of work, author or authors, editors where appropriate, publishing company and location, date of publication and from which page or pages of that publication this particular source originates. The sources have accompanying questions and are also used with the exam-style questions at the end of the chapters. The range of sources used will expose you to many different types of sources you may find in the examination.

Key debates

Historians often disagree on historical events and this historical debate is referred to as historiography. Knowledge of historiography is helpful in reaching the upper mark bands when you take your IB History examinations. The key debates in Chapters 3, 5 and 6 will help you to develop your understanding of historiography.

Theory of Knowledge (TOK) questions

Understanding that different historians see history differently is an important element in understanding the connection between the IB History Diploma and Theory of Knowledge. Alongside the key debates are Theory of Knowledge style questions which make that link.

Summary diagrams

At the end of each section is a summary diagram which gives a visual summary of the content of the section. It is intended as an aid for revision.

Chapter summary

At the end of each chapter is a short summary of the content of that chapter. This is intended to help you revise and consolidate your knowledge and understanding of the content.

Skills development

At the end of each chapter are the following:

- Examination guidance on how to answer different question types, accompanied by a sample answer and commentary designed to help you focus on specific details.
- Examination practice in the form of Paper 1 practice questions.
- Suggestions for learning activities, including ideas for debate, essays, displays and research which will help you develop skills needed for Paper 1 and a deeper understanding of the content.

These are all intended to help you develop the following skills in order to achieve examination success:

- *Source analysis.* This book allows you to become familiar with the works of many historians and a variety of primary source material. It teaches you to analyse all types of sources and gives you the opportunity to review their strengths, weaknesses, origins, purpose, values and limitations.
- *Integrating sources into essays.* Integrating sources into essays requires that you know how to write a good essay. This book gives guidance on writing good essays that integrate sources.

End of case study material

There are two case studies for Paper 1 prescribed subjects. At the end of each case study in this book you will find:

- a full set of Paper 1 practice questions focused on each case study
- a timeline of important events.

End of the book

The book concludes with the following sections:

Glossary
All key terms in the book are defined in the glossary.

Further reading
This contains a list of books, websites, films and other resources which may help you with further independent research and presentations. It may also be helpful when further information is required for internal assessments and extended essays in history. You may wish to share the contents of this area with your school or local librarian.

Internal assessment
A list of potential internal assessment questions for those students wishing to explore a particular topic in more depth.

Case Study 1

The Civil Rights Movement in the United States 1954–1965

CHAPTER 1

Racism and white supremacy

This chapter examines what life was like for African-Americans leading up to the Civil Rights Movement. It explains how, when and why white supremacy was re-established in the South despite the fact that equal rights for black people had been written into the Constitution after the Civil War. It analyses the impact of racism, segregation and violence against blacks and the origins and development of the Civil Rights Movement. Finally, it focuses on the Supreme Court's 1954 ruling on desegregation in schools. This was a significant breakthrough but provoked massive resistance in the South, as shown in Little Rock, Arkansas, in 1957. You need to consider the following questions throughout this chapter:

★ What was the background to the Civil Rights Movement?

★ How was white domination maintained after slavery was ended?

★ How important was the NAACP in the development of the Civil Rights Movement?

★ What was the impact of the Supreme Court decision of 1954?

 Before the Civil Rights Movement

▶ *Key question: What was the background to the Civil Rights Movement?*

When the United States was created in 1783, it was made up of thirteen states, from Massachusetts in the north to Georgia in the south (see the map on page 16). These states had been thirteen colonies of the British Empire. Most of the colonists were of British origin, together with upwards of 40 per cent from other European countries. In their Declaration of Independence of 1776, the American colonists declared their commitment to equality and liberty for the United States of America. The first words are: 'We hold these truths to be self-evident, that all men are created equal ... with certain inalienable Rights, that among these are Life, Liberty and the pursuit of Happiness.'

Yet large minorities of Americans were not entitled to these rights: they were neither equal nor free in the newly independent Unites States of America. One group was Native American. Another group consisted of the black slaves, mostly living in the South. The first three chapters of this book are about the struggle of these African-Americans, long after slavery ended, to gain equal, civil rights.

Negroes, blacks or African-Americans?

Until the 1960s, the term 'Negro' was acceptable and widely used by blacks and white people. This term is now derogatory. The word 'colored' was also used by many, although now it is outdated and potentially offensive. Most common are 'black' Americans or 'African-Americans', both of which are used interchangeably in this book. Some say that the term 'African-American' is divisive as it does not apply to black Americans today who originate from countries such as Cuba and Jamaica. 'Black' is therefore a more unifying term.

African-Americans today are nearly all descended from enslaved people whom Europeans, and the British in particular, trafficked to America. They were regarded as property and hundreds of thousands were enslaved in the colonies of the British Empire in America. These are today the southern states of the USA (see the map on page 16). Slaves were employed in hot, back-breaking work on white-owned plantations, often working in extreme heat, growing sugar, rice, tobacco and, above all, cotton.

After the creation of the United States of America in 1783, these African-Americans remained as slaves. Or, rather, the vast majority did. A small minority of them were able to buy their freedom, some escaped and some worked in the northern states of the USA where slavery was not so widely employed. But over 90 per cent of African-Americans still worked as slaves in the South.

The American Constitution

Civil rights are the rights of an individual to legal, political and social equality. In the USA, those rights are written into the **Constitution**. They include:

- the right to vote in elections
- the right to equal treatment under the law
- the right to a fair trial
- the right to free speech, religion and movement.

The **Civil Rights Movement** aimed to secure these rights through changes in the law or through changes in the way the laws were interpreted. Amongst other things, that meant winning the support of the government in Washington DC, the capital of the USA.

What are civil rights?

🔑 **KEY TERM**

Constitution The rules and regulations by which a country's government works.

Civil Rights Movement A range of social and political movements in the USA whose goal was to end racial segregation and discrimination against black Americans and ensure legal, social and political equality for them.

The American system of government

The rules and regulations for the government of the United States were set out in the Constitution of 1787. One of the primary aims of the men who drew up the Constitution was to establish a balance between the powers of the individual states and of the central government. The thirteen states that made up the United States had come together to fight for their freedom from Britain but did not want to replace one strong central government, that of the British monarch, with another in Washington, DC (1791). They were keen to retain their autonomy.

The solution was to create a **federal system of government**. This provided for a federal (national) government in the capital and for separate governments in each of the states. The head of the federal government would be the president. He would be elected by all the citizens, that is, white men. He could propose laws but these would have to be passed by an elected law-making body, the **Congress**. The Congress was to consist of two houses, as shown in the summary diagram opposite. One house, the Senate, would consist of two elected representatives, or senators, from each state. In this way, the smaller states could not be dominated by a few bigger states. The other house was the House of Representatives.

This system of government would be replicated in the individual states, each of which would have an elected governor and **legislature**. The states would be responsible for law and order, for education and many other matters.

There was much scope for dispute between the federal government and the states over their respective powers. It was the job of the **Supreme Court** to act as arbitrator in such disputes. As the highest court in the land, its job was to protect the Constitution and decide, when asked, if laws passed by the federal or state governments were constitutional or not. However, the Constitution was not set in stone. Changes could be made but they had to be passed by a majority of two-thirds in both houses of Congress *and* ratified, or approved, by the states. These changes were added as **Amendments** to the Constitution.

The campaign by African-Americans for their civil rights involved:

- demands for changes in federal law
- appeals to the Supreme Court for interpretations of the law that enabled them to secure their equal right (for example in the case of *Brown* v. *Board of Education of Topeka*, 1954 (see page 30).

 **KEY TERM**

Federal system of government A system in which power is shared between central and state governments.

Congress The national, or federal, law-making body.

Legislature The elected, law-making body in each state (the state equivalent of Congress).

Supreme Court The highest court in the USA. Its primary role was to interpret the Constitution.

Amendments Under the Constitution, Congress could make changes, in the form of new clauses, to the Constitution. Each Amendment required a two-thirds majority in Congress and approval by 75 per cent of the states.

Citizens vote for:

President (executive branch)

- Elected for four years
- Can propose laws
- Appoints the cabinet and federal judges

Congress (legislative branch)

- Made up of two houses: the Senate and the House of Representatives
- Each state elects two senators
- The number of representatives per state depends on the state's population
- Makes laws
- Approves federal judges

Supreme Court (judicial branch)

- Judges appointed by the president
- Approves laws and makes rulings about the interpretation of laws
- Can declare laws unconstitutional

The Civil Rights Movement aimed to secure equal rights for all, regardless of colour:

- The right to vote
- The right to equal treatment under the law
- The right to a fair trial

This was to be achieved by:
- Changing the law
- Securing implementation of the law

SUMMARY DIAGRAM

The US system of government and the Civil Rights Movement

2 Discrimination, segregation and violence against African-Americans

▶ *Key question: How was white domination maintained after slavery was ended?*

In the nineteenth century, as white Americans settled on land in the West, there was increasing friction between the North and the South about whether new states admitted into the Union (the states that had formed the United States of America, or USA) should be free or slave states. Most northerners wanted them to be free states so that there would be no slave

The USA at the time of the Civil War, showing Confederate and Union states. Nearly 95 per cent of blacks lived in the South. Three states – Louisiana, Mississippi and South Carolina – had black majorities.

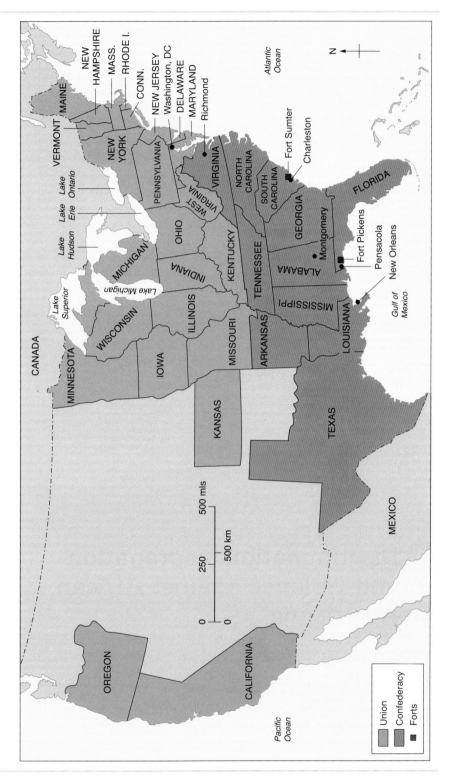

Look at Source A. In what ways was the Confederacy such a significant threat to the Union?

labour to compete with free men working their own land. Slave labour would undercut free men. The Republican Party, which emerged in the 1850s, represented these people. Disagreement over this matter formed the background to the Civil War. The fighting broke out in 1861, soon after the Republican Abraham Lincoln was elected president. Eleven slave-owning southern states seceded, or broke away, to form the **Confederacy**.

Civil war and the abolition of slavery

During the war, in 1863, in what became known as the Emancipation Proclamation, Lincoln promised to end slavery in the Confederate states. He hoped this would encourage even more slaves to disrupt the Confederates' war effort and, better still, to fight alongside Union forces, which many did. In 1865, the forces of the North, the Union, emerged victorious and the **13th Amendment** to the US Constitution was passed by Congress (of northerners). This abolished slavery. Now the big questions were: How were the defeated Confederate states to be treated? And how were the 4 million freedmen (freed slaves) to be provided for? This was the challenge of **Reconstruction**.

Reconstruction in the South

The freedmen had no money, land or property. Most left the plantations on which they had been employed. They looked for family and friends from whom they had been separated. After that, they wanted land, education and the vote. Lincoln spoke of granting the vote to educated freedmen and 'those who serve our cause as soldiers'. This was going too far for many people, even for many northerners, and Lincoln was assassinated by a Confederate sympathizer five days after General Lee surrendered to General Grant.

Meanwhile, the freedmen themselves set up schools and their own independent churches. They were helped by northern charities which provided food and clothing and also established hospitals and schools. But few freedmen were given land and most ended up working as **sharecroppers**. This meant that they worked for plantation owners, often ex-slave owners, who granted them land and basic housing and, in return, the freedmen shared their crop with the landowner. Whole families could work together, free from close supervision, and decide what hours they worked. In practice, they were enslaved by debt as they had to borrow money to buy seed and tools from the landowners or merchants. They were free to set up businesses but very few could afford to do so. Most remained as poor sharecropping labourers.

The Ku Klux Klan (KKK)

Most white southerners wanted blacks to remain subservient to, and dependent on, whites and to preserve **white supremacy**. Several southern states enacted laws which allowed whites to whip blacks for indiscipline, to

> What was achieved by Reconstruction in the South?

 KEY TERM

Confederacy A loose alliance of states that resented what they saw as increasing domination by the federal government and sought more autonomy. Their supporters were known as the Confederates.

13th Amendment This Amendment to the Constitution abolished slavery.

Reconstruction The process of rebuilding and reforming the Confederate states and restoring them to the Union.

Sharecroppers Ex-slaves (freedmen) who rented land and, in return, shared their crop with the landowner.

White supremacy The belief that whites are superior to other races.

? Why do you think members of the KKK, as in Source B, dressed in this way?

The White League, another white supremacist group (left), and the Ku Klux Klan (right). The painting from 1874 shows members of these organizations joining hands over a black family.

KEY TERM

Ku Klux Klan (KKK)
A secret terrorist society formed by ex-Confederate soldiers in 1865 in order to maintain white supremacy.

14th Amendment This guaranteed 'equal protection of the law' to all citizens.

send them back to their previous owners if they were thought to be 'vagrants', to prevent them being witnesses in court and to limit the areas where they could live. If this did not work, intimidation and terror usually did. Members of the **Ku Klux Klan (KKK)**, often on horseback, terrorized and killed many blacks for daring to rent or buy land, go to school or get a better job. White supporters of the Republican Party were also their victims.

'Equal protection of the laws'

For most Republicans, who had a huge majority in Congress after the elections in 1866, this situation was intolerable. It was an insult to those who had fought for freedom, whether black or white, and it was an insult to the murdered Lincoln. In 1868, Congress passed the **14th Amendment** which guaranteed 'equal protection of the law' for all citizens. The Amendment also declared that the federal government could intervene if any states tried to deny their rights, including the right to vote, to any citizen. The states could only be readmitted to the Union if they ratified the 14th Amendment. All except one of the eleven southern states refused to ratify the Amendment. Violence increased and many blacks who were active in politics were murdered. In one county in South Carolina, when whites lost an election, 150 freedmen and their families were driven from their homes. Thirteen people were killed, including a white judge who had been elected with black votes.

Congress then went further and enacted laws to establish military rule in the South and make sure southern states drew up constitutions that guaranteed black civil rights. These laws had the effect of hardening white supremacist feeling in the South even further. Most southerners resented northern domination and interference as much as they resented blacks exercising their civil rights. The third and most dramatic Amendment, the **15th Amendment**, was passed in 1870 and granted black male **suffrage**.

Black advancement during Reconstruction

During Reconstruction, certainly up until the mid-1870s, a number of black men gained political power. With the vote, they were able to elect senators and Congressmen, magistrates and sheriffs, especially in black majority areas in states like Mississippi and South Carolina. Sixteen were elected to Congress and hundreds to state legislatures. Some black people had set up businesses, including newspapers. They had established their own churches and schools. A black middle class of teachers, church ministers, businessmen and a small number of lawyers and doctors emerged. The black colleges of higher education, especially universities like Howard and Fisk, were to produce many of the black leaders who would carry on the struggle for civil rights into the twentieth century.

But this progress proved to be short lived. The North grew weary of its involvement in the South and its troops were withdrawn. It wanted the southern states to be reconciled, not alienated. After all, they had ended slavery and, by 1877, all the southern states had ratified the 14th Amendment to the Constitution and thus been readmitted to the Union. This was enough for most northern whites. Many northern politicians were now far more concerned about managing America's westward expansion and rapid industrial growth.

'Jim Crow' laws

The period of Reconstruction ended in 1877. With the removal of troops, and the loss of interest on the part of the North, a wide range of **'Jim Crow' laws** were passed by southern states. Jim Crow was a figure of fun, a character who had appeared in travelling **minstrel** shows in the South since the days of slavery. He was originally a crippled black stable boy, unsteady on his feet, slow and stupid. He was played by a white man with his face darkened by makeup (a practice known as 'blackface'). He came to represent a black stereotype. To keep black people in their place, supposedly legal means were found to impose **segregation**. The Jim Crow laws, passed by

KEY TERM

15th Amendment This granted the suffrage to black men. (Women, black and white, were granted the right to vote in 1920.)

Suffrage The right to vote.

'Jim Crow' laws Named after a comic, stereotypical character, these laws were passed by southern states in order to 'legalize' segregation.

Minstrel A member of a band of entertainers with blackened faces who performed songs and music ostensibly of black American origin.

Segregation The separation of people by race in schools, public spaces and transport.

How were black people treated in the South after the end of Reconstruction?

southern state legislatures, kept the races apart in schools and hospitals, hotels and restaurants, cemeteries and parks. Perhaps most aggravating of all, to black people, was segregation on public transport: blacks were forced to sit at the back on tramcars and to sit in separate carriages, usually older and dirtier, on railways. In order to avoid contravening the 14th Amendment, which guaranteed equal rights to all citizens, southern politicians claimed that these Jim Crow laws *did* ensure that blacks had equal rights. It was just that they were separate. However, it was rarely the case that blacks were treated equally, which was most obviously seen in education as was shown by the huge differences in spending on white schools and black schools. Older, unheated buildings, far fewer books, less well-qualified and poorly paid teachers were the norm in black schools. Not surprisingly, rates of black illiteracy remained far higher than those for whites.

KEY TERM

Poll tax A tax levied on would-be voters, which made it harder for blacks (who were usually poorer) to vote.

Disenfranchised Deprived of the right to vote.

Lynching Unlawful killing, mostly by hanging, usually of black people.

Southern states also developed 'legal' ways of preventing blacks from voting. The state of Mississippi introduced a **poll tax** in 1890 for those wishing to register to vote. Most poor blacks were unable to pay. Literacy and citizenship tests were also introduced: a voter had to prove that he could read and answer questions about the state constitution. Although the local registrar allowed many illiterate whites to pass this test, these laws did exclude a number of whites, so a 'grandfather clause' was enacted: a voter had to prove that his grandfather had been a free man before 1865. In Mississippi, the number of black voters fell from 190,000 in the 1870s to 8000 in 1890. Similar laws were passed by several southern states and blacks were effectively **disenfranchised**. By 1900, only three per cent of blacks were able to vote in much of the South. Since the states largely controlled the conduct of elections, these laws mostly went unchallenged.

In these ways, a seemingly legal and democratic foundation for white supremacy was laid in the Jim Crow South. Southern whites justified the system on the grounds that blacks were inferior and dangerous. In fact, many southern whites claimed that blacks had degenerated since the ending of slavery. No longer so closely supervised by whites, they had – according to the prejudiced white view – become lazy, incompetent, even criminal. Above all, many whites believed, black men's lust for white women led to increased incidences of rape. When, in 1898, a black newspaper editor in Wilmington, South Carolina, suggested that white women sometimes consented to have sexual relations with black men, whites went on the rampage: the newspaper offices were burnt down and 1400 blacks were forced to flee from the city, never to return.

Rape came to be the most common justification for **lynching**, that characteristically ritual form of execution in the South. In her autobiography, Ida Wells, the outspoken black journalist from Tennessee, said lynching was 'an excuse to get rid of Negroes who were acquiring wealth and property', a means to 'keep the nigger down'. Worst of all, whites knew they would not be arrested or punished for these and other forms of violence against blacks: police, lawyers, judges and juries were all white.

Plessy v. Ferguson 1896

Understandably afraid of white violence and the 'legal' consequences, few blacks challenged white supremacy openly. However, some did resist. One way was to challenge Jim Crow laws in the courts. The most famous case at this time was that of *Plessy v. Ferguson*, which was heard in the Supreme Court in 1896. It originated when, in 1892, Homer Plessy sat in a whites-only part of a train in Louisiana. Plessy looked white but, because he had one black grandparent, he was classed as a 'Negro' in Louisiana. When he bought a first-class rail ticket and sat in a 'white' carriage, he was asked to leave. He refused to move, and was arrested and jailed. The case was taken, by a group of blacks from New Orleans, to the Supreme Court in Washington, on the grounds that it contravened the 14th Amendment. It was hoped that the decision would be overturned in the highest court in the land. However, the Court stated that segregation was not unconstitutional as long as separate facilities were equal. (It left it to judges in local federal courts to decide on this matter. Subject as they were to state pressure, it was unlikely that they would defy state authorities.) It was to be 50 years before the Supreme Court changed its mind about the enforced separation of the races (see page 80).

SOURCE C

Excerpt from *Better Day Coming: Blacks and Equality, 1890–2000* by Adam Fairclough, published by Penguin, London, UK, 2002, p. 14. Professor Fairclough is a British historian specializing in American history.

Plessy v. Ferguson was an unmitigated judicial defeat for black Americans. Not only did the Supreme Court deny that 'enforced separation' discriminated against black people, it also implied that racial segregation was 'in the nature of things'. The Fourteenth Amendment did not require 'enforced commingling [blending together] of the two races'. In an argument that reeked of racism, the Court explained that 'if one race be inferior to the other socially, the Constitution of the United States cannot put them upon the same plane'.

What are the reasons why the author of Source C thinks the Court's decision was such a defeat?

The North's abandonment of black southerners

The Supreme Court decision appeared to epitomize the North's abandonment of southern blacks. The federal government was effectively endorsing white supremacy. Most northerners acquiesced in the South's solution of the 'Negro question'. With the blacks disenfranchised, Republican power in the South was demolished. Conservative Democrats were to dominate the South until the latter half of the twentieth century.

Slavery ended in 1865: Amendments to the Constitution guaranteed equal treatment for black people

BUT

Plessy v. *Ferguson* ruling in 1896 stated that separate but equal facilities were not unconstitutional	Jim Crow laws passed by Southern states to maintain white supremacy: • by enforcing segregation in public places, e.g. schools, public transport • by preventing blacks voting	The KKK terrorized blacks who sought equal treatment
Discrimination	**Segregation**	**Violence**

SUMMARY DIAGRAM

Discrimination, segregation and violence against African-Americans

 # The NAACP and the emergence of the Civil Rights Movement

▶ *Key question: How important was the NAACP in the development of the Civil Rights Movement?*

The majority of blacks in the South were forced to live with white domination. After all, the odds were stacked against them. Sitting in the wrong place on a tram or train or trying to register to vote could lead to the loss of a job or rented property. Worse still, it could lead to physical violence, even death. Most made no attempt to cross the 'color line', the barrier preventing them from participating in activities with whites. Some, however, attempted change.

What was the role of the NAACP?

The National Association for the Advancement of Colored People (NAACP)

In 1905, a group of mostly northern blacks met at Niagara on the Canadian side of the US border. They claimed that 'persistent, manly agitation is the way to liberty'. One of them was W.E.B. Du Bois. A highly educated black northerner, he had travelled extensively in the South and experienced discrimination firsthand. He was one of the founder members, in 1909, of the **National Association for the Advancement of Colored People (NAACP)**. This organization had both black and white members and set out to publicize injustice, for instance by sending out white members to investigate lynchings. (It was too dangerous for blacks to do that.) Such

🔑 KEY TERM

National Association for the Advancement of Colored People (NAACP) The oldest and largest civil rights organization. It is still active today.

atrocities were reported in *The Crisis*, the magazine which Du Bois edited for the NAACP. He was keen to reach a large number of blacks, to appeal to their hearts and minds. *The Crisis* had cartoons and striking covers. It published articles about black history and literature, proud to show what black Americans had achieved and to encourage voting. It was fearless in its reporting and published photographs of lynching. It advocated armed self-defence in the face of lynch mobs. By 1919, *The Crisis* had a circulation of over 100,000.

The NAACP also decided to employ the best lawyers and to take cases of discrimination to the Supreme Court in order to secure impartial enforcement of the Constitution, especially of those civil rights which were guaranteed by the 14th and 15th Amendments. This policy had some success: in 1915, the Supreme Court knocked out Oklahoma's 'grandfather clause'. Although white Oklahomans might find other ways of keeping blacks disenfranchised, this was the first time the Supreme Court struck down such a device. In 1917, the Court ruled that a Kentucky law on segregated residential zoning, keeping black and white houses apart, was unconstitutional. Again, it might make little difference to daily life as other ways of enforcing segregated housing would undoubtedly be found. But it showed that the NAACP could take the battle for civil rights to the centre of government in Washington and that the Supreme Court could be an ally.

African-Americans and the two world wars

At the start of the twentieth century, 90 per cent of black Americans still lived in the South. The majority worked on the land, trapped by poverty, lack of skills and all the obstacles raised by Jim Crow laws. A small but steady number continued to move to the cities of the South in order to find work and escape from the control of their rural, white landlords.

> What was the impact of the world wars on the Civil Rights Movement?

The First World War

Between 1914 and 1918, the 'Great Migration' began: over 350,000 black people migrated to the North, to cities like New York, Chicago and Philadelphia, attracted by the offer of better, well-paid jobs in the fast-expanding industries like automobiles and munitions. The latter grew particularly rapidly during the First World War as the USA was supplying armaments to the European powers, especially the British. Black people were also driven to escape all the daily humiliations of Jim Crow laws as well as the ever-present threat of lynching.

Many blacks joined the armed forces when the USA entered the war in 1917. However, many became embittered by their treatment in the army. Given menial jobs as cooks or labourers or forced to fight in segregated regiments, many returning veterans were impatient, determined to resist white supremacy and assert their rights. But, in the South, little had changed. Many whites in states like Alabama or Mississippi were still determined to keep them in their place and there was a big increase in lynchings in 1919.

In Texas, a white leader of the NAACP was beaten so badly that he died soon afterwards. One of his assailants was a county judge.

? How would you describe and explain the attitudes of the people in the crowd in Source D?

SOURCE D

This photograph shows the lynching of Thomas Shipp and Abram Smith that took place in Indiana, a northern state, in 1930. There was an increase in lynchings after the First World War.

The Second World War

The Second World War and its outcome had a similarly dramatic impact on the lives of black Americans. Nearly a million were called up to fight and a larger number left farms in the South to seek work in cities, both in the South and, more especially, in the North. Black Americans were eager to play their part in the war to defeat racist Nazi Germany. They were also determined to take advantage of the war in order to achieve their rights. Many supported the 'Double V' campaign, to win a double victory, conquering racism both abroad *and* at home. President Roosevelt responded by appointing the first black general, Benjamin O. Davis, and calling for equal opportunities for all in the armed forces.

It was easier said than done. Many army leaders had a low opinion of black soldiers and resisted pressure to enlist them in combat units, while many of the military training camps were situated in the South. Not only did black soldiers come up against racism within the camps but black soldiers from the North, unused to Jim Crow laws, were shocked by the treatment they received outside the camps. Insulted or refused service in shops and bars, they came up against segregation on public transport. Nowhere was this worse than on buses: there were numerous incidents where black soldiers were ordered by the drivers not to sit in 'white' seats and, when they refused, were arrested and, in a few cases, shot.

When the war ended, there were some signs of improvement for black Americans. For example, Congress passed a law which offered returning soldiers financial aid to attend college and gain qualifications. Many black army veterans benefited. Having fought for freedom and democracy against fascism and racism, returning soldiers were determined to enjoy their rights. One of them, an army corporal from Alabama, said: 'I went into the Army a nigger. I'm comin' out a *man*.' Yet, in the South, blacks were thrown off buses for sitting in the wrong place and could be shot for trying to vote. In 1946, Theodore Bilbo, seeking re-election as senator for Mississippi, called on 'every red-blooded American who believes in the superiority and integrity of the white race to get out and see that no nigger votes'.

Discrimination in the North

Generally, in the North (and the West, for example, Los Angeles), discrimination was not as extreme as in the South but it was still widespread. Black soldiers returning to the North met hostility too, especially as competition for urban housing led to overcrowding and the deliberate exclusion of blacks from white neighbourhoods. Chicago's black population doubled in the 1940s and was increasingly squeezed into unsafe, insanitary housing, sometimes ten to a room. There were numerous outbreaks of violence in northern cities, the worst being in Detroit. During the war, 50,000 blacks arrived in the city, lured by job opportunities in arms production. There were even more white immigrants, many from the South. In June 1943, rumours of a white woman having been raped by a black man triggered a race riot. Large mobs of whites entered the black **ghetto** to hunt for victims. By the time order was restored by federal troops, 34 had been killed, 25 black and nine white, and hundreds injured.

In the North and in the West, both during and after the wars, there were more job opportunities and better pay than in the South. Blacks usually voted freely and received fairer treatment in court. They were free to express their own views, even to protest. Black culture, epitomized by jazz musicians like Louis Armstrong and Duke Ellington, flourished in northern cities. However, northern whites kept their distance from blacks, not by law but by social pressure. There were no 'whites only' notices but estate agents, builders and local politicians used various, informal means to steer the black population away from the mainly white areas. Most urban northern blacks lived in ghettoes. They took the lowest paid jobs as domestic servants, cleaners, porters and waiters. In the factories, white-only unions effectively excluded blacks or, at any rate, ensured they only took the unskilled jobs. Unable to find work, some urban blacks took to gambling, prostitution or theft. In this way, the southern stereotype of the lazy, criminal, inferior black person was replicated in the minds of some northerners.

 **KEY TERM**

Ghetto An area inhabited overwhelmingly by (usually poor) members of one race or ethnic group.

The development of black activism

The black response to racial discrimination took many forms. One example was the campaign against racial discrimination that had started in Chicago in the 1930s and then spread to other cities: tens of thousands of black Americans implemented the slogan 'Don't buy where you can't work' and, in places, the boycotts led to blacks being employed in retail stores.

Another example of direct action was the plan by A. Philip Randolph, the leader of an all-black trade union, to organize a March on Washington in 1941. This was to be a demonstration by thousands of blacks in the heart of the American capital. The aim was to pressurize the federal government into banning all job discrimination in war industries; in other words, in all the shipyards, aircraft and weapons factories which were producing arms for the government's war effort. The mere threat of such a demonstration in Washington led to Roosevelt setting up the Fair Employment Practices Commission (FEPC) to ensure that blacks were employed in the war industries. This showed the impact which the threat of mass protest could have and it boosted the confidence of the emerging Civil Rights Movement. In reality, the FEPC had limited impact. There was widespread resistance in the South, where employers insisted that white workers would refuse to work alongside blacks and, even in the North, some unions organized 'hate strikes' where white workers walked out, refusing to work with blacks.

What was achieved by the NAACP in the 1930s and 1940s? →

The growing impact of the NAACP

The campaigns run by the NAACP and many local black organizations contributed significantly to the advancement of the cause of black civil rights. During the Second World War, NAACP membership leapt from 50,000 to 450,000. The organization attracted far wider support in the South, especially in the growing urban population, and gave its backing to numerous small-scale, local campaigns. More and more blacks gained the confidence to attend NAACP classes, where they learned the skills needed to pass literacy classes and pay the poll tax so that they could register to vote. The development of this sustained, **grassroots** activity marked a new development in the campaign for black civil rights in the South.

 KEY TERM

Grassroots An activity or a movement rooted in local, community politics.

Electoral register Before people were allowed to vote, they had to apply to be put on the electoral register (a list of names and addresses).

This movement was complemented by the gains of the NAACP lawyers, who took an increasing number of legal cases to the Supreme Court. The latter was now more receptive thanks to the appointment, by President Roosevelt, of several more liberal judges. In 1944, the Court outlawed the all-white Democratic primary election in Texas. A primary election is held in each state to decide who will be the candidate for that party in a general election, and white primaries (in which black people were banned from voting) had been common in the South before this. Now that black men could not legally be excluded, many more of them got to register to vote. Although many still faced intimidation if they attempted to register, the percentage of black men in the South on the **electoral register** rose from three per cent in 1940 to twelve per cent in 1950.

The NAACP and segregation in schools

The NAACP decided to focus on education in its legal campaign. Their chief lawyer was Charles Houston, professor of law at the all-black Howard University in Washington DC. He was mentor to a whole generation of black lawyers trained to fight civil rights cases. His star student was Thurgood Marshall. Although Houston, Marshall and their legal team wanted to abolish segregated schooling completely, they first set about achieving equality within the segregated system. In other words, they wanted to ensure that facilities in black schools were equal even if they were separate. In this way, the whole system of segregated schooling might become so prohibitively expensive that the dual system might have to be dismantled.

The NAACP achieved a significant victory in the late 1930s when the Supreme Court ruled that the states of Virginia and Maryland had to pay equal salaries to black and white schoolteachers. Victories in these border states of the upper south in the early 1940s would not necessarily lead to immediate compliance by states in the most racist states of the South but many did in fact fall into line in order to be able to maintain their separate schools. The salaries gap was virtually closed by the end of the war while the legal basis for segregated schools was being gradually undermined by the NAACP's legal challenges.

Despite these victories, however, the Jim Crow system of segregation was still entrenched in the South, bolstered by all-white courts, police and prison officers. Nevertheless, an increasingly educated and eloquent urban black population grew in the South, and growing awareness of the discrepancy between America's democratic values and white supremacy was helping to win wider support for an activist approach. With the emergence of more widespread, sustained and well-organized action, the foundations for the Civil Rights Movement of the 1950s and 1960s were being laid.

Presidential support for civil rights

The Democrat Franklin Delano Roosevelt (FDR), who became president in 1933, had given a huge boost to the campaign for civil rights. During the Great Depression of the 1930s, large numbers of black labourers were laid off in the South because the cotton plantations were badly hit, first by the boll-weevil (a particularly damaging pest) and then by a collapse in the market for cotton. Roosevelt introduced his New Deal to get the unemployed back to work. FDR took on many black advisers, his 'black cabinet', and his wife, Eleanor Roosevelt, advocated 'fair play and equal opportunity for Negro citizens'. For the first time, large numbers of black Americans in the North switched their support from the Republican to the Democratic Party. As the Democratic Party expanded its membership to include many immigrants and northern blacks, so the South lost some of its dominant influence in the party. These developments were to have a significant impact on the development of the Civil Rights Movement in the 1950s and 1960s.

President Truman

President Truman, who became president when Roosevelt died in 1944, was shocked by reports of attacks on black soldiers returning home at the end of the Second World War. In 1946, he appointed a Committee on Civil Rights to investigate the causes of such violence. Genuinely appalled though he was, both by the murders and by the fact that 'nothing is done about it', there were also electoral reasons for his action: the presidential election of 1948 was likely to be close and he feared that blacks might vote Republican. Although only twelve per cent of blacks were registered to vote in the South, black voters could have a significant impact in northern cities. After the Committee's report, *To Secure These Rights*, was published in 1947, Truman proposed a civil rights bill that would ban segregation in public transport, end poll taxes and make lynching a federal crime. In July 1948, he ordered the **desegregation** of the armed forces. He was showing far more commitment to civil rights than any of his predecessors. He won a close presidential contest over his Republican rival in 1948 but a combination of Republicans and southern Democrats killed his civil rights bill in Congress. It would take another twenty years of sustained pressure from the Civil Rights Movement to induce Congress to pass such a comprehensive bill.

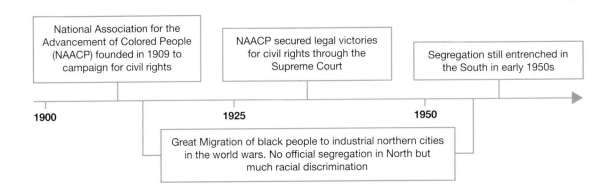

Brown v. Board of Education of Topeka, 1954

▶ **Key question:** *What was the impact of the Supreme Court decision of 1954?*

In the first half of the twentieth century, the NAACP set out to erode segregation. It filed many cases in court and succeeded in bringing about small-scale, piecemeal change. In 1950, Thurgood Marshall, now the NAACP's chief lawyer, argued before the Supreme Court that dual law schools at the University of Texas and segregated facilities at the University of Oklahoma had created separate but not equal facilities. These decisions suggested that increasing finance to upgrade separate facilities did not produce genuine equality.

The stage was set for what would become the NAACP's biggest challenge: the desegregation of all publicly funded schools. Although spending on black schools had increased in some areas, the disparity in provision was still very marked in much of the South. The following explains the situation in Clarendon County, South Carolina, in the 1950s.

SOURCE E

In 1950, about 32,000 people lived in Clarendon County. More than 70 per cent were African-Americans. Outside the towns of Summerton and Manning, the county was mostly rural and poor.

Use Source E to explain the impact of segregated schooling on black children in Clarendon County.

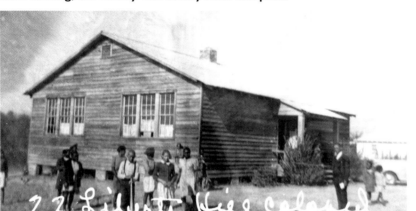

Because the school board refused to fund buses for black students, the county's 61 'colored' schools were scattered throughout the region. Most, like Liberty Hill Colored School (above), were small wooden structures that accommodated one or two classrooms.

The county provided 30 buses to bring white children to larger and better equipped facilities (above).

White children from the Summerton area attended this red-brick building, with a separate lunchroom and science laboratories. Most rural black schools had neither electricity nor running water. In the 1949–50 school year, for every dollar spent on a white child only 24 cents was allotted for a black student. Not surprisingly, black adults in the county averaged just over four years of education.

The NAACP and *Brown* v. *Board of Education of Topeka*

In 1952, the NAACP brought five cases to the Supreme Court, the first named of which was *Brown* v. *Board of Education of Topeka*. Linda Brown was an eight-year-old black girl who lived near an all-white school in Topeka, Kansas. Her father, Oliver Brown, had sued the Topeka Board of Education in Kansas, claiming that his child should be able to attend her local, all-white, school rather than have to cross town to go to an all-black school. The Court's Chief Justice, Earl Warren, finally delivered the Court's unanimous ruling in May 1954. He said that segregation was dehumanizing and that, even if the schools were equally good in material terms, the psychological effect of segregated schooling was to breed feelings of 'inferiority' in the 'hearts and minds' of young blacks and thus infringed their rights to 'equal protection under the law'. He called for the desegregation of schools in order to comply with the 14th Amendment to the Constitution.

SOURCE F

? Why does Earl Warren, in Source F, conclude that 'the doctrine of "separate but equal" has no place'?

Excerpt from Earl Warren's ruling on 17 May 1954.

Segregation of white and colored children in public schools has a detrimental effect upon the colored children. The impact is greater when it has the sanction of the law, for the policy of separating the races is usually interpreted as denoting the inferiority of the negro group. A sense of inferiority affects the motivation of a child to learn …

We conclude that, in the field of public education, the doctrine of 'separate but equal' has no place. Separate educational facilities are inherently unequal.

This was a dramatic result and gave great hope to the NAACP and its supporters, both white and black. It finally eliminated the legal basis for segregation in education by overturning the *Plessy* v. *Ferguson* decision. It certainly seemed to be a great victory for the NAACP's policy.

SOURCE G

? What, according to Source G, are the main reasons for the Supreme Court's ruling?

Excerpt from *Awakenings (1954–1956)* by Vincent Hardy, quoted in *The Eyes on the Prize Civil Rights Reader*, edited by Clayborne Carson and others, published by Penguin, New York, USA, 1991, p. 35. Harding was a civil rights activist in the 1960s, an adviser to Martin Luther King Jr and, later, the first director of the Martin Luther King Jr Memorial Center.

Just about everyone who was alive and black at the time realized that the long, hard struggles, led by the National Association for the Advancement of Colored People (NAACP), its often brilliant and courageous lawyers, and its lengthening line of risk-taking black plaintiffs [people who bring cases to court], had forced the Supreme Court to take a major stand on the side of justice in the Brown v. Board of Education of Topeka *decision.*

As the following two sources show, many newspapers praised the decision, but not all.

SOURCE H

The Washington newspaper, *Post and Times Herald*, praised the decision under the heading 'Emancipation' on 18 May 1954.

The Supreme Court's resolution yesterday of the school segregation cases affords all Americans an occasion for pride and gratification. The decision will prove, we are sure – whatever transient difficulties it may create and whatever irritations it may arouse – a profoundly healthy and healing one. It will serve – and speedily – to close an ancient wound too long allowed to fester. It will bring to an end a painful disparity between American principles and American practices. It will help to refurbish American prestige in a world which looks to this land for moral inspiration and restore the faith of Americans themselves in their own great values and traditions.

For what reasons, according to Source H, is the Supreme Court's decision a source of 'pride' for all Americans?

SOURCE I

Excerpt from an article headed 'Bloodstains on White Marble Steps' in the newspaper, *Daily News*, published in Jackson, Mississippi, on 18 May 1954.

Human blood may stain Southern soil in many places because of this decision but the dark red stains of that blood will be on the steps of the United States Supreme Court building …

White and Negro children in the same schools will lead to miscegenation [a derogatory, insulting term for sexual relations between people of different races]. Miscegenation leads to mixed marriages and mixed marriages lead to mongrelization [the mixing of breeds, usually applied to dogs] of the human race.

Compare and contrast how Sources H and I respond to the Supreme Court decision. How do you explain these differences?

Thurgood Marshall (see page 27) was confident that all segregation would be eliminated by 1963, the hundredth anniversary of Lincoln's Emancipation Proclamation. However, this was not to be the case, either in education or in other areas. One of the reasons for this was that the Supreme Court had, very unusually, not followed up its decision with a plan for implementation. No doubt this was partly to try to soften the impact of what was going to be seen as a controversial decision which would arouse much opposition. Opinion polls showed that the vast majority of white southerners were opposed to school desegregation. Even when, in 1955, the Court's '*Brown* II' ruling called for desegregation 'with all due speed', it did not set any timetable and it left it to lower federal courts to ensure that schools were desegregated. These courts were vulnerable to pressure from the ruling elites in the white supremacist South. As one commentator remarked, this ruling allowed the southern states 'to make haste slowly'.

President Eisenhower's response

Another reason why schools in the South were not immediately desegregated was that Republican President Eisenhower (elected in 1952) did not endorse, let alone express support for, the Court's decision. In fact, he later told friends that his appointment of Earl Warren as Chief Justice in 1953 had been 'the biggest damn fool decision I ever made'. He believed that deeply entrenched racial feelings, traditions and customs could not, should not, be changed by law. 'You cannot change people's hearts by law', he said. It is also likely that he wanted to reach out to white southerners who traditionally voted for the Democratic Party. Another explanation is that he was keen to maintain the comparative calm of mid-1950s' America and he knew that the Supreme Court's decision threatened to disrupt the social order and lead to violence in the South. Whatever his reasons, his obvious lack of enthusiasm for the ruling indicated that federal support for desegregation would not be forthcoming.

Deep South Used to denote the states which had been most dependent on plantation agriculture, sometimes referred to as the Cotton Belt, and which had formed the core of the Confederacy. It is usually thought to include states such as Alabama, Louisiana, Mississippi and South Carolina.

> Why, and in what ways, did southerners oppose the desegregation of schools?

Southern resistance to the desegregation of schools

By far the most significant reason for the lack of immediate desegregation, at any rate in the South, was widespread opposition from whites. There was *some* desegregation of schools in border states like Maryland, Missouri and Oklahoma and in areas where black children formed only a small proportion of the school population. However, in Virginia, which bordered Washington DC, by 1965, eleven years after the Brown ruling, fewer than 12,000 out of 235,000 black students went to desegregated schools. In the **Deep South**, some white moderates, in the churches, education and the press, called for acceptance of the ruling, although the majority kept quiet. But there was virtually no desegregation of schools in the states of Georgia, Alabama, Mississippi, Louisiana and South Carolina (see the map on page 16) and the Supreme Court decision was seen as an outright attack on the southern way of life, of long-standing customs and 'our Southern traditions'. Above all, it was an attack on **states' rights**, in this case the states' rights to organize education. Nearly all southern members of Congress went on to sign the **Southern Manifesto**, in March 1956, in order to condemn the Brown decision and unite the South in resistance.

 KEY TERM

States' rights The rights which the Constitution reserves for the states as opposed to the federal government.

Southern Manifesto A statement of defiance against the 1954 *Brown* ruling which was signed by most southerners in Congress.

?

What are the main grounds on which the Senators and Congressmen in Source J intend to resist the *Brown* decision?

SOURCE J

Excerpt from the 'Declaration of Constitutional Principles: The Southern Manifesto', 12 March 1956.

We regard the decisions of the Supreme Court in the school cases as a clear abuse of judicial power … and to encroach upon the reserved rights of the States and people …

This unwarranted exercise of power by the Court, contrary to the Constitution, is creating chaos and confusion in the States principally affected. It is destroying the amicable relations between the white and Negro races that have been created through 90 years of patient effort by the good people of both races. It has planted hatred and suspicion where there has been heretofore friendship and understanding.

We pledge ourselves to use all lawful means to bring about a reversal of this decision which is contrary to the Constitution and to prevent the use of force in its implementation.

We appeal to our people not to be provoked by the agitators and troublemakers invading our States and to scrupulously refrain from disorder and lawless acts.

Most southerners believed in white supremacy or, at least, in white superiority over blacks. They opposed any kind of racial integration in public places, above all any kind of interracial sex or marriage which, of course, integrated schooling might lead to. The state governments and local school boards, who were in charge of education, put up obstacles to desegregation: token admission of a few blacks to white schools in order to show compliance with the Court's ruling; teaching according to 'ability groups', a euphemism for racial groups; overcomplicated admissions procedures and paperwork for blacks seeking to enrol their children in white schools.

White Citizens' Councils

The KKK, with its lynchings, was revived. **White Citizens' Councils**, claiming to be non-violent (wearing 'suits not sheets') were set up and attracted widespread support. Many members were doctors, lawyers, farmers, businessmen and politicians. They used economic reprisals as well as cruder methods to deter integrationists: blacks who tried to admit their children to white schools were fired by their employers or evicted from their homes by their landlords. Often these Councils received state funding, while state laws required the NAACP to reveal lists of their members and addresses, thus exposing them to intimidation and violence. Firebombing the houses of black (and white) civil rights campaigners became common. Perpetrators were rarely arrested and, even when they were put on trial, the all-white juries nearly always acquitted the defendants. Juries, judges, police officers and politicians in the South nearly all supported, or turned a blind eye to, intimidation, threats and violence against those who made any attempt to disturb the continuation of white domination and strict segregation.

Little Rock, Arkansas, 1957

What happened at Little Rock, Arkansas, in 1957, highlights the reasons for the lack of desegregation in southern schools. When nine black students were enrolled at Central High School they were met on arrival by a white mob shouting abuse and threatening to lynch them. The students, led by Daisy Bates, president of the state's NAACP, expected to be protected and escorted into school by troops of the National Guard who had been sent, according to State Governor Orval Faubus, to safeguard law and order. In the

 **KEY TERM**

White Citizens' Councils
Organizations set up to maintain segregation. The first one was in Mississippi but they soon spread across the Deep South.

What was the significance of events at Little Rock?

event, the students were blocked by those troops ('to keep the niggers out', said one of them). A photograph of one particular student, fifteen-year-old Elizabeth Eckford, who had been harassed and abused in a frightening way, appeared on the front of national newspapers, both in the USA and abroad, and shocked liberal opinion.

SOURCE K

Black student Elizabeth Eckford tries to enter Little Rock Central High School on 4 September 1957. She was spat on and there were shouts of 'Nigger whore!' and 'Lynch her!'

In what ways might the photograph in Source K have been used to advance the cause of civil rights?

SOURCE L

Elizabeth Eckford explains what happened to her, located at www.facinghistory.org.

I walked further down the line of guards ... and I attempted to pass through there. But when I stepped up, they crossed rifles ... So, I walked toward the center of the street and when I got to about the middle and I approached the guard he directed me across the street into the crowd. It was only then that I realized that they were barring me, that I wouldn't go to school.

As I stepped out into the street, the people who had been across the street started surging forward behind me. So, I headed in the opposite direction to where there was another bus stop. Safety to me meant getting to that bus stop. It seemed like I sat there for a long time before the bus came. In the meantime, people were screaming behind me. What I would have described as a crowd before, to my ears sounded like a mob.

How, according to Source L, did the guardsmen and the crowd respond to Elizabeth Eckford's attempt to enter Little Rock High School?

These events showed the USA in a highly unfavourable light, not at all a beacon of freedom and democracy, which was the image which the government preferred to portray. Civil rights activists could use the **Cold War** context to their advantage, pointing out that the USA needed to be seen to uphold its ideals of liberty, equality and justice if it was to win friends and allies, especially in Asia and black Africa. Soviet diplomats at the United Nations in New York wasted no opportunity to publicize every lynching and race riot to help win allies among the non-white member states at the **United Nations (UN)**.

KEY TERM

Cold War The state of tension, primarily between the USA and the Soviet Union, that existed from the late 1940s to the late 1980s.

United Nations (UN) An organization formed in 1945, the main aim of which was to solve international disputes.

SOURCE M

Excerpt from *Cold War Civil Rights* by Mary L. Dudziak, published by Princeton University Press, USA, 2000, p. 131. Dudziak is professor of law at Emory University and a specialist in legal history with a particular interest in civil rights history.

The president's top aides emphasized the international impact of the Little Rock crisis. The US Ambassador to the United Nations, Henry Cabot Lodge, wrote President Eisenhower that, 'Here at the United Nations I can clearly see the harm that the riots in Little Rock are doing to our foreign relations. More than two-thirds of the world is non-white and the reactions of the representatives of these people is easy to see' … In addition Eisenhower wrote [in his memoirs], 'around the world it could continue to feed the mill of Soviet propagandists who by word and picture were telling the world of the "racial terror" in the United States.'

How does the author of Source M show the impact of the Cold War on the issue of civil rights?

Federal intervention

With the eyes of the world on Little Rock, President Eisenhower was forced to act, to show that the US Constitution was being upheld and justice done. He sent in 1200 paratroopers to escort the students into school. This action infuriated southern opinion: Governor Faubus said they were being 'occupied'. The troops could not protect the black students from bullying and other forms of intimidation once they were inside the school. Nevertheless, the students remained at school with the protection and support of some of their teachers and classmates, while the civil rights campaigners could claim to have won a huge victory as well as favourable publicity (outside the South, at any rate). Little Rock Central High School became a largely black school within a few years. The crisis at Little Rock won increased support for the Civil Rights Movement nationally and, above all, it had elicited the intervention of federal government troops in the South for the first time since Reconstruction, nearly 100 years before.

? What lessons, according to Source N, were learned by civil rights activists as a result of the Little Rock crisis?

SOURCE N

Excerpt from *Debating the Civil Rights Movement, 1945–1968* by Steven Lawson and Charles Payne, published by Rowan & Littlefield, Maryland, USA, 1998, p. 17. Both authors are professors at American universities.

Whatever reluctance to use force Eisenhower had shown, his resolution of the crisis had inspired optimism among African-Americans … Nevertheless this incident showed that the national government remained a tentative ally for African-Americans. Whatever rights the Constitution guaranteed and the courts affirmed, the federal government was likely to act only if pressured to do so … Appeals to moral conscience went only so far in persuading white officials to combat Jim Crow. Presidents and members of Congress responded to grievances more effectively when Blacks and their white allies exerted substantial political pressure or when their attempts to obtain equality provoked violence from white resisters … In this way, the government helped shape the logic for protest by signaling to Blacks the need to confront racism head-on before Washington would choose to intervene.

Although the outcome was a victory for desegregation in Little Rock, official, state-sponsored segregation remained predominant in the schools of the Deep South for several more years. Furthermore, the victory had encouraged the flight of many middle-class, white families to the suburbs in order to enrol their children in white suburban schools. This 'white flight', which also occurred in northern cities, led to a kind of unofficial segregation. Meanwhile, Governor Faubus became even more popular for his stand on racial segregation (and was re-elected as governor by a large majority) and was emulated by politicians in neighbouring states. By the end of the 1950s, very few schools in the Deep South had been desegregated.

Civil rights legislation

In the late 1950s, President Eisenhower's government responded to increasing black pressure and the need both to win the northern black vote and to improve America's international image, by passing two Civil Rights Acts. Both were diluted in Congress and Eisenhower himself was less than enthusiastic. The first one, in 1957, set up a Civil Rights Commission to monitor racial relations. The second act, in 1960, imposed criminal penalties for public officials obstructing black voters (although they would be tried by all-white juries if in the South!).

As the 1950s drew to a close, white supremacists still dominated the South. Only three per cent more blacks were added to the electoral registers as a result of the two Civil Rights Acts. Many cities ignored the Supreme Court rulings and continued to enforce segregation in schools and other public facilities. It would take new tactics and broader support to pressurize the federal government into ending segregation in the South.

| **1954** | Supreme Court ruled that 'separate but equal' schooling for blacks and whites was unconstitutional |

| Seen as a great breakthrough for civil rights | Massive opposition in the South:
• Southern Manifesto
• White Citizens' Councils
• Revival of Ku Klux Klan | Little support from President Eisenhower |

| **1957** | Little Rock, Arkansas, 1957:
• Highlighted opposition to desegregation of schools
• White resistance and huge publicity forced Eisenhower to send in troops
• Nine students admitted |

| **1959** | At end of 1950s, Jim Crow laws still preserved white supremacy in Deep South |

SUMMARY DIAGRAM

Brown v. Board of Education of Topeka, 1954

Chapter summary

Racism and white supremacy

Even after the end of slavery and three constitutional Amendments to safeguard the civil rights of African-Americans in the 1860s, white supremacy was maintained in much of the South by the passing of Jim Crow laws and by the terror spread by organizations like the Ku Klux Klan. Then, in 1896, the Supreme Court ruled, in the case of *Plessy* v. *Ferguson*, that enforced segregation was not unconstitutional.

In the two world wars, many black people migrated to the North. Although they were free of the Jim Crow laws, black people came up against discrimination in housing and employment in the cities of the North.

From the early twentieth century, the NAACP won several legal cases in the Supreme Court, culminating in the *Brown* decision of 1954, which declared segregated schooling to be unconstitutional. Nevertheless, little progress was made in the Deep South because of massive, organized white resistance. However, a victory for civil rights was achieved at Little Rock in 1957.

✓ Examination advice

Remember that questions for Prescribed subject 4 will be numbered 13, 14, 15 and 16 in the Paper 1 exam.

Paper 1 Question 13: how to answer direct questions

Question 13 on the IB History Diploma examination is in two parts, 13a and 13b. Each part involves reading comprehension and simply asks you to tell the examiner what the sources say. Each of the questions will ask only about one source. You will often see questions that ask you to convey the message or meaning of a source – to explain what the source is saying.

Question 13 requires no prior knowledge, just the ability to read and understand sources. When you start your examination, you will receive five minutes of 'reading time' when you cannot actually touch your pen and start writing. Use the time wisely and read Question 13 to see which sources it is asking about. Once you understand which sources the question is about, read the sources and then think of your response. When the five minutes are up, you may begin writing. You should be ready to answer the question immediately.

Question 13 is worth 5 marks out of the total of 24 for Paper 1. This means it is worth about twenty per cent of the overall mark. Answering Questions 13a and 13b should take five minutes or less of the actual examination time.

How to answer

In order to best answer the question, you first have to determine what the question is asking you about the source and what type of source it is. The vast majority of sources are fragments of speeches, quotes from various historians or historical figures, or any other type of written source. There are, however, visual sources that can be asked about as well, such as photographs, charts, maps, cartoons and diagrams.

When you start your answer, it is good practice to use the wording in the question to help you focus your answer. For example:

Question	Begin your answer with:
According to Source *N*, what was the impact of segregation in US schools?	The impact of segregation in US schools, according to Source *N*, was …
Why, according to Source *N*, did 'colored children' suffer more than white ones in public schools?	'Colored children' suffered more, according to Source *N*, because …
What was Chief Justice Earl Warren's view on the doctrine of 'separate but equal', according to Source *N*?	According to Source *N*, Warren's view on the doctrine of 'separate but equal' was …

After starting your answer, you should paraphrase what the original source stated. This means you should explain what the source says, but in your own words. Sometimes this is impossible because the words used in the source may be so specific that there is no other way to restate them. If this occurs, make sure you put quotation marks around the phrases which you are copying from the source.

The total number of marks available for Question 13 is 5. One part is worth 3 marks and the other 2. This will be clearly indicated on the examination. If a question is worth 3 marks, try to have at least three specific points to your answer. If you have made 4 points and one is incorrect, you will still score full marks. The same is true if a question is worth 2 marks: raise at least three points to help ensure that you score the maximum number of marks.

Example
This question uses Sources I (page 31) and K (page 34).

a) According to Source I, what would the results of desegregated schools in the US be? (3 marks)

b) What is the message conveyed in Source K? (2 marks)

It has just been announced that your reading time has begun on the IB History Paper 1 examination. Find the Paper 1 questions that refer to 'Rights and protest' and read Question 13a. It asks you to explain what Source I suggests the results of school desegregation will be. You cannot touch your pen during the reading period, so go to Source I in the booklet and read it. Once you are allowed to pick up your pen and start writing, do so. Below is a good sample answer for the questions for 13a and 13b:

13a) According to Source I, school desegregation will result in racial mixing, marriage between white and black people, and the unnatural blending of different races. This will mean the end of white purity. There will also be violence as a result of the Supreme Court's decision.

13b) The message conveyed in Source K is the lonely attempt of Elizabeth Eckford to enter the Little Rock High School in the face of an angry mob of white protesters, some of whom are screaming insults at her. A soldier or national guardsman does not appear to be protecting her.

Each answer repeats part of the question, using phrases such as 'According to Source I' and 'The message conveyed in Source K'. This helps the answer to focus on the question.

Both sources are paraphrased in the answers.

Both questions are answered in paragraph form and not bullet points.

Questions 13a and 13b are worth a combined 5 marks. Both answers indicate that the student read and understood what each source stated. Question 13a is worth 3 marks. The answer for 13a contains at least three different points to address the question. Question 13b is worth 2 marks. The answer has more than two points to answer the question. Mark: 5/5.

Examination practice

The following are exam-style questions for you to practise, using sources from Chapters 1 and 2. Sources can be found on the following pages:

1 Why, according to Source G, was the Supreme Court forced to take a stand?

2 What is the message of Source D?

3 What is the message of Source E?

4 What is the message of Source K?

5 What positive outcomes would there be as a result of the Supreme Court's decision, according to Source H?

6 What, according to Source J, was unconstitutional about the Supreme Court decision?

7 How, according to Source M, did the Little Rock crisis hurt the USA internationally?

8 Why, according to Source N, was the US government a 'tentative ally' for African-Americans?

9 What message is conveyed by Source F (in Chapter 2)?

10 What message is conveyed by Source K (in Chapter 2)?

Protests and action: from Montgomery to the Civil Rights Act

This chapter focuses on mass protest and the emergence of new leaders and new organizations. It examines the Montgomery Bus Boycott of 1955–6 and analyses the impact of the student sit-ins and the Freedom Rides. It assesses the importance of the campaign, led by Martin Luther King Jr, in Birmingham, Alabama, and the response which it elicited from the federal government. You need to consider the following questions throughout this chapter:

★ What was the significance of the Montgomery Bus Boycott?

★ What was the impact of sit-ins and Freedom Rides?

★ To what extent was the campaign in Birmingham a turning point?

★ How successful was the March on Washington in 1963?

The Montgomery Bus Boycott 1955–6

▶ *Key question: What was the significance of the Montgomery Bus Boycott?*

The Montgomery Bus **Boycott**, which took place in Alabama, is probably the best known event in the history of the Civil Rights Movement. It is closely associated with the names of Rosa Parks and Martin Luther King Jr. One was a middle-aged woman who refused to give up her seat on a bus to a white person and thus triggered a year-long protest. The other was a charismatic young preacher who became the most famous black man in the South and, arguably, in the world. There are many reasons why the boycott is so significant, especially given the context in which it happened.

 **KEY TERM**

Boycott A refusal to have anything to do with a person or an organization, in this case the Montgomery bus company.

Montgomery: the context

The city of Montgomery, in Alabama, had a population of 120,000, of whom a third were black. The black population suffered all the usual indignities of racial discrimination and segregation. None was more aggravating and humiliating than the insistence that they sit on the back seats of public buses and, if they were full, that they stand, even if the seats reserved for whites were empty.

← **What may have influenced Rosa Parks' defiance?**

Montgomery: a familiar story

On Thursday 1 December 1955, 42-year-old Rosa Parks climbed aboard one of Montgomery's segregated buses and sat immediately behind the white section. When the bus filled up, the driver ordered her to give up her seat to a white man. She refused and was arrested. Several factors may have had an impact on Rosa Parks' decision to stay in her seat.

Emmett Till

Emmett Till was a fourteen-year-old boy brought up in the northern city of Chicago. In 1955, he was sent by his mother to spend the summer with relatives in the South. He was a cheeky boy and his mother had warned him to show respect to white people. However, on leaving a shop in the small town of Money, Mississippi, in August 1955, he said 'Bye, baby' to the white female, older cashier. (There are several different accounts of what was actually said.) The woman's husband said Emmett had not just spoken but had wolf-whistled at his wife. He and his half-brother seized the boy and beat him to death before dumping his body in a nearby river. Emmett's mutilated body was dragged out after three days and flown to Chicago where, before the funeral, his mother had it placed in an open coffin to show 'what they did to my boy'. Thousands filed past his body and a photo was published in the black-owned magazine, *Jet*. The killers were acquitted by the all-white jury. Roy Wilkins, the NAACP leader, summed up the murder: 'Mississippi has decided to maintain white supremacy by murdering children'. The body of Emmett Till was shown around the world. It affected the lives of a whole generation of people and encouraged many to become civil rights activists. Rosa Parks later said she had Emmett Till on her mind at the time she refused to give up her seat on a bus to a white man.

Rosa Parks' status

Rosa Parks had been an active member of the NAACP for many years. She had joined in 1943, became branch secretary and worked on voter registration campaigns. She ran the NAACP Youth Council. She was particularly angered by the injustice of segregated public transport and, for many years, she had campaigned with other local, black, civil rights campaigners against the usually insulting, abusive behaviour of Montgomery's white bus drivers. Referring later to her arrest, she said, 'People always say that I didn't give up my seat because I was tired, but that isn't true. I was not tired physically, or no more tired than I usually was at the end of a working day … No, the only tired I was, was tired of giving in.'

The local civil rights leaders had wanted to take up the case of fifteen-year-old Claudette Colvin who, nine months earlier in March 1955, was thrown off a bus and arrested for refusing to give her seat to a white passenger. They decided against it and against publicizing her case when they discovered she was pregnant while not married, whereas Rosa Parks was a respectable, dignified, married woman and presented a more 'acceptable' face of the movement.

Organizing the boycott

Montgomery had seen years of grassroots activism which was sustained by a strong, well-organized black community. The local leaders, including Rosa Parks, were no longer afraid, despite years of intimidation.

- Foremost among those leaders was E.D. Nixon. He was a railway porter who had been inspired by A. Philip Randolph (see page 26). He had helped to organize the Montgomery Voters' League in 1940 and had led a march of 750 people to register to vote in Montgomery in 1944. Then, for many years, he was president of the Alabama state branch of the NAACP and had worked closely with Rosa Parks.
- Jo Ann Robinson was a professor of English at all-black Alabama State College and president of the Women's Political Council, a group of 300 educated black women who had been campaigning for voter registration and desegregation of the buses for several years. They had also persuaded the city authorities to employ black policemen.

Mobilization

When Rosa Parks was arrested, Nixon and the Women's Political Council took responsibility for mobilizing the blacks of Montgomery. Years of experience had given Nixon and Robinson the knowledge of who to contact and the skills to organize a city-wide boycott. They decided it should take place on the day of Parks' trial, Monday 5 December. They had just four days to organize it. Nixon called a meeting of church ministers, college professors and others whose leadership would be crucial. He persuaded them to announce the plans in their sermons on the Sunday before the boycott, to distribute leaflets and to persuade the black-owned taxi companies to transport people at bus-fare rates. Robinson and her colleagues stayed up half the night producing thousands of leaflets to publicize the boycott. They distributed them in shops, schools, churches and bars. The main aim of the boycott was to hit the bus company's owners in their pockets: black people constituted the majority of the bus company's users and a boycott would deprive the company of most of its income.

'People – don't ride the buses today. Don't ride it for freedom'

The slogan above, written on a piece of cardboard, appeared on a bus shelter in the centre of Montgomery at 5a.m. on the Monday morning, the day of the boycott. Nearly all of Montgomery's black population obeyed it. Usually 30,000 black people regularly used the buses, but not on this day. They walked or cycled to work or, if they knew someone with a car, they shared lifts. The boycott was a huge success. However, to force the bus company to agree to their demands, they would have to extend the boycott. Nixon called a meeting of 50 church ministers, the most influential leaders of the black community, and they set up the **Montgomery Improvement Association (MIA)** to co-ordinate it. They invited a 26-year-old Baptist minister to be

← How effective was the organization of the boycott?

 **KEY TERM**

Montgomery Improvement Association (MIA)
The organization that co-ordinated the Montgomery Bus Boycott.

president. His name was Martin Luther King Jr. He had only recently become pastor of Dexter Avenue Church so he was not associated with any one black faction. He was also known to be highly educated, a good speaker and independent-minded. In Nixon's words, King 'wasn't any white man's nigger'.

King was asked to address a mass meeting to be held at the Holt Street Baptist Church on the evening of the initial boycott. Nearly 5000 turned up for the meeting, most standing outside, listening on loudspeakers. Buoyed up by their success, they voted unanimously to continue the boycott.

When King rose, he immediately struck a chord with his listeners, 'We are tired! Tired of being segregated and humiliated!' It was time to protest. He praised American democracy with its right to protest. He also appealed to Christian values and reminded everyone of Jesus' call to 'Love your enemies'. He instilled in his listeners a belief in their moral authority: 'We are not wrong in what we are doing. If we are wrong, the Supreme Court is wrong. If we are wrong, the Constitution of the United States is wrong. If we are wrong, God Almighty is wrong.' The impact of his speech was to inspire and galvanize the thousands who attended.

SOURCE A

? Use Source A to explain why you think there was such confidence at the meeting.

Excerpt from *Bus Ride to Justice* by Fred Gray, published by New South Books, Montgomery, Alabama, USA, 2013, p. 61. Gray was the MIA's black lawyer.

Not only were there thousands of African-Americans crowded in and around Holt Street Baptist Church but also a few whites … There was an electricity in the air. Such a feeling of unity, success and enthusiasm had never been before in the city of Montgomery, certainly never demonstrated by African-Americans. The people were together. They were singing. They were praying. They were happy that Mrs. Parks had refused to give up her seat and they were happy that they were part of a movement that ultimately would eradicate segregation on city buses and would set a precedent for the elimination of segregation in almost every other phase of American life. They clapped and shouted 'Amen' as the boycott leaders entered the auditorium … The high point of the meeting was the speech by Dr. King. This was the first time he had spoken to so many people. It was the first speech of his career as a civil rights leader.

Extending the boycott

At the church meeting, three objectives for the boycott were agreed:

- more courteous treatment of black passengers
- seating on a first-come, first-served basis with whites filling the bus from the front and blacks from the back
- the employment of some black drivers.

SOURCE B

Martin Luther King Jr speaking to advisers and organizers of the bus boycott in 1956. Rosa Parks is seated in the front row.

What kind of a leader does the photograph in Source B suggest King was?

Martin Luther King Jr

Martin Luther King Jr was born in 1929 and brought up in Atlanta, Georgia, where both his father and grandfather were Baptist ministers. He encountered racial discrimination and segregation on a daily basis and later admitted it made him 'determined to hate every white person'. He went to theological college in Philadelphia and completed a doctorate in Boston. In 1953, he married Coretta Scott, a fellow black activist from the South. King became convinced of the need for a mass movement against racial discrimination founded on the Christian belief in reconciliation through love. He was also influenced by Mohandas K. Gandhi's belief in non-violent, mass action which had been put into practice in campaigning against British rule in India. King, like Gandhi, believed that one should win over one's enemies by persuasion, by moral force and by appealing to their consciences so that they become convinced of the rightness of one's cause.

The objectives of the boycott (see page 44) did *not* include the demand for the desegregation of Montgomery buses; they simply sought to make it less harsh. Nevertheless, the bus company refused to compromise. The company rejected all the demands for fear that 'the Negroes would go about boasting of a victory'. Besides, most whites thought the boycott would not last long. They did not think the blacks had the organizing ability to sustain it. They thought they would start using the buses again once it rained. But the boycott did last: black people walked, shared lifts, cycled and hitchhiked instead.

Rosa Parks, who had been fined $10 for her offence, was fired from the white-owned store she worked for and received death threats. Yet the boycott was sustained for 381 days. The MIA organized a car pool, effectively a black taxi service, that charged only a few cents for each journey.

As the boycott continued, blacks became more determined, more confident. Thousands attended evening meetings in churches and the ministers played a crucial role in sustaining the boycott. The bus company suffered huge financial losses. Abuse was hurled at black pedestrians and car pools were bombed but the effect was only to harden blacks' resolve. When Martin Luther King Jr's house was bombed, in January 1956, with his wife and baby daughter inside, thousands of blacks surrounded the house to protect King, many with guns and knives, ready to take revenge. King came out and told the crowd to put away their weapons. 'We must love our white brothers no matter what they do to us. We must meet hate with love.' The courage and self-discipline shown by King and others, in facing this and other forms of white resistance, strengthened the resolve of the black boycotters and enhanced their determination to continue their action. The white supremacists of Montgomery had thought that they could break King and cripple the boycott. Instead they made him into a hero, a symbol of black resistance.

The initial results of the boycott

The bombings and the arrests of church leaders attracted huge publicity, both in America and abroad. Donations poured in and more cars were purchased for the car pool. Organized in a highly disciplined way, the car pool enabled blacks to get to work all over the city.

In June 1956, with the support of Thurgood Marshall (see page 27) and the NAACP, the MIA agreed to challenge the segregation laws in a federal court. That court ruled that the bus company's segregated transport was unconstitutional as a violation of the 14th Amendment, which guaranteed 'equal protection of the laws' for all citizens. The city of Montgomery appealed to the Supreme Court, which upheld the lower court's decision on 20 December 1956. Then, on 21 December, the Court's order came into effect and the bus company finally backed down. King, Nixon and other local leaders took their first ride on a desegregated bus. The year-long boycott had more than achieved its goal.

The success of the boycott

← Why was the boycott so important?

The boycott was a local action, started and sustained by Montgomery's black population. There had been similar bus boycotts before, in Louisiana and elsewhere, but none had been sustained for so long or been so successful. Black solidarity remained firm in the face of intimidation and terror. That in itself instilled huge confidence and pride in the black community and made black people yet more determined to continue their campaign. Furthermore, the boycott was successful in eliciting a Supreme Court ruling in the blacks' favour as well as a climbdown by the bus company. Montgomery's blacks had shown they could exploit their economic power (they constituted the majority of the bus company's users) as a weapon in their battle and that organized, collective action – local, popular and sustained – could achieve advances in civil rights. It set a precedent and, soon afterwards, over twenty other southern cities desegregated their bus transport after boycotts.

SOURCE C

Excerpt from *Becoming King – Martin Luther King Jr. and the Making of a National Leader* by Troy Jackson, published by the University Press of Kentucky, USA, 2008.

In his memoir of the boycott, King claimed that 'The Montgomery story would have taken place if the leaders of the protest had never been born.' In many respects, this is true. The boycott idea preceded King's arrival in the city, and the first few days of the protest would have occurred had King not been on the scene at all … The MIA [Montgomery Improvement Association] had many resolute leaders who were committed to staying the course. Even the emphasis on love and non-violence would have emerged as a dominant theme without King's presence. The commitments to loving your neighbor and turning the other cheek were deeply rooted in the African-American Christian tradition.

For what reasons does the author of Source C suggest that the Montgomery Bus Boycott would have taken place even without King?

Yet King's role was vital. The ground may have been laid and the momentum of the boycott established by others but, once he became the leader and spokesman of the MIA, he became the symbol of the whole movement, a unifying figure who could connect with the professional classes and the poor, the highly educated and the illiterate. His charisma and his broad appeal allowed him to project the message of the Civil Rights Movement far beyond Montgomery. His church, and the other churches, provided the organizing centres for the boycott. His response to the bombing of his house calmed down the crowd who might otherwise have resorted to violence and it won nationwide respect, particularly among northern whites. This support would be crucial, in bringing pressure to bear on the federal government, in the future.

? For what reasons does the author of Source D see Montgomery as 'the birthplace of the Civil Rights Movement'?

SOURCE D

Excerpt from *Better Day Coming, Blacks and Equality, 1890–2000* by Adam Fairclough, published by Penguin, New York, USA, 2001, p. 234. Fairclough is a British historian specializing in African-American history.

If Brown was the legal turning point in the struggle for black equality, the Montgomery bus boycott was the psychological turning point ... Unity really had brought strength; the paralyzing fear of white persecution lifted ... The spiritual and institutional strength of the black church proved to be a powerful force. For the first time since Reconstruction, the fight for equality became a true 'movement' – a people's affair that directly engaged the masses of everyday, ordinary folk. Montgomery truly was the birthplace of the Civil Rights Movement.

🔑 **KEY TERM**

Southern Christian Leadership Conference (SCLC) A non-violent civil rights organization founded by Martin Luther King Jr.

The Southern Christian Leadership Conference (SCLC)

The boycott also led to the formation of the **Southern Christian Leadership Conference (SCLC)** in January 1957. It was formed by King and other church ministers in order to exploit the power of the black churches and mount sustained mass demonstrations against racial discrimination and segregation. Being based on the black churches, it was less vulnerable to state repression than the NAACP, which was a political organization. The churches also provided meeting places, a stable base of support and a network of communications. Several of the SCLC leaders helped to develop the philosophy of peaceful confrontation, of non-violent, direct mass action which would be developed, taught and practised widely and successfully in the early 1960s.

? What qualities, according to King in Source E, would mass action need to demonstrate in order to be successful?

SOURCE E

Excerpt from an article by Martin Luther King Jr entitled 'The Social Organization of Non-Violence' in the magazine *Liberation*, October 1959, quoted in *The Eyes on the Prize Civil Rights Reader* edited by Clayborne Carson and others, published by Penguin, New York, USA, 1991, p. 12.

There is more power in socially organized masses on the march than there is in guns in the hands of a few desperate men. Our enemies would prefer to deal with a small armed group rather than with a huge, unarmed but resolute mass of people. However, it is necessary that the mass action method be persistent and unyielding. Gandhi said the Indian people must 'never let them rest,' referring to the British. He urged them to keep protesting daily and weekly, in a variety of ways. This method inspired and organized the Indian masses and disorganized and demobilized the British ... All history teaches us that like a turbulent ocean beating great cliffs into fragments of rock, the determined movement of people incessantly demanding their rights always disintegrates the old order.

However, in its first years, the SCLC achieved little. In Montgomery itself, schools and hospitals, restaurants and hotels remained segregated. After the boycott, there were further attacks on King's house and four black churches were bombed. The SCLC failed to enlist massive, grassroots support and, in 1960, its executive director, Ella Baker, complained that the organization was failing to 'develop and use our major weapon – mass resistance'. That was about to change.

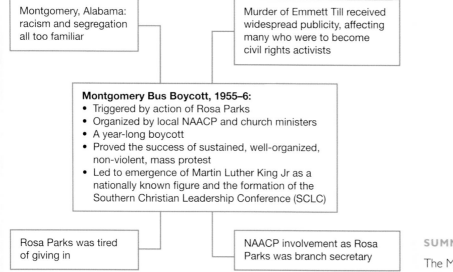

Montgomery, Alabama: racism and segregation all too familiar

Murder of Emmett Till received widespread publicity, affecting many who were to become civil rights activists

Montgomery Bus Boycott, 1955–6:
- Triggered by action of Rosa Parks
- Organized by local NAACP and church ministers
- A year-long boycott
- Proved the success of sustained, well-organized, non-violent, mass protest
- Led to emergence of Martin Luther King Jr as a nationally known figure and the formation of the Southern Christian Leadership Conference (SCLC)

Rosa Parks was tired of giving in

NAACP involvement as Rosa Parks was branch secretary

SUMMARY DIAGRAM

The Montgomery Bus Boycott 1955–6

② Sit-ins and Freedom Rides

▶ *Key question: What was the impact of sit-ins and Freedom Rides?*

On 1 February 1960, four smartly dressed black students walked into a Woolworth's store in Greensboro, North Carolina. They bought some stationery and then sat down at the whites-only lunch counter and asked to be served. They were refused. They sat there, reading the Bible and carrying on with their studies, until closing time. Next day, 29 students followed their example and, on the third day, all except two of the 65 seats were occupied.

The students were pushed, kicked and punched by young whites. They had tomato ketchup poured over them and cigarettes stubbed out on their bodies. But they did not retaliate and, when the police arrived, they were arrested for trespass or for disorderly conduct. They themselves were not disorderly but, on this and succeeding days, white mobs arrived to abuse them and caused a disturbance. News of the sit-ins spread fast, to other college campuses and to other cities. Soon similar sit-ins were taking place in the cities of several neighbouring southern states. By August 1960, 70,000 students, both black and white, had followed the example of the four original Greensboro students and about 3600 had been arrested. The Greensboro students provided the spark that launched a new wave of protest.

What impact do you think the photograph in Source F would have on the public?

SOURCE F

Sit-in students (black and white) sit quietly while white people pour food over their heads at a Woolworth's lunch counter in Jackson, Mississippi, in May 1963.

Why did the sit-ins take place in 1960?

The rise of the sit-ins

The actions of the first four students were not *completely* spontaneous. They had wanted to take some kind of direct action, to make an impact. They had felt the effects of racial discrimination all their lives. They had read about Gandhi's non-violent campaign against British rule in India and had heard Martin Luther King Jr's speeches. They knew of the Montgomery Bus Boycott and similar actions. And they were determined to take some form of non-violent, direct action in order to further the cause of civil rights. Theirs was not the first ever sit-in: such tactics had been tried before. However, it was *their* idea to do something in Woolworth's, in Greensboro, and it had the effect of reigniting the Civil Rights Movement. The students' example spread across the South. Soon there were wade-ins on white-only beaches, read-ins in white-only libraries and 'piss-ins' in white-only toilets.

A growing impatience

As the new decade started, the Civil Rights Movement had seemed to lose momentum. The *Brown* decision of 1954 (see page 30) had not led to widespread desegregation of schools in the South, nor of cafés and restaurants, hotels and cinemas, parks and swimming pools. Church organizations and the SCLC were continuing to hold rallies and to train people in the art of non-violent direct action, yet only modest changes had been achieved in the Jim Crow South (see page 19), where segregation was still intact.

Many educated young people from the black universities and colleges in the South were growing impatient, especially when they learned of fellow blacks in African countries gaining their independence. In 1957 Ghana had won its independence from Britain and, in 1960, twelve more African nations gained their independence from European powers. The student leader, John Lewis, said: 'We identified with the blacks in Africa. They were getting their freedom, and we still didn't have ours in what we believed was a free country.' The novelist James Baldwin wrote: 'at the rate things are going here, all of Africa will be free before we can get a lousy cup of coffee'. The US vice president at that time, Richard Nixon, had been invited to attend the independence celebrations in Ghana in 1957. When he asked a black guest what it was like to be free, he replied: 'I wouldn't know. I'm from Alabama.'

Another reason why the sit-ins started at this time was because there was a growing *national* movement. In the North, in Philadelphia, a young church minister, Leon Sullivan, formed a new organization to target retail stores that refused to employ blacks yet which relied on black customers. In the first few months of 1960, about a quarter of a million black Americans joined 'Don't Buy Where You Can't Work' boycotts. Martin Luther King Jr later invited Sullivan to speak at the SCLC conference. Furthermore, activists in the North and South sang the same protest songs and listened to similar music and read similar magazines.

Nashville, Tennessee

One of the other cities where students started sit-ins was Nashville, Tennessee. Here, a church minister, James Lawson, who was also a member of SCLC, had been holding workshops in civil disobedience for some time. A number of highly motivated Christian students there had even held sit-ins before 1960. Now, in February 1960, they targeted various stores in the city. Meanwhile, older black people began to boycott the main stores in a city where blacks spent $50 million annually. Although a boycott was a less confrontational form of action, it could have huge economic impact just as the boycott of Montgomery city buses had done. The students who sat in at the lunch counters in Nashville were arrested by the police only to be replaced by waves of more students who arrived to take their places.

The 'Rules of Conduct' produced by two of the students instructed: be friendly, be courteous; stay non-violent; sit straight and face the counter; don't retaliate or leave or laugh. They followed these rules and, even when they were spat at and punched, they did not hit back. When the police asked them to move, they remained still, so they were dragged out. The students adopted a policy of 'Jail, no **bail**'. As the prisons filled up, bail was reduced to $5 but the students still refused to pay, so many of them had to be released as there was not enough room for them. Black adults offered food, money and prayers to their new leaders. Three weeks later, the bus station finally served blacks at the lunch counter in Nashville and, in May, the city centre stores decided to desegregate their lunch counters. However, it was to be another four years before Nashville officially desegregated its hotels, cinemas and fast-food outlets.

Although the gains in Nashville may have been modest, they were replicated in many other southern cities. The disruption caused by the sit-ins and the economic effects of consumer boycotts hit southern businesses. Woolworth's profits fell drastically and, within a year, they desegregated the lunch counters in all of their stores across the South.

The response of the NAACP and the SCLC

At first, the NAACP was critical of the sit-ins, preferring to continue the more orderly route of taking legal action. The SCLC also feared that the students were being too confrontational. They hoped the students would come under the wing of their elders but they did not and they would not. Nevertheless, both the NAACP and SCLC offered support, in legal aid and training as well as finance, which the students accepted. Television, now widespread in American homes, played its part in publicizing the campaign. Journalists flocked to report the disturbances that took place in and outside stores across the South. Most Americans, especially whites, may not have approved of the sit-ins, but they could not help noticing the difference in behaviour between the students and their white attackers. Even the segregationist editor of a North Carolina newspaper contrasted the smart dress and peaceful, dignified behaviour of the students with the 'ragtail rabble, slack-jawed, black-jacketed, grinning fit to kill' white mobs who taunted them.

SOURCE G

For what reasons does the author of Source G see the sit-ins as 'a watershed in the history of black protest'? Compare this source with Source D on page 48. Which do you see as more significant: the Montgomery Bus Boycott or the sit-ins?

Excerpt from *Sweet Land of Liberty? – The African-American Struggle for Civil Rights in the Twentieth Century* by Robert Cook, published by Pearson, Harlow, UK, 1998, pp. 114–15. The author is professor of American history at the University of Sussex, UK.

The student demonstrations were a watershed in the history of black protest in the United States. In effect, they kick-started the civil rights movement into action by revealing the extent of grass-roots dissatisfaction with segregation and by providing the existing protest organisations with a mass constituency in the South.

The Student Nonviolent Coordinating Committee (SNCC)

Why was the SNCC set up?

One of the most significant results of the sit-ins was the formation of the **Student Nonviolent Coordinating Committee** (or **SNCC**, pronounced 'snick'). This originated in April 1960, just two months after the start of the Greensboro sit-in. It was the result of an initiative by Ella Baker. Baker was one of the few leading female figures in the SCLC and had been a civil rights activist since the 1920s. She joined the NAACP in 1940 and helped to set up new branches. Keen to mobilize ordinary blacks rather than rely on **litigation**, she left the NAACP in 1946. She campaigned against segregated schooling and police brutality in New York. She raised funds for the Montgomery Bus Boycott and became executive director of the SCLC.

Baker called on student leaders to attend a meeting in Raleigh, North Carolina, over the Easter weekend. Altogether, there were 126 students from 56 colleges from twelve southern states. Although most of those attending came from black colleges in the South, there were also some northerners, including whites. Baker challenged the students to find bigger targets, 'bigger than a hamburger or even a giant-sized Coke'. For instance, she encouraged them to take direct action against discrimination in voting, housing and jobs.

KEY TERM

Student Nonviolent Coordinating Committee (SNCC) The student-run organization formed after the 1960 sit-ins.

Litigation Taking a case to a court of law.

SOURCE H

Ella Baker (1903–86), one of the most active, long-serving civil rights campaigners speaking in Mississippi in 1964 after the murder of three civil rights workers there.

What impression do you get of Ella Baker from Source H?

Martin Luther King Jr, the SCLC leader, also spoke at the meeting, but Baker steered the students towards setting up a completely independent organization. In a dig at King, she advised them to adopt 'group-centered leadership' rather than a 'leader-centered group'. She said that 'strong people don't need strong leaders'. They did not need much prompting: they were idealistic, committed and determined to be independent of the SCLC. The majority were under 21 years of age and they were proud of what they had achieved. At the end of the meeting, the SNCC was formed. The SNCC was to remain highly democratic, with no obvious or dominant leader emerging. Also, it was far less male-dominated than the SCLC: many women were to play a leading role. One of them, Diane Nash, had been the leader of the Nashville sit-in movement.

The Nashville minister James Lawson, also a member of SCLC, urged the students to adopt non-violence as their main weapon. He also criticized the NAACP for their overreliance on the courts, as the historian Robert Cook writes in Source I.

SOURCE I

? Of what does Lawson, in Source I, accuse the NAACP?

Excerpt from *Sweet Land of Liberty? – The African-American Struggle for Civil Rights in the Twentieth Century* by Robert Cook, published by Pearson, Harlow, UK, 1998, p. 119.

Lawson also caused a minor furore [controversy] by criticising the NAACP for its preoccupation with 'fund-raising and court action rather than developing our greatest resource, a people no longer the victims of racial evil who can act in a disciplined manner to implement the constitution'. He was also reported to have attacked the Association's [NAACP's] magazine, The Crisis, *as an organ of the black bourgeoisie [affluent middle class].*

This was an early sign of the splits that were to bedevil the Civil Rights Movement. Nevertheless, the SNCC was committed to non-violent, grassroots, direct action and white members were welcomed. SNCC activists were to be the 'shock troops' of the movement.

SOURCE J

? Identify three or four ways in which, according to Source J, the formation of the SNCC was significant.

Excerpt from *Ain't Scared of Your Jails (1960–1961)* by Clayborne Carson, quoted in *The Eyes on the Prize Civil Rights Reader* edited by Clayborne Carson and others, published by Penguin, New York, USA, 1991, p. 108. Carson is an African-American professor of history at Stanford University, in California, and director of the Martin Luther King Jr Research and Education Institute.

The formation of SNCC … not only solidified student involvement in the movement but placed students in leadership roles … What emerged was a coordinating committee that operated independently of other established civil rights organizations and relied on strong local leadership. The formation of SNCC helped transform the student movement from one that emphasized small-scale protests to a sustained force that would challenge racism throughout American society.

Civil rights and the election of President Kennedy 1960

All the main civil rights groups agreed on the importance of the presidential election in November 1960. The two candidates, Richard Nixon for the

Republicans and John Kennedy for the Democrats, both supported civil rights reform, although neither made it a priority.

In his campaigning, John Kennedy said segregation was immoral and damaged America's international image. He sounded as if he would do far more for black civil rights than President Eisenhower had done. Then, in October 1960, when Martin Luther King Jr was sentenced to four months of hard prison labour for joining a sit-in in Atlanta, Kennedy called King's pregnant wife on the phone and expressed sympathy while his brother, Robert, phoned the judge and managed to secure King's release. The increase in black support which this earned him may well have made all the difference in the November election, which Kennedy won by the closest of margins. Certainly, black Americans had high hopes of the new, young president.

At first, Kennedy gave the impression he would be a great champion of civil rights. He maintained contact with several leaders of the Civil Rights Movement, especially King. He appointed more blacks to official positions than any previous president, including five black federal judges, one of whom was Thurgood Marshall. However, he also appointed some segregationists as judges in the South: one of them referred to black people in court as 'niggers' and 'chimpanzees'. Furthermore he had promised, before his election, to get rid of segregation in federal housing projects 'at the stroke of a pen', but it was only after two years and the receipt of thousands of pens from protesters that he passed what was a very diluted measure.

Kennedy realized that racial discrimination was a serious problem that would not go away and needed constant attention. But he treated it as an irritant rather than a major priority, and he delegated day-to-day responsibility for civil rights questions to his brother Robert, whom he appointed **attorney general**.

Freedom Rides 1961

In May 1961, thirteen volunteers, seven black and six white, set off on a bus journey from Washington DC to New Orleans. They planned to sit together, not in the separate black and white sections of the bus. When they stopped at bus terminals, they planned to ignore 'White' and 'Colored' signs in toilets, waiting rooms and restaurants. Blacks would go to 'White' toilets and vice versa.

The inspiration for these 'Freedom Rides' came from James Farmer, leader of the **Congress of Racial Equality (CORE)**. As a boy, Farmer had seen his father, a college professor, cruelly humiliated by whites. He vowed he would never allow himself to be treated in such a way. He was one of the founders of CORE in 1942 and he pioneered the sit-in technique during the Second World War. Now, in 1961, he decided to challenge segregation in **interstate transport**. This had been declared unconstitutional in a Supreme Court

KEY TERM

Attorney general Head of the Justice Department in the federal government.

Congress of Racial Equality (CORE) An interracial civil rights group founded by James Farmer and other students in Chicago in 1942.

Interstate transport Transport which crossed state boundaries and was therefore the responsibility of the federal government, specifically the Interstate Commerce Commission.

Why were the Freedom Rides launched in 1961?

ruling in 1946 and, again, in December 1960 but most southern states continued to enforce segregation. Now Farmer set out to test that ruling. His intention was to create crises at bus terminals in the South by provoking the extremists, which would in turn attract publicity and, he hoped, force the federal government to intervene and enforce the law. This was not civil disobedience, he said. The riders were not *disobeying* any law. They were claiming their legal right to sit together and to use desegregated facilities.

As the Freedom Riders' bus arrived in Anniston, Alabama, it was firebombed by a mob of 200. When the riders, fearful of being asphyxiated by the smoke, staggered out of the bus, they were beaten up. When a second bus arrived, the police stood by as thugs ordered the black riders to sit at the back. They refused. When two white riders attempted to intervene, they were beaten up. One of them, a retired professor, spent the rest of his life in a wheelchair because his injuries were so severe. When those who were not hospitalized travelled on to Birmingham, Alabama, the police told the local Ku Klux Klan leader that they would give his men fifteen minutes before they intervened. Police chief 'Bull' Connor said he was quite happy for the riders to look like 'a bulldog got hold of them' by the time his forces restored order. Alabama Governor Patterson was unsympathetic too: 'when you go looking for trouble, you usually find it'.

SOURCE K

? What impact do you think the image in Source K would have both in the South and other parts of the USA?

A mob firebombed this Freedom Ride bus in Anniston, Alabama, on 14 May 1961. This dramatic photograph attracted immediate publicity, both nationally and internationally.

The response of the federal government

For the new government of Democratic President John Kennedy, the Freedom Rides were, according to a presidential adviser, 'a pain in the ass'.

The president was about to meet the Soviet leader, Nikita Khrushchev, and the last thing he wanted was bad publicity about race relations in the USA. Besides, he depended on some very powerful southern Democratic senators to steer his legislation through Congress. If the federal government intervened, it could alienate southern Democratic opinion, particularly the senior Democratic senators who chaired important committees in Congress, and divide his party. He was reluctant to use federal troops but his brother, Robert, the attorney general, threatened to send in US marshals unless the local authorities agreed to provide protection for the riders.

Despite the beatings, the riders continued. They were now joined by SNCC volunteers, one of whom, Diane Nash, said, 'If they stop us with violence, the movement is dead. We're coming.' When they arrived in Montgomery, they were attacked by Klansmen. And it was not just the riders themselves who were beaten up. Reporters and photographers were also clubbed, with iron bars and bats as well as fists. When a large meeting, addressed by Martin Luther King Jr, was held in the Baptist church in Montgomery, the building was surrounded by an angry mob and stones and Molotov cocktails (homemade bombs) were thrown in. With a very real danger that those inside could be burned alive or, if they tried to escape, savaged by the mob, King phoned Robert Kennedy in Washington. Kennedy immediately ordered 400 US marshals to step in. They used tear gas to disperse the mob, the first show of federal force since Little Rock in 1957 (see page 35).

Robert Kennedy now asked for a 'cooling-off period' but Farmer replied: 'We've been cooling off for a hundred years. If we got any cooler we'd be in a deep freeze.' He was determined to carry on: he did not want the riders to be seen as having given in to white violence. Over 1000 more activists, mostly black but also whites, including clergy, professors and trade union members, defied segregation on the Freedom Buses and in the bus terminals. They filled the jails. It was not only in the South that there were demonstrations: in Chicago, 2500 blacks rode 46 buses to City Hall with banners demanding better housing and jobs.

Eventually, in November 1961, Robert Kennedy compelled the Interstate Commerce Commission to enforce desegregation on their buses and in their bus terminals. The old signs on the buses and in the toilets and waiting rooms (for example, 'Whites Only' and 'Colored Waiting Room') had to be replaced with new ones. Fifteen years after the Supreme Court first ruled, in 1946, that segregation on interstate transport was illegal, the federal government finally enforced the Court's decision. The Freedom Rides had forced the federal government to intervene and this led to the end of segregated public transport.

'The Battle of Ole Miss' 1962

Less than a year after the Freedom Rides, the Kennedy government was again forced to intervene in the South, this time with military force. In June 1962, a federal court ruled that black student James Meredith should be admitted to the University of Mississippi (known as 'Ole Miss'), which no black person had previously attended. Playing to white segregationists, the governor, Ross Barnett, obstructed repeated attempts by the federal government to secure Meredith's admission. By the time Meredith was finally escorted, under armed guard, into the university, on 30 September 1962, the campus had become a battleground. Three thousand whites, using rocks, lead pipes and smoke bombs, fought with 400 federal marshals throughout the night. Two people, a French journalist and a bystander, were killed before Kennedy ordered 13,000 troops to restore order.

Sit-ins, 1960	Freedom Rides, 1961
• Were non-violent protests by students in the South • Thousands were jailed but refused bail, thus filling the prisons • Reignited the Civil Rights Movement and led to formation of SNCC	• Launched by CORE to test Supreme Court ban on segregation in interstate transport • Blacks and whites, travelling together through the South, were met by violence • Kennedy government reluctant to intervene but was forced to because: the Rides were extended and violence continued, bringing adverse publicity • Federal government enforced desegregation on interstate transport Kennedy sent troops to restore order at the University of Mississippi, 1962

③ Project Confrontation: Birmingham 1963

▶ *Key question: To what extent was the campaign in Birmingham a turning point?*

Before the campaign in Birmingham, activists tried to challenge segregation in Albany, Georgia. It was a town in which the city authorities resisted any moves to desegregation.

The Albany Movement 1961–2

In the autumn of 1961, SNCC and local activists led a broad attack on racial discrimination and desegregation in Albany. Activists from the SNCC and the local branch of the NAACP decided to challenge segregation, not only in transport facilities but also in parks, hotels and restaurants. Students from the local college were enlisted and local adults formed the Albany Movement. In November 1961, hundreds were arrested for sit-ins at bus and rail stations and for entering white hotels and cinemas. But the city authorities stood firm and refused to implement any change. At this point the movement's leader invited Martin Luther King Jr, an old friend, and the SCLC to come to Albany. The campaign was reinvigorated by both the presence of King and the foot-stamping, hand-clapping protest meetings. Also, the campaign became famous for the singing of songs that became the hallmark of the Civil Rights Movement. One of those songs, 'We Shall Overcome', became the anthem of the movement and of many protest movements around the world.

SOURCE L

Excerpt from *Better Day Coming, Blacks and Equality, 1890–2000* by Adam Fairclough, published by Penguin, New York, USA, 2001, p. 268.

'We Shall Overcome' was easy to sing and had a majestic melody that endowed the verses with nobility. Sung slowly with swelling harmonies, it beautifully exemplified the idealism and optimism of the Civil Rights Movement … Freedom songs melded naturally with the tradition of church singing. They encouraged the active participation of ordinary people, and made the audience, rather than the speakers, the center of attention. They made the mass meetings in Albany some of the most enthusiastic and inspirational occasions of the entire Civil Rights Movement.

What, according to Source L, was the importance of singing in the Civil Rights Movement?

However, the police chief, Laurie Pritchett, outwitted the protesters throughout the campaign. He knew that violence, either by local whites or by his police, would attract media attention and that, in turn, might invite federal intervention, as it had with the Freedom Rides. So he trained his officers to be non-violent towards the demonstrators. He would play King at his own game. He also hired jails in other parts of the county so that there was no limit to the numbers arrested. At one time, over 700 were under arrest. This was the first time that such large numbers of adults went to jail. The president of the Albany Movement later said, 'These were common, ordinary, everyday people, housewives, cooks, maids, laborers, children out of school.' Although some of those arrested might have been subjected to rough treatment in jail, none was on the streets. Furthermore, when King led a march on City Hall and was himself arrested, Pritchett made sure he did not spend long in jail and thus attract publicity. Instead, he arranged for an 'anonymous' person to pay bail for King so that he had to be released.

There was *some* federal government pressure on the authorities to negotiate a settlement with the Albany Movement. They agreed to desegregation, King left town and the campaign petered out. Pritchett and the city authorities thus avoided the intense publicity which the Freedom Rides had attracted. However, for the Albany Movement, as well as for King and the SCLC, the campaign was largely a failure because the authorities refused to implement the changes they had agreed to and, even when the demonstrations started up again, they were unable to bring about an end to segregation in transport and other public places.

There were other reasons why, for the Civil Rights Movement as a whole, the Albany campaign was a setback. First, they had not planned their campaign thoroughly and their targets were dispersed. Maybe they would have had more chance of success if they had just focused on segregated transport. Second, there was much distrust and rivalry between the different civil rights groups. The NAACP leaders in Albany resented the SNCC presence and the SNCC workers disliked the SCLC's tendency to 'take over' and King's high profile. The SCLC had no base of local support in Albany and departed once an agreement had been made with the city authorities. Above all, the police response had ensured that there was no violence and thus little national attention even when the authorities refused to implement the agreement they had made. King and the SCLC, in particular, had learned many lessons. They did not make the same mistakes in Birmingham.

Why did King decide to launch a campaign in Birmingham?

Fred Shuttlesworth, Martin Luther King Jr and the campaign in Birmingham

At his inauguration as governor of Alabama in 1963, George Wallace vowed 'I say segregation now, segregation tomorrow, segregation forever!' He had come to power, determined 'never to be outniggured again' after having lost in a previous election contest to a rival with large Klan support. Martin Luther King Jr saw him as 'the most dangerous racist in America today'. Birmingham, the capital of Alabama, was the largest industrial city in the South and it was reputed to be 'the most segregated city in America'. It had a history of racial tension and police brutality, with a high rate of black unemployment and poor housing. With members of the Klan tormenting its black neighbourhoods, carrying out burnings, mutilations and bombings, it had become known as 'Bombingham' to its black citizens.

In 1956, after the state of Alabama had banned the NAACP, the black Baptist preacher Fred Shuttlesworth established the Alabama Christian Movement for Human Rights. He worked closely with the SCLC to challenge segregation on buses and in schools in Birmingham. In retaliation, the Klan burnt his home and his church, and the police infiltrated his organization and tapped his phones. When he enrolled his children at a white school near his home, a mob stabbed his wife and attacked him as police looked on. They survived the attack. In 1963, he pleaded with King to come to Birmingham.

The time was right: the recent campaign in Albany, Georgia, had fizzled out with no visible gain. King and the SCLC had not made a major breakthrough since the Montgomery Bus Boycott. The movement was losing momentum and the non-violent approach of the SCLC was losing ground, especially in the North, to more militant, **black nationalists**. Above all, the government had done little, despite all Kennedy's promises, to improve civil rights. The SCLC had a strong base in Birmingham, and a significant campaign, which would attract widespread media attention and boost support for civil rights, was needed to put pressure on President Kennedy.

 **KEY TERM**

Black nationalists Those who believed that black people should seek separation from, not integration with, whites. Many of them criticized the policy of non-violence.

Birmingham was a suitable target for a new campaign because of its history of segregation and racial violence, and the groundwork had already been laid by Shuttlesworth and his movement. The Klan was known to be large and guaranteed to resort to violence in the face of public demonstrations while the police chief, 'Bull' Connor, could be relied on to resort to physical force, as he had shown with the Freedom Riders (see page 56). The resulting violence and police brutality would attract widespread publicity and public outrage and force the federal government to intervene. If civil rights actions could be successful here, in one of the biggest and most segregated cities, then maybe Jim Crow laws throughout the South could be swept away.

Project Confrontation

King and his SCLC colleagues now devised a plan, 'Project C' (C for 'confrontation'). They used this codename because they feared their phones were tapped and their plan would be leaked. They aimed to desegregate businesses, such as the large retail stores, to force them to employ blacks and integrate their facilities for customers: blacks were not allowed to use the same toilets as whites or try on clothes before buying them. The plan was for a peaceful march, from the Baptist church to the city centre, to disrupt traffic and carry out a very public boycott of city centre stores in the busy few shopping days leading up to Easter.

The demonstrators were met by police with batons and dogs. This show of force attracted media attention, which in turn attracted more marchers, more police violence and more publicity. Many were arrested and then the state authorities secured a court injunction (a special court order) forbidding further protests. With money for bail running out and some black businesses calling for a retreat by the demonstrators, King came under intense pressure to obey the injunction and call off the campaign. If he carried on, he risked losing the support of key allies, especially in Washington, and the long-promised civil rights bill might be further delayed. Then on Good Friday, King announced that he had received an 'injunction from heaven' calling on him to disobey immoral, man-made laws and carry on leading the demonstrations until 'Pharaoh lets God's people go'. He saw it as his duty, as an American Christian, to obey a higher law, God's law, as the evil of segregation and racial injustice was so great. He marched to City Hall, was arrested with his deputy, Ralph Abernathy, and put in solitary confinement.

'Letter from Birmingham City Jail'

A group of white church ministers now placed a big advertisement in the *Birmingham News*, in which they criticized Project Confrontation, saying it was illegal and led by 'outside agitators'. Reading a copy of the paper in his jail cell, King scribbled his response in the margins. He explained his non-violent philosophy, saying he was not an outside agitator but a dutiful Christian fighting 'injustice'. He also warned that if peaceful demonstrators were dismissed as 'rabble rousers', millions would turn to black nationalism and a 'frightening racial nightmare' would ensue. The first source below is from the white clergymen and the second is from King's 'Letter from Birmingham City Jail'.

SOURCE M

? What are the criticisms which the clergymen make in Source M?

Excerpt from *Letter to Martin Luther King*, a statement by eight white Alabama clergymen, located at: http://teachingamericanhistory.org/library/document/letter-to-martin-luther-king/.

We are now confronted by a series of demonstrations by some of our Negro citizens, directed and led in part by outsiders. We recognize the natural impatience of people who feel that their hopes are slow in being realized. But we are convinced that these demonstrations are unwise and untimely ...

Such actions incite hatred and violence ...

We strongly urge our own Negro community to withdraw support from these demonstrations and to unite locally in working peacefully for a better Birmingham. When rights are consistently denied, a cause should be pressed in the courts and in negotiations with local leaders, and not in the streets.

SOURCE N

? How does King, in Source N, refute the criticisms made in Source M?

Excerpt from 'Letter from Birmingham City Jail', a reply to the letter in Source M, from the American Friends Service Committee, May 1963. The complete text can be found at: www.loveallpeople.org/birminghamjail.pdf.

I cannot sit idly by in Atlanta and not be concerned about what happens in Birmingham. Injustice anywhere is a threat to justice everywhere ...

For years now I have heard the word 'Wait!'. It rings in the ear of every Negro with piercing familiarity. This 'wait' has almost always meant 'never' ... We must come to see with the distinguished jurist of yesterday that 'justice too long delayed is justice denied'. We have waited for more than three hundred and forty years for our constitutional and God-given rights ...

I guess it is easy for those who have never felt the stinging darts of segregation to say wait. But when you have seen vicious mobs lynch your mothers and fathers at will and drown your sisters and brothers at whim; when you have seen hate filled policemen curse, kick, brutalize, and even kill your black brothers and sisters with impunity ... then you will understand why we find it difficult to wait.

You spoke of our activity in Birmingham as extreme. At first I was rather disappointed that fellow clergymen would see my nonviolent efforts as those of the extremist... Was not Jesus an extremist in love? 'Love your enemies, bless them that curse you, pray for them that despitefully use you.' ... Was not Abraham Lincoln an extremist – 'This nation cannot survive half slave and half free.'

The Children's Crusade

A week later, King was released on bail, but it seemed that the demonstrations might die out. There were not many more demonstrators willing to risk jail. Then an SCLC official had a novel idea: he called for a 'children's crusade', for school students to take the place of their elders. After all, it was their future. Besides, they had no jobs to lose – and they could take time off school!

In May, hundreds of school children gathered at the Baptist church. They watched an inspiring film about the sit-ins and then they set off, marching, singing and praying. They were arrested and carted off to jail. Impressed by their bravery and shocked by the behaviour of the police, many more adults joined the demonstrations. Television reporters came from all over the country. With demonstrations continuing, police chief 'Bull' Connor now resorted to the use of high-pressure fire hoses, which knocked people over and threw them against walls. Pictures of this action and of police using German Shepherd dogs against teenagers appeared on television stations all over the USA and in newspapers around the world. Millions were sickened.

> **What was the effect of the Children's Crusade?**

SOURCE O

Police dogs being used to attack peaceful demonstrators in Birmingham, Alabama, 1963.

> What is the value, as historical evidence, of the photograph in Source O?

With thousands jailed, sometimes 60 to a cell, and America's image at home and abroad severely damaged, the federal government was forced to act. Senior federal officials were sent to initiate talks between King and Birmingham businessmen. The latter were losing business because of the boycott and disorder and, under huge pressure from Washington, they gave in and agreed to desegregate stores, cinemas, restaurants and other privately owned places. King proclaimed a 'magnificent victory for justice'.

Meanwhile, white extremists threw bombs into the house of King's brother and the hotel where King himself was staying. The resulting black rage led to attacks on white businesses and the police, and President Kennedy prepared to send in federal troops before King was able to pacify the angry blacks with his call for non-violence. Most importantly, the mayor and city council agreed to desegregate schools.

The impact of the Birmingham campaign

In the summer of 1963 there were sit-ins and demonstrations, partly inspired by Birmingham's example, in many cities and small towns in the South. In the next few months, 50 cities in the South agreed to desegregation in order to avoid the chaos and disorder of Birmingham. Across the USA as a whole, 100,000 demonstrated in the summer of 1963, against segregation, job discrimination and police brutality. Some of the biggest demonstrations were in northern cities like Detroit and Philadelphia. When the attorney general, Robert Kennedy, hosted a meeting of black writers and other intellectuals, he was met by a storm of criticism for not doing enough. The writer James Baldwin warned of *The Fire Next Time* (the title of his book) if there was not 'total liberation' soon. King warned President Kennedy that black Americans were at 'breaking point'.

King and the other SCLC leaders had assessed correctly how Connor would react to the Birmingham campaign and how the media would depict his reactions. As one SCLC member said: 'There never was any more skillful manipulation of the news media than there was in Birmingham.' There was an upsurge in support for civil rights and donations poured into the SCLC. An opinion poll in 1963 found that 42 per cent of Americans thought race was the most pressing American problem whereas only four per cent had thought so a year earlier. For many Americans, both black and white, Birmingham and the subsequent demonstrations and disturbances were a major turning point in the campaign for civil rights.

Kennedy's response

With demonstrations being held in many cities across the North and West, as well as the South, and public opinion increasingly calling for federal intervention, Kennedy faced mounting pressure. This pressure not only originated within the USA. The secretary of state (foreign minister), Dean Rusk, said that white supremacy was 'the biggest single burden that we carry on our backs in foreign relations'.

The prime minister of Uganda, supported by several black African leaders, sent an open letter to Kennedy in which he condemned the attacks on 'our own kith and kin'.

For the historian Manning Marable there was an additional reason why Kennedy finally came out in support of a major civil rights bill.

SOURCE P

Excerpt from *Race, Reform and Rebellion* by Manning Marable, published by University Press of Mississippi, USA, 1991, p. 73. Marable was professor of American history at Columbia University, New York, USA.

Kennedy was not unmoved by the carnage and the ordeal of blacks, but the racial crisis alone would not have prompted him to act. Many corporate [business] leaders, always looking at the social costs of doing business in the South, had concluded that desegregation was inevitable; that the federal government's appropriate role was to ensure the civil order that was essential to business expansion. For both moralistic and economic reasons, then, big business had come to accept the death of Jim Crow, and a number of corporate and financial leaders urged the administration to do the same.

> Explain, in your own words, what the author of Source P sees as the main reason for Kennedy's 'conversion'? What do *you* think?

On 11 June 1963, Kennedy went on television and said that civil rights was 'a moral issue' and admitted: 'It is time to act'. A few days later, he sent a civil rights bill to Congress. It guaranteed equal access to public buildings, schools and jobs. It threatened a loss of federal funds for state and local agencies which continued to practise segregation and discrimination. He had finally committed himself to the cause of civil rights and broken with southern Democrats.

SOURCE Q

Excerpt from Kennedy's *Report to the American People on Civil Rights*, 11 June 1963, quoted on the website of the John F. Kennedy Presidential Library and Museum, located at: www.jfklibrary.org/Asset-Viewer/ LH8F_0Mzv0e6Ro1yEm74Ng.aspx

We preach freedom around the world, and we mean it. And we cherish our freedom here at home. But are we to say to the world – and much more importantly to each other – that this is the land of the free, except for Negroes; that we have no second-class citizens, except Negroes; that we have no caste or class system, no ghettos, no master race, except with regard to Negroes.

> How convincingly do the words of Source Q show Kennedy had been converted to the cause of support of civil rights?

The writer and journalist Todd Purdum said that, with his speech, 'Kennedy had done what no other American president, not even Abraham Lincoln, had ever done: he had committed his country to assuring full equality for black Americans in the eyes of the law, and had declared that doing so was a moral imperative.'

Albany Movement, 1961–2

Seen as a setback for the Civil Rights Movement, especially for King's SCLC

Birmingham campaign, 1963:
- King launched SCLC campaign to desegregate white-owned stores
- Peaceful marches met by police violence and received nationwide publicity
- King's defied a court order ('Letter from Birmingham City Jail') and marches continued
- Children's Crusade led to increased police violence and media attention
- Increasing support for civil rights led to Kennedy's promise of a civil rights bill

 ## The March on Washington, August 1963

> ▶ *Key question: How successful was the March on Washington in 1963?*

Civil rights leaders knew the pressure on the federal government would have to be maintained if Congress was to pass Kennedy's bill. One of these leaders was A. Philip Randolph, who had planned a 'March on Washington' as far back as 1941 (see page 26). Martin Luther King Jr and other civil rights leaders now approached Randolph with the aim of organizing such a march in order to show mass support for, and put pressure on Congress to pass, the civil rights bill.

SOURCE R

Excerpt from an article in the *New York Times* by historian David Garrow on 15 August 2013.

'We are on the threshold of a significant breakthrough, and the greatest weapon is the mass demonstration,' King told his close friend Levison in a telephone call wiretapped by the F.B.I. Because of Birmingham, King went on, 'we are at the point where we can mobilize all of this righteous indignation into a powerful mass movement'.

The year 1963 would be the centenary of Lincoln's Emancipation Proclamation, and a march that ended with speeches from the steps of the Lincoln Memorial in Washington would be highly symbolic. Roy Wilkins of the NAACP was initially not keen, fearing that such a demonstration might not persuade Congress. John Lewis, who had participated in sit-ins and Freedom Rides, and was now leader of the SNCC, would have preferred mass sit-ins in Washington. However, a compromise agreement was reached, to which *all* the main civil rights leaders subscribed, for a national protest. Two of the main demands would be for jobs and freedom (and the formal

? What do the words from King, quoted in Source R, tell you about the means which King adopted to pursue the goal of civil rights?

name of the demonstration was to be 'The March on Washington for Jobs and Freedom') but passing the civil rights bill was to be the priority. The veteran civil rights leader, 74-year-old Randolph, would be the director and SCLC's Bayard Rustin the key organizer.

Organizing the march

At first Kennedy, like most Americans, was opposed to the march: there was already much opposition to his bill in Congress and Kennedy felt his opponents might dig their heels in and attract more support if subjected to force. However, when he realized that all the key civil rights leaders were determined to go ahead, Kennedy decided to stamp his mark on the march. He told his advisers: 'If we can't stop it, we'll run the damn thing'. He would make sure it increased support for *his* civil rights bill. The following agreements were made with the organizers:

- The date would be set for a Wednesday, not a weekend.
- The organizers would try to attract as many whites as possible, including church and trade union leaders.
- Demonstrators would be encouraged to dress conservatively.
- They would arrive by train and bus in the morning and depart the same day.
- Detailed programmes would outline the day's events, where to go and so on.
- The 'march' would consist of a short walk with speeches at the end.

It was even said that government officials planned to play 'He's Got the Whole World in His Arms', a popular gospel song, through the loudspeakers, if any speech became too inflammatory. In effect, the government converted the demonstration from a protest against federal inaction into a rally in favour of its own civil rights bill. John Lewis, the SNCC leader, complained that the march was becoming a 'march *in*, not *on* Washington'.

Bayard Rustin was an organizing genius. He had helped to organize the Montgomery Bus Boycott and later to set up the SCLC. He and a team of organizers now spent weeks planning the march. Hundreds of volunteers were recruited to act as marshals and it was agreed with the authorities that white police would be stationed round the edges to deter any white extremists. Hundreds of drinking fountains, toilets and first aid stations would be set up (Washington in August is very hot and humid). A New York church agreed to send 80,000 cheese sandwiches.

The march was to be the first time that America (and the world) had seen such a massive black protest, so it had to be well organized. Congress was worried that there might be too many black protesters in one place, Rustin was worried that there might be too few (less than 100,000) and Robert Kennedy felt that a low turnout would not be good for the president as it was *his* civil rights bill that needed support. Rustin and King brought in

> **Who were and what was involved in organizing the march?**

Protestant ministers, Catholic priests and Jewish rabbis who would be at the front of the march, as well as musicians to entertain the crowds before the speeches. The churches organized 'freedom' buses and trains: 2000 buses and 30 special trains. Police leave was cancelled, federal troops were to be on standby and liquor stores closed.

The march, 28 August 1963: 'I have a dream'

In the event, the march passed off peacefully. A quarter of a million arrived: from northern cities like Chicago, Detroit and New York as well as from Birmingham and other cities in the South. Most were middle class and black, but a quarter were white and there were clergy of all faiths. It was the biggest demonstration in US history. There was two hours of live music, mostly freedom songs (many of which were now popular among all classes and colours) sung by folk singers like Bob Dylan and Joan Baez. Placards, all approved by the organizers, demanded 'Jobs for All', 'End Segregation' and 'Voting Rights Now'.

All the main civil rights leaders spoke. When John Lewis's speech was leaked the day before, there was enormous pressure on him to tone it down. The speech was critical of the civil rights bill as 'too little, too late' and it spoke of marching through the South, burning down Jim Crow and 'leaving a scorched earth.' It was only when Randolph, the elder statesman of the movement, interceded with him that he agreed to delete the more inflammatory statements. Thus, the veneer of unity was preserved. Although no women spoke, Randolph introduced the heroines of the movement, including Rosa Parks, Daisy Bates and Diane Nash. Last to speak was Martin Luther King Jr. He evoked the memory of Lincoln and the promises of freedom and equality which were enshrined in the Declaration of Independence. And he delivered the famous 'I have a dream' sequences, conveying his vision of a colour-blind America:

SOURCE S

? Why do you think these sentences, quoted in Source S, are so effective?

Excerpt from Martin Luther King Jr's speech of 28 August 1963 given at the Lincoln Memorial in Washington, DC. For the complete text and an audio version of the speech see: www.americanrhetoric.com/speeches/mlkihaveadream.htm.

I have a dream that one day … the sons of former slaves and the sons of former slave owners will be able to sit down together at a table of brotherhood.

I have a dream that one day even the state of Mississippi … will be transformed into an oasis of freedom and justice.

I have a dream that my four children will one day live in a nation where they will not be judged by the color of their skin but by the content of their character.

King brought to his speech all the passion, charisma and electrifying oratory that were his hallmark. It was inspiring, spine-tingling, uplifting. At the end, there was a stunned silence – and then cheering and weeping.

The result of the march

Most historians have seen the march as a resounding success. It was peaceful and it was celebratory. It was broadcast live for three hours on US television and was widely covered in many other countries. Many Americans saw (some for the first time) blacks and whites united, marching together in support of a cause that they might not have understood, and they saw that it was not threatening. That evening, the television networks all focused on King's speech in their news programmes and, from that point onwards, the American public saw King as *the* leader of the Civil Rights Movement. However, this was not the case. As Ella Baker, a one-time colleague of King, complained, 'The movement made King, he didn't make the movement.' The SCLC was only involved in a few campaigns. Local leaders did not need him. Some SNCC members mocked him as 'De Lawd'. Furthermore, many black militants were critical. The black nationalist Malcolm X (see page 99) described the march as the 'Farce in Washington … subsidized by white liberals and stage-managed by President Kennedy'.

> **What was the impact of the march?**

SOURCE T

Excerpt from *The Autobiography of Malcolm X*, published by Penguin, London, UK, 1968, p. 388. This book was published shortly after the death of Malcolm X and was jointly written with Alex Haley. Here Malcolm X comments on the March on Washington.

In a subsequent press poll, not one Congressman or senator with a previous record of opposition to civil rights said he had changed his views. What did anyone expect? How was a one-day 'integrated' picnic going to counter-influence these representatives of prejudice rooted deep in the psyche of the American white man for four hundred years?

The very fact that millions, black and white, believed in this monumental farce is another example of how much this country goes in for the surface glossing over, the escape ruse, surfaces, instead of truly dealing with its deep-rooted problems.

What that March on Washington did was lull Negroes for a while.

> In what ways and why is Malcolm X, in Source T, so critical of the March on Washington?

SOURCE U

Excerpt from *The Struggle for Black Equality, 1954–1992* by Harvard Sitkoff, published by Hill & Wang, New York, USA, 1993, p. 152. Sitkoff is professor of history at the University of New Hampshire, USA.

King's dream had buoyed the spirit of African-Americans and touched the hearts of whites … King's eloquence and vision offset the ugly images of black violence that the demonstrations had started to evoke, replacing them with an inspiring picture of the movement at its benevolent best. To the extent that any single public utterance could, [King's] speech made the black revolt acceptable to white America.

> How do you account for the different conclusions which the authors of Source T and Source U arrive at?

As Malcolm X suggests, the march did not lead to a swift passing of the civil rights bill. Many in Congress were unmoved, while southern Democrats

'And remember nothing can be accomplished by taking to the streets', an editorial cartoon by Herb Block, published in the *Washington Post*, 6 September 1963.

? What did the cartoonist mean by the word 'restricted' in Source V?

were disappointed that Kennedy had supported the march. The bill became bogged down in Congress. In the South, segregationists remained as entrenched as ever. Less than three weeks after the march, a bomb was thrown into a church in Birmingham. It killed four young black girls at Sunday school. Millions were shocked and sickened by it. Angry blacks rioted in Birmingham, attacking white shops and the police. The FBI launched a huge investigation, but it was not until 1977 that anyone was convicted.

However, an even greater shock was the assassination of President Kennedy in November. His successor, Lyndon Johnson (LBJ), appealed to Congress to pass the bill as a tribute to the memory of Kennedy and he used all his years of experience as a senator to steer the civil rights bill through Congress. It was eventually passed in July 1964. Exactly how he managed this and what the Act achieved is explained in the next chapter.

March on Washington, August 1963
• To win public support and maintain pressure on Congress to pass civil rights reform • Led by Randolph and organized by Rustin • All the main civil rights leaders spoke, culminating in King's 'I have a dream' speech • Live TV coverage of march by 250,000, both black and white

No immediate increase in Congressional support	Four girls killed in bomb at church in September	Civil Rights Act still stuck in Congress when Kennedy assassinated, November 1963

SUMMARY DIAGRAM

The March on Washington, August 1963

Chapter summary

Protests and action: from Montgomery to the Civil Rights Act

The Montgomery Bus Boycott of 1955–6 showed how successful an organized, sustained, non-violent, mass protest could be. It also led to the emergence of Martin Luther King Jr and of the SCLC. After a lull in the late 1950s, the Civil Rights Movement was re-energized by the student sit-ins of 1960 and the Freedom Rides in 1961. After Albany, which some saw as a failure, the SCLC campaign in Birmingham in 1963 led to a huge increase in public support and to Kennedy's commitment to civil rights reform.

The March on Washington and King's 'I have a dream' speech further bolstered public, if not Congressional, support. The Civil Rights Act was eventually passed in July 1964, eight months after Kennedy's assassination.

✅ Examination advice

Remember that questions for Prescribed subject 4 will be numbered 13, 14, 15 and 16 in the Paper 1 exam.

Paper 1 Question 14: value and limitations based on origin, purpose and content

Question 14 on the IB History Diploma examination requires to you to discuss the origin, purpose and content of one source and then to use that information to determine its potential value and limitations. The question always asks you to refer to the origin, purpose and the content provided to assess the source's value and limitations for historians. Some knowledge of the topic, the value of types of sources, or of historians can be useful, although this is not required.

Question 14 is worth 4 marks out of the 24 total for Paper 1. This means it is worth seventeen per cent of your overall mark. Answering Question 14 should take approximately ten minutes of your examination time.

How to answer

Read Question 14 carefully. You will notice that it is asking you to analyse the value and limitations of a source for historians studying a particular event or action in history. These are to be determined by referencing the origin, purpose and content of the source. You should address Question 14 in a paragraph.

Structure will help you in answering the question. Incorporate the words origin, purpose, content, value and limitation into your answer:

- 'The origin of this source is …'
- 'the purpose of this source is …'
- 'the value of this source is …'
- 'the content of this source indicates …'
- and 'a limitation of this source may be …'.

This keeps you focused on the task, making sure you cover all the required elements, but also helps the examiner to understand your answers by providing a framework that he or she can follow.

It is important to remember that you are to use the origins, purpose and content to determine the value and limitations of the named source for historians studying a particular topic.

Origin

The origin of a source is the author, the type of publication, the year it was published and, sometimes, the country it originates from. If there is biographical information included as part of the source's introduction, this may also be used in addressing the source's origin. If only the author is stated, then the origin is that author or authors.

Purpose

The purpose of a source is usually indicated by the source's title, the type of source, the writer or speaker, if it is a speech, or the location of the source, such as in a newspaper, an academic book or a journal. Purposes can range from speeches that try to convince certain groups or nations that what the speaker is saying is the truth or should be heeded, to explaining the history of a certain period. If a book's title is *The History of the Civil Rights Movement*, the purpose of this particular source is likely to provide a sweeping overview of the Civil Rights Movement. If you are making a hypothesis regarding the purpose, use words such as 'perhaps', 'likely' or 'possibly' instead of stating your theory as a fact. The content of the source may help to determine the purpose.

Content

The content of a source, especially if the source is a speech, a cartoon or an official document of some sort, may help to determine the purpose as well as any value or limitation. A public speech by Martin Luther King Jr could potentially include important details for a historian studying the Southern Christian Leadership Conference (SCLC) in the 1950s.

The content of larger works by historians may be more difficult to use to determine the source's value and limitations. Historians tend to discuss historical events, emphasizing various pieces of evidence while ignoring or explaining away other details. Use the content to help explain the value and limitations of the source for historians, but do so with care. Use words like 'possibly' and 'perhaps' if you are not completely sure about your hypothesis.

Value

The value of a source flows naturally from the origins, purpose and content. For instance, imagine there is a book called *Memories of the Boycott* that was written by a participant in the Montgomery Bus Boycott. The value will be that the author probably witnessed or participated in certain important events during the long boycott. He or she may have been one of the organizers. This individual would have met and spoken with other participants, including those who made important decisions. This would give the author first hand knowledge regarding the organization and running of the 1955–6 protest.

If the author wrote about the boycott 50 years later, it could be that this individual had access to records from that period. This would mean that the author may have a less emotional and more objective view of the racial tension in Alabama in the 1950s and therefore be better able to determine the long-term effect of decisions and actions of the period.

Your answer will have to be determined by the origin, purpose and content of the source you are asked to discuss. Do not state that primary sources have more value than secondary sources; this is not necessarily true.

Limitations

The limitation of a source is determined in much the same way you determined the source's value. If the writer of *Memories of the Boycott* was an active participant in the boycott, his or her views may reflect only one side of the event. The author may not have known of the broader context of the boycott, regionally and nationally, which could possibly affect the accuracy of what he or she wrote. Here one could use the word 'possibly' because the limitations may only be theoretical unless other information is present to clarify the point of view of the author.

There are other ways to determine possible limitations of a source:

- The title of the source may be of a limited nature or too broad for the topic.
- The date of publication, if given, may be limiting if it is too close to or far from the historical events.
- A source that is political in nature may be trying to advocate a certain view or policy instead of being objective.
- The content of the source may clearly indicate bias, such as advocating a specific view while possibly attacking another potential view of the historical event or individual.

Do not state that sources are limited because they are secondary sources; this may not always be true.

Visual images

Visual sources will have information explaining their origin; the content of a photograph is critically important as well. Remember that photographs can capture a single moment in time so that they can show exactly what happened, but they can also be used to send a particular message.
A photograph of black protesters being set on by police dogs may have been a rare event rather than standard police procedure. Cartoons, posters and even photographs often have a political message. The purpose of any of these could potentially be to convince the viewer of a certain point of view. Another purpose could be to make fun of a particular idea or person for some other reason. Further information on visual sources can be found on page 111.

Example

This question uses Source E (see page 48).

> With reference to its origin, purpose and content, analyse the value and limitations of Source E for historians studying non-violence in the Civil Rights Movement. (4 marks)

You will immediately turn to Source E and read that it is an excerpt from an article written by Martin Luther King Jr. There is no need to brainstorm or outline for this question, so get started.

The <u>value</u> of Source E for historians studying non-violence is that it is an account written by Martin Luther King Jr, a man personally involved in the non-violent struggle against an oppressive system, as indicated by the stated <u>origin</u> and <u>purpose</u>. As such, he would have potentially witnessed and/or participated in events regarding the social organization of the masses. The <u>content</u> of the source clearly indicates that Dr King had analysed the power of non-violence practised in India by Gandhi and how the British were unable to resist the persistence of the Indian masses. King thought this strategy would work in the United States as well.

A <u>limitation</u> of Source E for historians is that the <u>origin</u> of the extract is from the magazine Liberation, a possibly non-objective source. The <u>purpose</u> of King's article is to promote non-violence so he is unlikely to hold counterviews. The <u>content</u> supports this because King contends that concerted efforts against oppression will 'always' result in success. The <u>content</u> also suggests that the Indian non-violent and unyielding struggle for freedom against the British was a good guide for the United States even if the two situations might be very different.

> The terms origin, purpose, content, value and limitation are used throughout.

> There are two values and they are connected to the origin, purpose or content.

> There are two limitations and they refer to the origin, purpose or content.

> Use of words such as 'possibly' and 'potentially' indicates where hypotheses are being stated.

> Question 14 is worth 4 marks. The answer indicates that both values and limitations have been addressed using the origin, purpose and content of the source. There are at least two values and two limitations discussed with reference to the usefulness of the sources for historians studying non-violence in the Civil Rights Movement. Mark: 4/4.

Examination practice

The following are exam-style questions for you to practise, using sources from this chapter. Sources can be found on the following pages:

Source A: page 44   Source Q: page 65
Source J: page 54   Source U: page 69
Source M: page 62

1 With reference to its origin, purpose and content, assess the value and limitations of Source A for historians studying the Montgomery Bus Boycott.

2 With reference to its origin, purpose and content, assess the value and limitations of Source J for historians studying importance of the Student Nonviolent Coordinating Committee (SNCC).

3 With reference to its origin, purpose and content, assess the value and limitations of Source M for historians studying white reactions to Project Confrontation.

4 With reference to its origin, purpose and content, assess the value and limitations of Source Q for historians studying President Kennedy's civil rights legacy.

5 With reference to its origin, purpose and content, assess the value and limitations of Source U for historians studying the impact of the March on Washington on altering long-held views of race relations in the USA.

Activities

1 In groups, using Sources B (page 45), C (page 47), D (page 48), L (page 59), N (page 62), P (page 65), S (page 68) and T (page 69), create Paper 1-type questions. Try to create at least two different questions per source. Exchange your questions with other groups and take eight minutes to answer one of the questions from another group. Once questions have been answered, review the answers and assign marks. Be sure to indicate what was successful and appropriate and what might be improved.

2 There are thousands upon thousands of sources that cover this important period in US history. Try to come up with several primary and secondary sources on your own that deal with the SCLC, sit-ins, Freedom Rides, Ella Baker, 'The Battle of Ole Miss', 'Project C', the March on Washington and Malcolm X. You can search for good sources on the Library of Congress website (www.loc.gov), as well as in your school library. You can create your own questions along the lines of Questions 13a, 13b and 14. These can be shared with your classmates.

3 Create an illustrated timeline of the events covered in this chapter or focus on one particular topic. How do the photographs or illustrations you chose try to influence those who view them?

CHAPTER 3

The achievements of the Civil Rights Movement

This chapter assesses the passing and the impact of the Civil Rights Act and Voting Rights Act and examines the importance of the Selma campaign in the passing of the latter. It explores the nature and success of the SNCC's campaign in Mississippi, particularly the Freedom Summer of 1964. It then evaluates the career of Malcolm X. Finally, the importance of Martin Luther King Jr in the Civil Rights Movement is debated. You need to consider the following questions throughout this chapter:

★ How successful was the Civil Rights Act 1964?

★ What was the significance of the SNCC's campaign in Mississippi and what was achieved?

★ Why did Martin Luther King Jr go to Selma in 1965 and what was achieved?

★ What was the impact of Malcolm X on the Civil Rights Movement?

★ How important was Martin Luther King Jr in the Civil Rights Movement?

 # The passing of the Civil Rights Act 1964

▶ *Key question: How successful was the Civil Rights Act 1964?*

Lyndon Baines Johnson (see page 70) was determined to push through Kennedy's civil rights legislation. He had his own vision of the **Great Society** and of 'an end to poverty and racial injustice'. Furthermore, as a southerner, he was determined to prove his liberal credentials. He had started his working life teaching poor Mexican-Americans and he saw the damage that poverty, prejudice and poor schooling could do.

President Johnson's role in passing the Act

Johnson had even more direct experience of the impact of segregation when he was vice president. When his black cook, Zephyr Wright, and her husband were driving the vice president's official car from Washington DC to his home state of Texas, they could not use the toilets in a petrol station. Instead, as Johnson later recounted, 'they would … pull off on a side road, and Zephyr Wright, the cook of the vice president of the United States, would squat in the road to pee.' There were other reasons too:

 **KEY TERM**

Great Society Johnson's plan to decrease poverty and inequality in the USA.

? How, according to Johnson in Source A, would civil rights reform benefit the South?

SOURCE A

Excerpt from *Lyndon B. Johnson, Portrait of a President* by Robert Dallek, published by Penguin, London, UK, 2005, p. 164. Dallek is professor of history at Boston University, USA.

At the same time, Johnson saw civil rights reform as essential to the well-being of his native region. He had known for a long time that segregation not only separated blacks and whites in the South but also separated the South from the rest of the nation, making it a kind of moral, political and economic outsider … An end to southern segregation would mean the full integration of the South into the Union, bringing with it economic progress and political influence comparable to that of other regions.

Johnson knew that an end to racial tension would attract business investment and that desegregation would bring economic improvement to the South. He had supported the Supreme Court ruling in the *Brown* case in 1954 (see page 30) and was one of the few southern politicians who had not signed the Southern Manifesto (see page 32). Even if it meant alienating southern Democrats, he was determined to exploit the grief following Kennedy's assassination and, as a tribute, to pass his civil rights bill. Years later, Johnson said: 'history books taught me that martyrs have to die for causes. John Kennedy had died. But his "cause" was not really clear. That was my job. I had to take the dead man's program and turn it into a martyr's cause.'

Kennedy's civil rights bill stalled in Congress. Johnson now infused it with a sense of urgency and purpose, zeal and decisiveness. A highly experienced politician (he had been the senator of Texas for fifteen years), Johnson was skilled at negotiation and persuasion. Many politicians were subjected to what journalists called the 'Johnson Treatment': he moved in close, with a grip of the hand or the shoulder, a hand on the knee or a nudge in the ribs. He flattered, he twisted arms and made deals: he promised federal help, to an Arizona senator, for a water project in his desert state and offered emergency aid to one of the Alaska senators after an earthquake. Both of these senators were Republicans.

Republican support

Johnson knew that he would need Republican Party support in Congress because many southern Democrats would vote against the bill. In fact, eighteen southern Democratic senators took it in turns to make prolonged speeches, hoping to talk the bill to death. Meanwhile, outside Congress there was increased public support for civil rights and a wide cross-section of religious leaders – Protestant ministers, Catholic priests and nuns, rabbis – lobbied Congress.

Johnson saw Everett Dirksen, the Republican leader in the Senate, as the key. He told Democrat senator Hubert Humphrey, 'You've got to let him [Dirksen] have a piece of the action', to convince him that he, Dirksen, could persuade fellow Republicans to pass the bill and go down in history as a great statesman. Johnson knew that there would be opposition, maybe major resistance, in the South, so he was keen 'to make this an American bill and not just a Democratic bill.' Johnson's Democratic allies in the Senate accepted some of Dirksen's changes to the bill as long as they did not significantly weaken it. Dirksen loved being in the limelight and the sound of his own voice. He had the last word before the Senate voted, referring to the reform as 'an idea whose time has come'.

Eventually, on 2 July 1964, just over a year after Kennedy sent his bill to Congress, the Civil Rights Act was passed. All except one of the southern Democrat senators voted against the bill. (In the House of Representatives, 110 out of 400 had voted against the bill.) The vast majority of northern senators, both Republican and Democrat, voted in favour. Johnson said to one of his advisers, 'I think we delivered the South to the Republican Party for your lifetime and mine.'

SOURCE B

The Johnson Treatment: Lyndon Johnson (right) lobbies Republican Leader in the Senate, Everett Dirksen (left).

What does the photograph in Source B tell you of Johnson's methods of persuasion?

The Civil Rights Act 1964

SOURCE C

Excerpt from the Civil Rights Act 1964 quoted in *From Slavery to Freedom* by John Hope Franklin and Alfred A. Moss Jr, published by McGraw-Hill, New York, USA, 1994, p. 624.

(a) All persons shall be entitled to the full and equal enjoyment of the goods, services, facilities, and privileges, advantages, and accommodations of any place of public accommodation, as defined in this section, without discrimination or segregation on the ground of race, color, religion, or national origin.

(b) Each of the following establishments which serves the public is a place of public accommodation within the meaning of this title:

(1) any inn, hotel, motel, or other establishment which provides lodging to transient guests, other than an establishment located within a building which contains not more than five rooms for rent or hire and which is actually occupied by the proprietor of such establishment as his residence;

(2) any restaurant, cafeteria, lunchroom, lunch counter, soda fountain, or other facility principally engaged in selling food for consumption on the premises, including, but not limited to, any such facility located on the premises of any retail establishment; or any gasoline station;

(3) any motion picture house, theater, concert hall, sports arena, stadium or other place of exhibition or entertainment … .

?
Why do you think so many places of 'public accommodation' are listed specifically in the extract from the Act in Source C?

The Civil Rights Act virtually wiped out Jim Crow laws at once. Businesses which employed more than 100 people were forbidden from practising racial discrimination and, within three years, the same provisions would apply to smaller businesses as well. It established an Equal Employment Opportunity Commission to act as a permanent watchdog agency and investigate claims of racial discrimination. The Supreme Court moved quickly to uphold the Act to pre-empt challenges to its constitutionality.

However, Johnson recognized that legislation alone could not ensure equality:

SOURCE D

Excerpt from Johnson's commencement address at Howard University 'To Fulfill These Rights', 4 June 1965, located at: www.lbjlibrary.org/.

Freedom is not enough. You do not wipe away the scars of centuries by saying: Now you are free to go where you want, and do as you desire, and choose the leaders you please.

You do not take a person who, for years, has been hobbled by chains and liberate him, bring him up to the starting line of a race and then say, 'you are free to compete with all the others,' and still justly believe that you have been completely fair.

?
Explain why Johnson believes, in Source D, that you could not be 'completely fair' simply by passing laws?

Thus it is not enough just to open the gates of opportunity. All our citizens must have the ability to walk through those gates.

This is the next and the more profound stage of the battle for civil rights. We seek not just freedom but opportunity.

Johnson knew that much racial segregation and discrimination had been illegal for many years but that laws had often not been enforced. His government now took steps to ensure the new laws *were* enforced. For instance, black Americans would no longer have to file suits in the law courts to stop segregation. Instead, it was the responsibility of the federal government to ensure it was eliminated and now there was a greater guarantee of legal action being taken quickly and effectively. There were also other ways in which the government could act: Johnson used federal funding to force the pace of school desegregation in the South. One of the most effective ways was by withdrawing federal funds from schools that failed to integrate and by injecting money to support those that *were* integrating. Pockets of resistance still remained: for instance, in Virginia, which bordered Washington DC, a number of schools closed down rather than allow blacks to attend. Nevertheless, by September 1965, 88 per cent of school districts in the South had complied.

Johnson's Higher Education Act of 1965 targeted poor black colleges with extra funding and it was largely due to action taken by his government that the number of black college students increased by 400 per cent in the 1960s. Although unemployment among blacks remained higher than among whites, a prosperous, black middle class emerged in the 1960s. This was partly a result of better educational and economic opportunities, some of which were enhanced by the Civil Rights Act and the federal government's greater willingness to enforce it.

Even in what had been arguably the two most racist states, Alabama and Mississippi, nearly two-thirds of cities had desegregated their public accommodation (such as hotels, restaurants, libraries and parks) by the end of 1965. By 1970, opinion polls suggested that the majority of southerners accepted the integration of public accommodation in the South. Great improvements for blacks undoubtedly took place and whites adjusted to many of the changes brought about by the Civil Rights Movement relatively easily. In the USA as a whole, interracial marriage between blacks and whites (which had been such a **taboo**, certainly in the South) became far more accepted, at least in theory. Source E (page 82) is a speech by John Lewis (the former leader of the SNCC and now a Congressman), commemorating the fiftieth anniversary of the March on Washington:

 **KEY TERM**

Taboo Something which custom or convention prohibits.

Give three reasons why, according to Source E, Lewis believes that the Civil Rights Act led to great change.

SOURCE E

Excerpt from John Lewis's speech, quoted in _An Idea Whose Time Has Come: Two Presidents, Two Parties, and the Battle for the Civil Rights Act of 1964_ by Todd S. Purdum, published by Henry Holt & Co., New York, USA, 2014, p. 331.

Sometime I hear people say nothing has changed, but for someone to grow up the way I grew up in the cotton fields of Alabama to now be serving in the United States Congress makes me want to tell them, 'Come and walk in my shoes'. Fifty years later, we can ride anywhere we want to ride, we can stay where we want to stay. Those signs that said 'white' and 'colored' are gone. And you won't see them any more – except in a museum, in a book, on a video.

Nevertheless, despite undoubted improvements in the South, the Civil Rights Act made little difference to the lives of black people in the ghettoes of cities like New York, Chicago, Detroit and Los Angeles. Although they were free to vote (and had been for many years), they remained stuck in poor housing, with poor schools and high unemployment in economically depressed ghettoes. In practice, they were no less segregated after the legislation of the mid-1960s than they had been before.

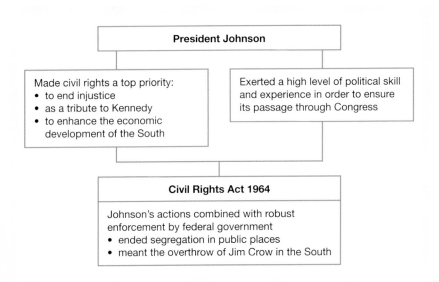

SUMMARY DIAGRAM

The passing of the Civil Rights Act 1964

Campaigning for the vote in Mississippi in the early 1960s

▶ *Key question:* What was the significance of the SNCC's campaign in Mississippi and what was achieved?

The Civil Rights Act banned segregation in schools and all public places but it did little to remove the obstacles that prevented blacks from voting. In Mississippi, the SNCC had been campaigning since 1962 to increase voter registration among rural blacks. This campaign was the most sustained and intensive of the whole Civil Rights Movement and it carried on despite intimidation, bombing, killing and lack of federal government support. It also highlights the importance of local struggles and the role of 'ordinary' people in the Civil Rights Movement.

Mississippi and civil rights

In the early 1960s, Mississippi was the poorest state in the USA. Nearly half of its population was black, more than in any other state. It also had the most incidences of racist beatings and lynchings. Only five per cent of black people were registered to vote and no black person had been elected to any office in the state since 1877, when Reconstruction ended (see page 19). However, for most black people, poverty was a far more pressing problem than not being able to vote. Most lived in small, isolated, rural communities and many had lost their jobs on the land with the increased use of chemical fertilizers and mechanization. Most of their children received only very basic, primary school education as much less was spent on black schools than on white ones.

Mississippi was where Emmett Till had been killed in 1955 (see page 42). Like a whole generation of African-Americans, Anne Moody was stunned by the news of his murder.

◀ **What had civil rights campaigners already done before the SNCC's campaign?**

SOURCE F

Excerpt from *Coming of Age in Mississippi* by Anne Moody, quoted in *The Eyes on the Prize Civil Rights Reader*, edited by Clayborne Carson and others, published by Penguin, New York, USA, 1991, p. 43.

Anne Moody was brought up in Mississippi where, from a young age, she worked as a maid for white families. She later participated in the sit-ins and became a full-time civil rights worker. She wrote her autobiography in 1968. She was fourteen when Till was killed.

Before Emmett Till's murder, I had known the fear of hunger, Hell and the Devil. But now there was a new fear known to me – the fear of being killed just because I was black. But I didn't know what one had to do or not do as a Negro not to be killed. Probably just being a Negro … was enough, I thought.

How, according to Source F, did the murder of Emmett Till change Anne Moody?

I was fifteen years old when I began to hate people. I hated the white men who murdered Emmett Till and I hated all the other whites who were responsible for the countless murders which Mrs. Rice [her teacher] had told me about and those I vaguely remembered from my childhood. But I also hated Negroes. I hated them for not standing up and doing something about the murders. In fact, I think I had a stronger resentment towards Negroes for letting the whites kill them than toward the whites.

Medgar Evers

Medgar Evers was one black Mississippian who was determined to change things. He was a veteran of the Second World War (white veterans were usually highly respected) but had still been prevented from registering to vote, by a white mob with knives and guns. Refused entry to the white-only University of Mississippi, he worked for the NAACP, investigating violent crimes against blacks and campaigning for desegregation and voter registration.

In the late 1950s, he organized a voter registration drive. He knew that once blacks were registered to vote in Mississippi, they could wield great power. Making up nearly half the population of the state, they would be able to elect Congressman and local legislators and officials. However, the forces of white supremacy were both well organized and well financed. Lawyers, judges and politicians were often members of the white Citizens' Council (see page 33). Fear of unemployment deterred many blacks from attempting to register to vote; those applying had to state the name of their employer which meant, in the words of one activist, 'you would be fired by the time you got home'. The authorities employed informers and spies, and published racist articles in the newspapers. Not surprisingly, very few blacks tried to register to vote.

Medgar Evers' work was brought to a sudden, tragic end: just a few hours after Kennedy spoke on television on 11 June 1963 (see page 65), Evers was murdered in front of his home.

What form did the SNCC campaign in Mississippi take?

The SNCC campaign in Mississippi 1961–3

In 1961, the local NAACP group invited SNCC leader Bob Moses to recruit and send in volunteers. Many of them had experience of sit-ins and the Freedom Rides. Many gave up their studies in order to be full-time activists. The idea was that they would live alongside poor, rural blacks, developing local leaders according to local needs. This was very much the approach favoured by Ella Baker ever since the first student sit-ins in 1960.

SNCC activist Charles Cobb explains how it was done:

SOURCE G

Excerpt from Scholars Online, part of The Choices Program, Brown University, USA, located at: www.choices.edu/resources/scholars_ civilrights.php. Charles E. Cobb, currently professor of history at Brown University in the USA, was a SNCC activist, mostly in Mississippi, from 1962 to 1967.

We embedded ourselves … encouraging locals to take control of their own lives, assert their rights. We chose to work with the people that nobody else worked with, the people at the very bottom of society … It takes a long time. You have to stay. That's what grass roots organization is.

> What, according to the author of Source G, was the key to grassroots organizing?

This campaign would be one of many rural projects, part of a national movement financed by the Voter Education Project (VEP), which had been set up by Robert Kennedy in order to channel student energies away from the more highly publicized sit-ins and Freedom Rides and relieve the pressure on the federal government to intervene.

The SNCC volunteers, and some from CORE, went from house to house encouraging people to register to vote. They organized literacy classes to help blacks pass the literacy and other tests that were imposed by the state authorities for those wishing to register. Above all, they tried to help local blacks to overcome their fear: fear of losing a job, fear of being hurt, fear of being killed. They had some successes: Fannie Lou Hamer, from Ruleville, Mississippi, came from a poor, sharecropping background and, aged 44, she met Moses. 'I didn't know that a Negro could register and vote.' Later, 'I could just see myself voting people outa office that I know was wrong and didn't do nothin' to help the poor.' She went on to work as a field secretary for SNCC and became a popular, highly respected figure in the movement.

Nevertheless, these grassroots activists were constantly in danger. Fannie Lou Hamer lost her job and was beaten up by the police for her work. Moses was knifed, shot at and imprisoned. Local activists and SNCC volunteers faced regular threats and had their phones tapped. Those arrested were subjected to police beatings while black churches and the houses of SNCC workers were firebombed by the Klan.

When the SNCC appealed to the federal government to intervene, the authorities in Washington insisted that law enforcement was a state responsibility. Besides, the Kennedy government was very reluctant to antagonize southern Democrats, several of whom held important positions in Congress. Robert Kennedy, as attorney general, pressed the **Federal Bureau of Investigation (FBI)** to be more active but, under the leadership of its powerful boss, J. Edgar Hoover, the FBI provided very little protection. Not surprisingly, the voter registration campaign bore little fruit, few new voters were registered and the VEP cut off funding in Mississippi.

 **KEY TERM**

Federal Bureau of Investigation (FBI)
The main investigative branch of the federal Department of Justice.

The FBI's dirty tricks

The SNCC no doubt felt let down by a lack of support from the Kennedy government. However, the FBI was arguably even less supportive of civil rights. The director, J. Edgar Hoover, saw Martin Luther King Jr as a Communist sympathizer and some civil rights workers had undoubtedly been members of the Communist Party. In Kennedy's time, Hoover had secured permission to tap King's phone, from the attorney general, Robert Kennedy. (Both Kennedys believed they had to be seen as being strongly anti-Communist. Also, they suspected that Hoover knew of President Kennedy's extramarital affairs, which could be seen as a security risk and open the president to blackmail by Hoover.) Hoover had also gone ahead and bugged the hotel rooms in which King had stayed. When King was awarded the Nobel Peace Prize in 1964, Hoover called him 'the most notorious liar in the country' and plotted his death. In November 1964, the FBI sent King a parcel with recordings (supposedly of illicit sexual behaviour) from his hotel room with an unsigned note recommending suicide.

SOURCE H

A SNCC cartoon criticizing the FBI and its director, J. Edgar Hoover, from *Student Voice*, 25 November 1964, p. 2, Ruth Koenig Collection, Archives Centre, National Museum of American History, Behring Center, Smithsonian Institute.

Scenes of the South by Weaver

WELL, MURDER IN THIS CASE IS A LOCAL MATTER WOULD YOU LIKE TO CONTEND THAT THE SHERIFF DENIED THIS NEGRO SOME CIVIL RIGHT IN KILLING HIM?

J EDGAR STANDBY (FEDERAL OFFICER)

?
What is the message of the cartoon in Source H? How does it convey this message?

Freedom Summer 1964

What was the impact of the 1964 Freedom Summer?

In the summer of 1964, Bob Moses decided that a much bigger operation was needed and more publicity was required in order to force the federal government to act. He called for hundreds of northern volunteers to come to Mississippi during their university vacation to help get blacks to register to vote and to run summer schools for their children. The majority of these students were white, often from privileged backgrounds. Several later went on to hold high office, such as governor of California and mayor of New York. Moses realized that attacks on whites would attract far more publicity than attacks on blacks, which were commonplace and often went unreported. Most of the volunteers came from liberal Democratic families. One of them said: 'I'm going because the worst thing after burning churches and murdering children is keeping silent'. Six hundred of them headed south for Mississippi's 'Freedom Summer'.

For white Mississippians, this was an invading northern army. In response, the 6000-strong White Knights of the KKK went into action with a campaign of arson and murder. The state police force was doubled in size and brought in more guns and gas masks. Meanwhile, on the civil rights side, the churches taught their members how to register, how to behave non-violently in the face of attack, and 'Freedom Schools' were set up to teach children.

'Mississippi Burning'

In June, the students received a week's training and were warned: 'you may be killed'. The Klan targeted three of the first volunteers to arrive in Mississippi. One was a black Mississippian, the other two were whites from New York. When the three of them went to investigate the burnt-out remains of a black church they were arrested by police. The police took them in for questioning (on speeding charges) and informed the Klan. When the volunteers were released, they were followed by three vehicles and no more was seen or heard of them. There was a national outcry, President Johnson called for a huge manhunt and sent 200 sailors to help in trawling the river and swamp where the bodies were thought to have been dumped. Thousands were questioned by FBI agents in an operation codenamed 'Mississippi Burning'. A month-and-a-half later the bodies were found. Nineteen people were implicated but the state refused to prosecute. Three years later, in 1967, the deputy sheriff, Cecil Price, and six others were convicted of a lesser charge. This was the first time a Mississippi jury had convicted Klansmen in connection with the death of a black man.

Despite the continuing violence, the voter registration drive went on. The students wrote press releases, answered phones and taught lessons in 'Freedom Schools' for black children as well as organizing black voter registration. For these volunteers, it was a transforming experience, a summer vacation that changed them forever. According to black activist Fannie Lou Hamer, many black Mississippians came to see that some 'white folks are human'.

That summer three more civil rights workers were killed and many more were beaten or shot at. There were numerous bombings but none of the white racists was convicted. Three thousand black children attended Freedom Schools but only 1600 of their parents succeeded in registering to vote. Fear prevented most from making the attempt.

Freedom Summer and disillusionment

Freedom Summer caused a certain amount of divisiveness amongst civil rights workers. In particular, the involvement of northern, white student volunteers engendered resentment amongst some SNCC field workers. They saw the students as 'fly-by-night freedom fighters', privileged whites only there for the summer while, for the SNCC workers and the black population of Mississippi, the bombings and lynchings would continue all year. Some objected that the whites took over many of the jobs that local blacks had done, undermining their self-confidence and perpetuating the stereotype of black inferiority. In other words, some SNCC workers began to criticize the integrationist approach and the need for blacks and whites to work together.

Furthermore, as white violence continued, some SNCC workers were losing faith in non-violent protest. Feeling that violence should be met with violence, some of them decided to carry guns. In many rural areas, the local black population did so anyway. When Klansmen attacked his home and wounded his wife, Mississippian Robert Howard retaliated with his shotgun, 'but I don't figure that I was violent, All I was doin' was protectin' myself'.

Some, even if only a minority, of the civil rights workers on the ground were becoming disillusioned with the non-violent, integrationist approach to gaining civil rights. What crystallized the disillusionment of many SNCC workers was what happened to the Mississippi Freedom Democratic Party (MFDP).

What happened to the MFDP?

Mississippi Freedom Democratic Party (MFDP), 1964

It was election year in 1964 and President Johnson hoped to be elected in November. But first of all, he would have to be chosen as the Democratic Party's candidate. The process of selecting the candidate would culminate in the Democratic National Convention in Atlantic City, New Jersey. Each state would send a delegation of its Democratic Party members. Not surprisingly, all of Mississippi's 68 delegates were white, so SNCC and other activists established the Mississippi Freedom Democratic Party (MFDP) in order to provide an alternative to the all-white official delegation. Some 80,000 members were enrolled and the MFDP's delegation, containing blacks *and* whites, was then freely elected and claimed to be the truly *democratic* delegation. As such, it demanded its right to represent the state's Democratic Party at the convention.

The MFDP delegation backed Johnson as their candidate, but Johnson was worried about losing white support right across the South if he supported the Freedom Party. He expected to be chosen as presidential candidate and the last thing he wanted to spoil his victory was a race row. Besides, he was confident that America's blacks would vote for him in the election anyway. His Civil Rights Act had just passed Congress while his Great Society programme would help millions of poor black people.

Eventually, the MFDP was pressured into agreeing that the all-white Democrats should be the official delegation, but that two of the MFDP would be given non-speaking, non-voting seats at the convention. (Blacks in Mississippi and other states were promised free elections before the Democratic Party convention in 1968, but were refused the representation they demanded at this convention. Thus, they were being compensated with the promise of being able to vote, and thus elect black representatives, in four years' time.)

Worse still, from the point of view of many activists, was that Martin Luther King Jr and other SCLC leaders agreed to the 'compromise', confident that the continuing non-violent campaign and the policy of working with, not against, the Democratic government in Washington would bring more reform, particularly on voting rights. For many SNCC activists, however, this was a sell-out and they felt betrayed by 'fake friends'.

SOURCE I

Excerpt from *Mississippi at Atlantic City* by Charles M. Sherrod, quoted in *The Eyes on the Prize Civil Rights Reader* edited by Clayborne Carson and others, published by Penguin, New York, USA, 1991, p. 187. Sherrod was a SNCC leader who attended the convention in Atlantic City. Here he recounts the reaction of one MFDP delegate, Annie Devine.

… ain't no Democratic party worth that. We have been treated like beasts in Mississippi. They shot us down like animals. We risk our lives coming up here … politics must be corrupt if it don't care none about people down there … these politicians sit in positions and forget the people put them there.

How do you account for the bitterness of the words in Source I?

For another SNCC worker, this 'was the end of innocence'. Many in the SNCC lost faith in the Democratic Party, in white liberals and in King. Some began to be drawn towards black nationalists like Malcolm X (see page 99).

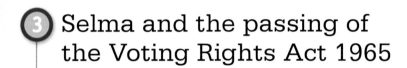

```
┌─────────────────────┐      ┌─────────────────────┐      ┌─────────────────────┐
│ Mississippi was the │      │ Grassroots          │      │ Freedom Summer 1964 │
│ poorest state in    │      │ campaigning by SNCC │      │ recruited northern, │
│ USA with highest    │──────│ in Mississippi in   │──────│ white students as   │
│ percentage of blacks│      │ early 1960s was met │      │ civil rights        │
│ yet lowest          │      │ with violence, often│      │ activists in        │
│ percentage of black │      │ condoned by state   │      │ Mississippi         │
│ voters              │      │ authorities         │      │                     │
└─────────────────────┘      └─────────────────────┘      └─────────────────────┘
```

┌─────────────────────┐   ┌─────────────────────┐
│ Attracted greater   │   │ Integrationist,   │
│ publicity but very │   │ non-violent   │
│ limited gains in   │   │ approach criticized │
│ voter registration │   │ by some SNCC   │
│   │   │ activists,   │
│   │   │ especially after   │
│   │   │ rejection of   │
│   │   │ MFDP at Democratic │
│   │   │ National Convention │
└─────────────────────┘   └─────────────────────┘

SUMMARY DIAGRAM

Campaigning for the vote in Mississippi in the early 1960s

③ Selma and the passing of the Voting Rights Act 1965

▶ *Key question: Why did Martin Luther King Jr go to Selma in 1965 and what was achieved?*

Although some SNCC activists had become disillusioned, especially after the Freedom Summer and the rejection of the MFDP at the Democratic National Convention, most carried on campaigning. Meanwhile, in November 1964, Lyndon Johnson won a landslide victory in the presidential election (even if he *had* lost the states of Alabama, Mississippi, Louisiana, Georgia and South Carolina in the Deep South). He gained 94 per cent of the black vote. He asked his new attorney general, Nicholas Katzenbach, 'to write the goddamndest toughest voting rights act that you can devise'. It would require a sustained effort, eliciting national publicity, in order to persuade Congress to pass such an act.

Voter registration in Selma, Alabama

What happened in Selma?

Alabama, like neighbouring Mississippi, was a highly segregated society. The Civil Rights Act made little *immediate* difference. It took time for schools, buses, hotels, restaurants, parks and swimming pools to be desegregated. Generally, the blacks were much poorer than the whites and, for example, the roads were paved in white neighbourhoods while, in black neighbourhoods, there were dirt roads. And, of course, the Civil Rights Act had not secured the right to vote. In fact, in Dallas County, where the town of Selma was situated, only one per cent of black people were registered to vote. The registration office was only open on two Mondays per month and the hours were very irregular: the office often opened late, shut its doors for long lunch hours and closed early. Even if applicants did turn up when the office was open, they were subject to long delays and had to answer lengthy questionnaires such as in Source J.

SOURCE J

Excerpt from the Mississippi Voter Registration Form, quoted in *The Civil Rights Movement* by Bruce Dierenfield, published by Pearson, Harlow, UK, 2008.

19 Write a reasonable interpretation (the meaning) of the section of the Constitution of Mississippi which you have just copied.

20 Write a statement setting forth your understanding of the duties and obligations of citizenship under a constitutional form of government.

Why might it prove virtually impossible for anyone to give a satisfactory answer to the questions posed in Source J? **?**

Even the slightest mistake meant disqualification. The registrar had the final say and he would always ask the question: 'Does your employer know you are here?' This kind of intimidation kept most black people away.

In 1963, the SNCC had organized a voter registration campaign here as they had in parts of Mississippi. Not surprisingly, it led to job dismissals and beatings, especially when photographs of applicants appeared in the papers. When the authorities forbade public gatherings of more than three people, even an orderly queue of a few people became illegal. Then, in January 1965, local activist Amelia Boynton invited Martin Luther King Jr to come to Selma. King saw Selma as a 'symbol of bitter-end resistance to the Civil Rights Movement in the Deep South'. Selma already had a large, well-organized local campaign and attracted hundreds of people to its meetings. Furthermore, it had a sheriff, Jim Clark, a hot-tempered racist who could be relied on to act violently and attract the media. King and other SCLC leaders were confident that they could provoke the kind of crisis that would attract the nationwide publicity needed to pressurize the federal government into passing a Voting Rights Act. Such a law, giving the federal government powers to override state authorities, could demolish all the obstacles which prevented blacks from voting.

Violence and imprisonment

In January 1965, King and SNCC leader John Lewis led a march to the courthouse in Selma where voter registration took place. At first, the sheriff herded the marchers peacefully into line but, the next day, he shoved a woman and the photograph appeared in the *New York Times* on the following day. A week later, he elbowed a middle-aged woman, who hit him back before she herself was clubbed. Again, the photograph appeared in the press on the next day. Every day, a new wave of demonstrators arrived at the courthouse, singing 'Ain't Gonna Let Nobody Turn Me Around', and every day hundreds were arrested for gathering without a permit. As planned, King was one of those arrested.

The prisoners were kept in cold, cramped conditions but they sang and clapped to keep their spirits up. All was reported in the press. Just as he had done in Birmingham, King wrote a letter from jail. He sent it to the *New York Times* in the form of an advertisement. One of the sentences was written out in capitals: 'THIS IS SELMA, ALABAMA. THERE ARE MORE NEGROES IN JAIL WITH ME THAN ON THE VOTING ROLLS'. At a nearby church in Selma, Malcolm X made a speech in which he warned whites that many blacks were less patient than King; in other words, the alternative to King was more threatening. Although he was seen as a critic of King, he was, in effect, endorsing the non-violent approach to civil rights.

The demonstrations continued and, by February, 3000 were in jail in Selma. Even the black teachers, normally the most conservative of the black professional classes, were persuaded to march and that, in turn, encouraged many more to march, especially their students. A federal judge now intervened, barring the registrar from using complicated registration tests and ordering him to enrol 100 people per day when the office was open. Meanwhile, the violence continued: when the campaign was extended to a neighbouring county, state troopers smashed heads and ribs and shot dead a black army veteran, Jimmie Lee Jackson, who was trying to protect his mother from a beating. The outrage caused by this event led to the decision to organize a march from Selma to Montgomery, the state capital, a distance of 54 miles (86 km).

What was the impact of Bloody Sunday?

Bloody Sunday, 7 March 1965

The march took place on Sunday 7 March and was led by the SCLC and SNCC. King was keen to be seen to work with the SNCC, who had done all the initial groundwork in Selma. The leaders of both organizations wished to show a united front to strengthen their case for a Voting Rights Act. Over 500 people set off, but they were blocked at the bridge leading out of town by state police with batons and gas masks. The marchers were ordered to 'turn around and go back to your church!' Two minutes later the police charged. Men and women, young and old, were mown down and gassed. Police on horseback then charged into the fleeing, falling demonstrators. John Lewis sustained a broken skull and five women were left unconscious. In all, 57 were taken to hospital for treatment. Most significant of all, as far as the organizers were concerned, the press and television cameras were present in large numbers. Television programmes were interrupted to show scenes from what became known as 'Bloody Sunday' and 50 million viewers heard Sheriff Clark shout out: 'Get those goddammed niggers! And get those goddamned white niggers!'

SOURCE K

Police attack demonstrators on Bloody Sunday, 7 March 1965. SNCC leader John Lewis, on the ground, sustained a broken skull.

What does the photograph, shown in Source K, tell you of the police response to the march?

The outcry was heard nationwide. Thousands of petitions were sent to the president demanding action. Demonstrations took place in over 80 cities across America. Over 100 senators and Congressmen spoke out in favour of voting rights. To keep up the momentum and maintain the pressure on the federal government, King called on religious leaders, of all denominations, to join him in 'a ministers' march' to Montgomery two days later. A thousand blacks and 450 whites, led by King, set off on the march. When the marchers reached the town bridge, they were again met by state police. They stopped to pray and then, following instructions from King, they turned around and walked back. King had secretly agreed with the federal government that the marchers would not confront the police but would turn back at the bridge. The reason for this was that State Governor Wallace had banned the march and a federal judge had refused to overturn the ban. Nevertheless, when the SNCC marchers saw this happening, they were furious.

SOURCE L

Excerpt from *Race, Reform and Rebellion* by Manning Marable, published by University Press of Mississippi, USA, 1991, p. 80. Marable was a professor at Columbia University and the director of its Center for Contemporary Black History.

In subdued anger, the amazed SNCC leaders and others walked back into Selma singing 'Ain't Gonna Let Nobody Turn Me Around.' … the damage to King's reputation was incalculable … For five difficult years, King had been the glue which kept the civil rights united front intact … Now the myth was shattered and the politician was something far less than what many … had hoped he was.

What do you think the author of Source L meant by 'the myth was shattered'? A critic at the time denounced King as an 'accomplice of the white power structure'. Do you think either of these judgements can be justified?

Many did indeed accuse King of a climbdown and SNCC activists called it Turnaround Tuesday, but there was no loss of momentum or of publicity in the campaign. That very evening, a white mob attacked three clergymen and one of them, a white northern minister, was so badly beaten that he died in hospital. The assailant (with a record of 26 arrests for assault) was found not guilty and rumours were circulated, by Sheriff Clark, that the murder had been staged by a civil rights worker in order to win sympathy for the cause.

What action did President Johnson take?

The response of the federal government

The impact of the murder of a white minister was massive. The nationwide outrage was such that President Johnson was forced to address Congress. In his televised speech, watched by 70 million, he spoke with far greater passion than ever before. He said of the marchers: 'Their cause must be our cause too. Because it is not just Negroes, but really, it is all of us, who must overcome the crippling legacy of bigotry and injustice.' And then, in the words of the most popular freedom song, he ended his speech, 'We *shall* overcome.' Martin Luther King Jr's colleagues reported that the speech brought tears to King's eyes as they watched on television.

Just as events in Birmingham in 1963 had forced Kennedy's hand, so now Selma forced the pace over voting reform. Two days after his speech, Johnson presented his voting rights bill to Congress. When Alabama Governor Wallace tried to ban the proposed march from Selma to Montgomery, on the grounds that it would disrupt traffic and cause disorder, a federal judge overrode him and authorized the march to go ahead. Johnson sent 2000 troops to protect the marchers, as well as planes and helicopters to deter bombers and snipers. Not all of this was due to King. The situation in Washington was changing: the mass media were now hugely supportive of the civil rights campaign; southern Democrats were no longer as strong in the Senate: black voting power in the North was greater; and the Cold War context meant that the US government had to be seen to act in order to maintain America's credentials as the home of liberty and democracy. Nevertheless, the Selma campaign put the voting rights issue right at the top of the political agenda and opinion polls showed that there was widespread support for reform.

The march from Selma to Montgomery

The march (at the third attempt!) set off on Sunday 21 March, two weeks after Bloody Sunday. There were 3000 marchers, led by Martin Luther King Jr and many other civil rights leaders. They included the veteran A. Philip Randolph and long-standing NAACP leader Roy Wilkins. There were religious leaders representing Protestants, Catholics and Jews. Priests and nuns, preachers and rabbis marched together. Along the road the usual abuse was hurled at the marchers but troops and army vehicles prevented outright violence. The Alabama legislature declared unanimously that the marchers were conducting wild interracial sexual orgies at their camps. SNCC leader John Lewis said; 'All these segregationists can think of is fornication and that is why there are so many shades of Negroes.' The marchers covered about 16 miles (26 km) a day, singing and clapping for much of the time, and slept in camps on the side of the road overnight. Volunteers drove out from Selma with supplies of food and drink.

On the last night, many celebrities turned up to show their support. A makeshift stage was erected and singers, comedians and actors – black and white – entertained the marchers. The next day there were rumours of snipers out to shoot King as he entered Montgomery so a dozen similarly dressed black men, of similar height, were sent to the front of the march to surround King. It was hoped that no would-be assassin would be able to identify the real Martin Luther King Jr. For King, Rosa Parks and many others, entering Montgomery meant a triumphant return to where the protest movement had begun, with the bus boycott, ten years previously.

In the centre of the state capital, King made a speech, characteristically uplifting and optimistic, to 25,000 people, the biggest civil rights gathering in southern history. But there was still a nasty white supremacist backlash: a white mother of five from Detroit was shot dead at the wheel of her car as she gave a lift back to Selma to some of the marchers. Later, an Alabama state jury acquitted the murderers.

The Voting Rights Act 1965

> **What difference did the Voting Rights Act make?**

The march from Selma to Montgomery put increased pressure on both the main political parties, while opinion polls showed 75 per cent in favour of a Voting Rights Act. The presidential signature was finally added, in August 1965, in a ceremony held in the same place that Lincoln had signed the Emancipation Proclamation in 1863. John Lewis said that the Act was 'as momentous as the Emancipation Proclamation.'

The Act ensured that blacks were not prevented from registering to vote and thus enforced the 15th Amendment to the Constitution of 1870. In states where less than half of the adults had voted in the 1964 election, the law automatically suspended the use of literacy and other tests. Also, if too few blacks were registered after the tests were suspended, the federal government was empowered to send in federal registrars: in this way, Alabama, Georgia, Louisiana and Mississippi were soon brought under federal supervision.

Within a month, 60 per cent of Selma's blacks were registered to vote. Across the South as a whole, the percentage of blacks who were registered to vote rose from 35 per cent in 1964 to 65 per cent by 1969. The figures for four states in the South are shown in Source M, overleaf:

? In which state, according to Source M, was the most dramatic progress made? How do you think this might be explained?

Percentage of black people registered to vote (based on data from Manning Marable, *Race, Reform and Rebellion*, published by University Press of Mississippi, USA, 1991, p. 82).

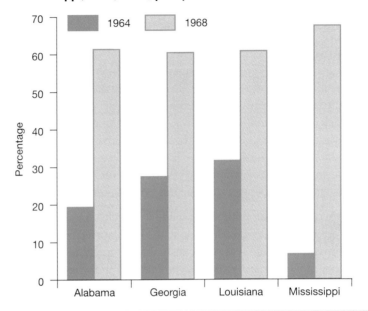

The whole tone of electoral politics changed in the South: there were no more open declarations of race hatred and white supremacy. Men like Sheriff Clark of Selma were voted out and most white politicians became more conciliatory.

Voting power also brought political power. There was a huge increase in the number of blacks elected to public office across the whole of the USA, not just in the South. The Act seemed to be reinforcing the change in public opinion about the participation of blacks in public life throughout America.

Not all historians have painted a completely favourable picture of the impact of the civil rights legislation in the South, as the two sources below show.

SOURCE N

? What, according to Source N, were the limitations of the civil rights legislation in the South? How far do you agree that the limitations were greater than what it achieved?

Excerpt from *Race, Reform and Rebellion* by Manning Marable, published by University Press of Mississippi, USA, 1991, p. 85.

Jim Crow was legally finished, yet black workers and sharecroppers were still victims of bombings, lynchings and rapes ... Black southerners had the electoral franchise; but what of economic security, housing and the right to live without fear?'

In an interview about what was achieved by the Civil Rights Movement as a whole, historian Francoise Hamlin said:

SOURCE O

Excerpt from Scholars Online, part of The Choices Program, Brown University, USA, located at: www.choices.edu/resources/scholarsonline/ hamlin/fh15.php. Hamlin is associate professor of history at Brown University, USA.

The Civil Rights Movement changed African-Americans' sense of what is possible. It empowered a generation. It showed that ordinary people can change the world, they can change their society and their community, that they can have a positive impact. It also shows that these laws have to be enforced, that when the laws are enforced, it works and change can happen. But the minute you take away the enforcement process, the people in power will fall back on the traditions and habits that were there before. Laws can't change people's attitudes.

[The following table accompanies Hamlin's online interview.]

Accomplishments of the Civil Rights Movement	Challenges still remaining
• Empowered a generation	• Laws can't change people's attitudes
• Showed that ordinary people can change the world	• Racism still deeply entrenched in US society
• Change can happen if laws are enforced	• Balance of power in government has not changed
• Increased and elevated a black middle class	• Huge segment of the black population left behind

What does Hamlin, in Source O, see as the key to effective legislation?

SNCC voter registration campaign in Selma, Alabama, since 1963

↓

SCLC targeted Selma for campaign in 1965 to gain maximum publicity and force federal government to pass Voting Rights Act

↓

Police violence on Bloody Sunday and killing of a white clergyman caused national outcry and increased pressure on president and Congress

↓

Voting Rights Act led to huge increase in black voting and election of black officials across the South within a few years

SUMMARY DIAGRAM

Selma and the passing of the Voting Rights Act 1965

Malcolm X and black nationalism

> ▶ **Key question:** What was the impact of Malcolm X on the Civil Rights Movement?

Five days after President Johnson signed the Voting Rights Act in 1965, a riot erupted in the black ghetto of Watts district in Los Angeles. It was triggered by an arrest for drink driving and an ensuing argument in which a black woman was roughly handled by the police. A crowd gathered, blows were exchanged and stories spread of a woman having been beaten up by the police. This was a city in which 65 blacks had been shot and killed by police in the previous two-and-a-half years. There followed five days of rioting, often accompanied by chants of 'Burn, baby, burn!', which were eventually suppressed by police and national guardsmen. Thirty-four people, mostly black, were killed, 4000 arrested and millions of dollars' worth of damage done. A journalist, Robert Conot, wrote of the riot: 'In Los Angeles the Negro was going on record that he would no longer turn the other cheek. That, frustrated and goaded, he would strike back, whether the response of violence, was an appropriate one or no.'

The riot was widely described as the work of a mindless minority. Yet it was not mindless: most of the property destroyed was white-owned shops that were thought to charge exorbitant prices for their goods. Like millions of others, Martin Luther King Jr was shocked. He flew to Los Angeles to try to calm the situation, only to be heckled by black teenagers who told him to 'go back where you came from.'

The background to the Watts riots in Los Angeles 1965

There had been riots in New York in 1964 but this was on a far larger scale. It showed, very starkly, what little effect the recent civil rights legislation had on the lives of many urban blacks. About 4 million had left the South for cities in the North and West between 1940 and 1965. They may have been able to vote in Los Angeles and other cities in the North and West for several decades, but many lived in huge ghettoes, far bigger and more segregated (even if not by law) than in any city in the South.

In the Watts district of Los Angeles, much of the old industry had declined, leading to high unemployment, while the new factories were being built on the outskirts. Male unemployment was six times as high in Watts as in the city as a whole. Public transport (in a city where the majority, but not the poorest, had cars) was wholly inadequate, making it difficult to travel to the outer suburbs where most of the new jobs were available. There was massive overcrowding, partly because a large amount of land had been given away to the Los Angeles baseball team for a new stadium. Many of the black residents, having emigrated from the rural South, were poorly educated, either because they had only had a very basic schooling in the old segregated South or because inner-city schools were overcrowded and poorly-resourced. The sewers stank in the hot summers because there was not enough water pressure to flush the toilets and there was no local hospital.

This pattern of urban poverty and deprivation was replicated in many cities of the North and West. So was the existence of segregated housing and of all-white neighbourhoods. Many publicly-funded housing projects were either all-black (in the ghetto) or all-white. In the field of private housing, estate agents steered black home-buyers away from white areas and, if a black family *did* move into an all-white neighbourhood, they came up against verbal and often physical abuse.

Splits develop in the Civil Rights Movement

By the time of the Watts riots, SNCC and CORE were becoming less committed to non-violence and integration with whites. In the South, the bombings and lynchings continued and one SNCC worker expressed what many felt: 'The days of singing freedom songs and the days of combating bullets and billy clubs with love are over.' While the NAACP and the SCLC felt that the federal government was finally delivering on its promises, the SNCC was distancing itself both from the Democratic government and from mainstream civil rights groups. Furthermore, increasing opposition to American involvement in the Vietnam War was also causing further fracturing of the Civil Rights Movement. In July 1965, SNCC declared that blacks should not 'fight in Vietnam for the white man's freedom until all the Negro people are free in Mississippi'.

The only civil rights leader who could maintain any kind of unity between the different civil rights organizations was Martin Luther King Jr. The non-violent kind of protest espoused by King and most civil rights leaders could only be sustained by hope and optimism yet, in the cities of the North and West, by the mid-1960s, bitterness and disillusionment were widespread. A student in Harlem, New York, told some visitors from Mississippi: 'Turning the other cheek is a load of trash. Up here we understand what snake is biting us.' This was the language of Malcolm X, not Martin Luther King Jr.

The emergence of Malcolm X

> ← **What was the message of Malcolm X?**

Malcolm X had more impact on America in the late 1950s and early 1960s than any other black leader apart from Martin Luther King Jr. No black leader instilled more fear in white America and no black leader voiced the anger and despair of urban blacks, especially the young, more effectively than Malcolm X. Yet, when he was killed in 1965, he left behind no programme or plan of action, no mass-based, lasting organization to carry on his work. So how significant *was* he? What was his legacy?

Malcolm X was born Malcolm Little in 1925 and was brought up in the Mid-West. In contrast to Martin Luther King Jr, he had a disrupted, insecure and unhappy childhood. His father was killed when Malcolm was six. The cause was said to be a tram accident but Malcolm later believed it was the work of white racists. His mother had a mental breakdown and was later admitted to an asylum. Fostered by a white family, Malcolm was a bright child but, when he said he wanted to become a lawyer, his English teacher told him: 'A lawyer – that's no realistic goal for a nigger.' This undoubtedly dented his self-esteem and contributed to his increasing rebelliousness. At fifteen, he was expelled from school and went to live with his half-sister in Boston. He took the usual jobs of the unskilled blacks in the ghetto – shoeshine boy and waiter – before drifting into a life of drugs, pimping and gambling. In 1946, he was jailed for burglary.

 **KEY TERM**

Nation of Islam (NOI)
A religious movement founded in 1930. Its leader was Elijah Muhammad and its main stated goal was to improve the lives of African-Americans in the USA.

Prison changed him. He read a lot, especially on the history of black people in America, and he became converted to the **Nation of Islam (NOI)**, a black-American religious organization often referred to as the Black Muslims. His reading and his new faith gave him a sense of purpose and also the firm belief that all his personal failures and family tragedies were caused by white racists. Released from prison in 1952, he called himself Malcolm X, with the X representing the African name he could never know. In his autobiography he later wrote that, 'For me, my "X" replaced the white slavemaster name of "Little" which some blue-eyed devil named Little had imposed upon my paternal forebears.' He launched himself into preaching and recruiting people to the NOI. He went into bars, clubs and back alleys 'fishing' amongst the 'poor, ignorant, brain-washed black brothers', he said. He portrayed himself as the spokesman of the oppressed black masses, especially in the urban ghettoes: 'I'm one of those 22 million black people who are the victims of Americanism.'

SOURCE P

Excerpt from a speech by Malcolm X to a predominantly black audience in the northern city of Detroit in 1963, quoted in *The Eyes on the Prize Civil Rights Reader*, edited by Clayborne Carson and others, published by Penguin, New York, USA, 1991, p. 248.

So we're all black people, so-called Negroes, second-class citizens, ex-slaves. You're nothing but an ex-slave. You don't like to be told that. But what else are you? You are ex-slaves …

We have this in common: We have a common oppressor, a common exploiter, and a common discriminator. But once we realize we have a common enemy, then we unite – on the basis of what we have in common. And what we have foremost in common is that enemy – the white man. He's an enemy to all of us. I know that some of you all think that some of them aren't enemies. Time will tell.

? What, according to Malcolm X in Source P, do all black people have in common?

Malcolm X criticized the 'so-called Negro leaders' and their policy of non-violent integration with white people: 'the black man in America will never be equal to the white man as long as he attempts to force himself into his house.' In the same speech as in Source P, he said:

SOURCE Q

Excerpt from a speech by Malcolm X to a predominantly black audience in the northern city of Detroit in 1963, quoted in *The Eyes on the Prize Civil Rights Reader*, edited by Clayborne Carson and others, published by Penguin, New York, USA, 1991, p. 248.

You don't have a peaceful revolution. You don't have a turn-the-other-cheek revolution. There's no such thing as a non-violent revolution. The only kind of revolution that is non-violent is the Negro revolution. The only revolution in which the goal is loving your enemy is the Negro revolution. It's the only revolution in which the goal is a desegregated lunch counter, a desegregated theater, a desegregated park, and a desegregated public toilet; you can sit down next to white folks – on the toilet. That's no revolution.

Why is Malcolm X, in Source Q, so critical of the 'Negro revolution'?

Malcolm X called for what he saw as revolutionary change. He said that the only way to overcome 300 years of domination by 'white devils' was for black Americans to take control of their own lives, to rely on self-help and defend their own communities. They should stop 'begging' the system for 'jobs, food, clothing and housing'. In expressing the anger and frustration of urban blacks, he made some highly provocative outbursts: he predicted racial warfare and a 'day of slaughter for this sinful white world'. Lashing out at black Christian leaders, he said, 'churches should be bombed and preachers killed'.

The Hate that Hate Produced

In 1959, a television documentary about the Nation of Islam was shown. Entitled *The Hate that Hate Produced*, it showed how the anti-black feelings of white supremacists had led to the backlash represented by people like Malcolm X. The NOI was portrayed as virulently racist, an army of black fanatics. When challenged about teaching 'racial hatred', Malcolm X said he was not teaching 'hatred but the truth, that the "black man" has been enslaved in the United States by the "white man"'. The media spotlight focused on the threat of violence. Very few whites learned of the Black Muslims' success in rescuing and rehabilitating poor blacks from lives of crime and persuading them to embrace such traditional American values as hard work, discipline and self-respect.

Malcolm X never came up with any specific programme, partly because the NOI claimed to be a religious organization, not a political one, but he instilled a sense of racial pride in urban blacks by teaching and preaching about African history and the emerging nations of black Africa. He urged black people to set up their own businesses and to defend their neighbourhoods against police brutality and white thugs. This was the ideology of black nationalism (see definition on page 60).

Malcolm X and the Civil Rights Movement

On the surface, Malcolm X was utterly different from mainstream civil rights leaders. He opposed their non-violent approach and asked how you could have a revolution by turning the other cheek or putting children in the front line, as in Birmingham (see page 63). He criticized the policy of working with whites in order to persuade the federal government to pass reform. He described the March on Washington as the Farce in Washington, an event that had been taken over by Kennedy's government to keep the blacks compliant. Even when the Civil Rights Act was passed, he claimed it made no practical difference, especially to blacks in the ghettoes. He was probably right: most urban blacks were still trapped by poor housing, poor schools and high unemployment. He talked of black separation, not integration, but failed to come up with any coherent programme of how to put this into action.

Malcolm X was heavily criticized by other civil rights leaders. James Farmer, the founder of CORE, said that 'Malcolm has done nothing but verbalize'. However, Farmer respected Malcolm X (who had outclassed him in a public debate) while Roy Wilkins, the NAACP leader, acknowledged that he 'helped us enormously by cataloguing the wrongs done to Negroes in such powerful language'.

Indirectly, he may have supported the Civil Rights Movement by pressurizing its leaders to be bolder, while his radicalism made the Civil Rights Movement seem responsible and moderate by comparison. He undoubtedly scared some whites into believing that, if they did not accept the demands for civil rights, then the alternative of a black uprising would be much worse. Certainly, Martin Luther King Jr used the threat of this 'nightmare' to pressurize white opinion into supporting civil rights.

Departure from the Nation of Islam 1964

In March 1964, Malcolm X left the NOI. He disagreed with the group's non-political stance, believing it should be politically active. He was also critical of the lifestyle of its leader, Elijah Muhammad, especially his fathering of children by different mistresses. Elijah Muhammad wished to silence him partly, no doubt, because he felt threatened by Malcolm's popularity and high profile. One example of this is how Malcolm X had publicly befriended the boxer Cassius Clay, who went on to become a member of the NOI and rename himself Muhammad Ali.

Malcolm X certainly felt freer once he had left the NOI. He set up the Organization of Afro-American Unity and began to develop specific proposals. He advocated voter registration drives and the election of black candidates for public office, like the mainstream civil rights leaders – but, unlike most other leaders, he said that urban blacks should set up all-black community schools and called for the setting up of rifle clubs so that black people could defend themselves and their families against police brutality and the violence of white vigilantes. He compared the presence of white police in the ghettoes to an occupying army under colonial conditions.

After he left the NOI, Malcolm X went on a pilgrimage to Mecca, to the holiest site of Islam. Here he saw Muslims of many different colors and nationalities. 'Islam brings together in unity all colors and classes', he wrote in his diary. Soon after his return to the USA, he made overtures to the mainstream Civil Rights Movement and no longer saw all whites as 'devils'. He toned down his language and sounded more conciliatory. He said, 'I believe that a man should not be judged by the color of his skin but rather by his conscious behavior, by his actions and his attitudes towards others.' These words could have come straight from Martin Luther King Jr.

We will never know what else he would have achieved in his life because, in February 1965, at the age of 39, Malcolm X was assassinated by members of the NOI. They had succeeded in silencing him forever. His body was laid out in a funeral parlour for four days and over 30,000 people came to pay their respects.

Malcolm X and Martin Luther King Jr

King understood the appeal of Malcolm and other black nationalists and he praised their emphasis on self-esteem and on instilling black pride. Nevertheless, he remained constant in his demand for non-violence and for integration with whites, which black nationalists like Malcolm X challenged.

SOURCE R

Malcolm X (right) meeting Martin Luther King Jr in 1964.

For whom do you think the meeting shown in Source R would have been more challenging and why? Explain your view.

Not surprisingly, Malcolm X has often been contrasted with Martin Luther King Jr. There were undoubted similarities. Both were powerful orators and gifted debaters. Both were fearless, despite death threats, in championing the rights of black people. Both believed that black people should be proud to be black, should assert themselves and should confront white racism. Malcolm himself, according to historian Clayborne Carson, was 'a peaceful man who never used violence to achieve his goals'. Yet both were prepared to *exploit* the use of violence: in Birmingham in 1963, King had set out to provoke violence from Bull Connor's police, while Malcolm X justified violence in self-defence. In a speech in 1965, he said, 'I don't advocate violence, but if a man steps on my toes, I'll step on his.' However, the historian Manning Marable has pointed out significant differences.

? What does Marable, in Source S, see as the key differences between King and Malcolm X?

SOURCE S

Excerpt from *Malcolm X, A Life of Reinvention* by Manning Marable, published by Allen Lane, London, UK, 2011, pp. 482–3.

King saw himself … first and foremost as an American, who pursued the civil rights and civic privileges enjoyed by other Americans … Malcolm perceived himself first and foremost as a black man, a person of African descent who happened to be a United States citizen … Malcolm perceived black Americans as an oppressed nation-within-a-nation, with its own culture, social institutions, and group psychology.

King presented a narrative to white Americans that suggested that Negroes were prepared to protest non-violently, and even die, to realize the promise of the nation's Founding Fathers [such as 'life, liberty and the pursuit of happiness']. By contrast, Malcolm proposed that the oppressed had a natural right to armed self-defense.

King was a southerner, and as a Baptist minister, a member of the educated, professional black elite. When, after 1965, he moved his campaign to the North, he was shocked by the plight of blacks living in the urban ghettoes. Malcolm X, by contrast, had direct experience of the poverty and discrimination which black people faced in cities like Chicago and New York. He drew attention to the harsh conditions and he voiced the anger and bitterness which many northern ghetto-dwellers felt. When King spoke of his 'dream' during the March on Washington, Malcolm responded, 'While King was having a dream, the rest of us Negroes are having a nightmare.'

The legacy of Malcolm X

Judgements of Malcolm X have varied enormously. Even among the mainstream civil rights leaders there were contrasting views. Historian Manning Marable explains in Source T (opposite) that Bayard Rustin, a close ally of King, was one of the most critical.

SOURCE T

Excerpt from *Race, Reform and* Rebellion by Manning Marable, published by University Press of Mississippi, USA, 1991, p. 91.

From the moment of his death … most of the mainstream civil rights leaders attempted to eradicate Malcolm's political influence among young blacks … The most vitriolic [bitter] yet articulate assaults on Malcolm came from Rustin. 'Now that he is dead we must resist the temptation to idealize Malcolm X, to elevate charisma to greatness … Malcolm is not a hero of the movement, he is a tragic victim of the ghetto.' Rustin insisted that Malcolm was a political failure; that having 'blown the trumpet, he could summon, even at the very end, only a handful of followers'.

Yet, by contrast to Rustin, John Lewis commented that Malcolm 'more than any single personality' was able to 'articulate the aspirations, bitterness, and frustrations of the Negro people'.

Historian Harvard Sitkoff believes that Malcolm X struck a deep chord with many urban blacks who felt that they were trapped in the ghettoes.

> ? For what reasons might Rustin, in Source T, say that Malcolm X was 'not a hero of the movement, he is a tragic victim of the ghetto'?

SOURCE U

Excerpt from *The Struggle for Black Equality 1954–1992* by Harvard Sitkoff, published by Hill & Wang, New York, USA, 1993, p. 197.

Malcolm's rejection of Gandhian non-violence and condemnation of integrationist ideals fit the mood of African-Americans whose hopes had been dashed … Malcolm's black nationalism crystallized the feelings of those whose expectations had been frustrated, and of those whose lives the civil rights movement had hardly touched … Malcolm instilled a positive sense of black identity among his followers. His ideas of racial pride … and African-American control of black community institutions both expressed and shaped the changing consciousness of young, black activists.

> ? Identify two of Malcolm X's achievements referred to in Source U.

Many of those activists, especially from SNCC and CORE, came to see that insisting on interracial cooperation did not lead to the end of anti-black violence whether in the rural South or urban North. For them, in the words of Sitkoff, 'the struggle for desegregation [would become] a battle for self-determination'.

A few months after Malcolm X's death, *The Autobiography of Malcolm X*, an account of his life and beliefs, was published. In the book, he explored his feelings of rejection and his search for his identity: the book was to have a huge impact on young, black Americans and on the emergence of the **Black Power** movement.

Postscript: the assassination of Martin Luther King Jr, 1968

After the passing of the civil rights legislation in 1964–5, Martin Luther King Jr continued his non-violent campaign of direct action to secure civil rights. In particular, he spoke out about the extent of inequality in American society and the lack of opportunities for all poor people, black or white.

 **KEY TERM**

Black Power A movement that emphasized black racial pride and the importance of blacks creating their own political and cultural institutions.

He also became an outspoken critic of the Vietnam War, pointing out that 'the US spent half a million dollars to kill an enemy soldier in Vietnam but only $35 to help a poor American'.

On 3 April 1968, King gave a speech in Memphis, Tennessee, in support of black rubbish collectors who were demanding equal treatment to white workers. The next day, on 4 April, he was shot dead by a lone white racist.

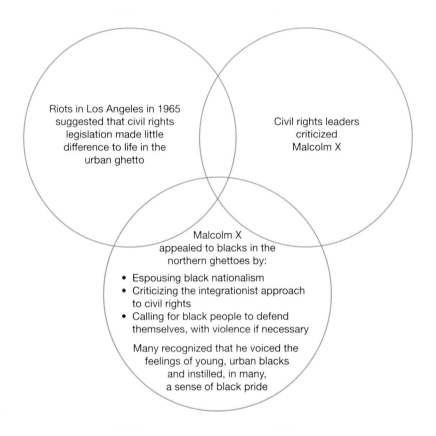

SUMMARY DIAGRAM

Malcolm X and black nationalism

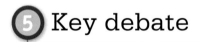

⑤ Key debate

▶ **Key question:** *How important was Martin Luther King Jr in the Civil Rights Movement?*

In the eyes of the vast majority of Americans, both black and white, Martin Luther King Jr was not only the most effective leader of the Civil Rights Movement but, for many, he was *the* leader of the movement. The same interpretation has shaped much teaching in US schools in subsequent decades. Yet Ella Baker, the veteran civil rights campaigner, famously said

'The movement made King, he didn't make the movement.' She rejected the 'top-down' view of the movement, as have many historians since then.

The importance of King: the top-down interpretation

The traditional interpretation of the Civil Rights Movement focuses on national institutions and national leaders. In this view, the Supreme Court's ruling in the 1954 *Brown* case triggered a protest movement in which King emerged as the heroic leader. As the historian Charles Payne writes, 'The narrative goes something like this':

SOURCE V

Excerpt from *Debating the Civil Rights Movement, 1945–1968* by S. Lawson and C. Payne, published by Rowman & Littlefield, Maryland, USA, 1998, p. 108.

Inspired by the Court, courageous Americans, black and white, took protest to the street, in form of bus boycotts, sit-ins and freedom rides. The protest movement, led by the brilliant and eloquent Dr. Martin Luther King, aided by a sympathetic federal government, most notably the Kennedy brothers and Lyndon Johnson, was able to make America understand racial discrimination as a moral issue … [and to] to remove racial prejudice and discrimination from American life, as evidenced by the Civil Rights Acts of 1964 and 1965.

According to Source V, who were the key figures and what were the key institutions in achieving civil rights for African-Americans?

There are many reasons for saying that King was a heroic and indispensable leader. Even Ella Baker, who criticized the fact that so much praise was heaped on King rather than on the thousands of civil rights workers all over America, admitted that his contribution to the movement was massive.

King led by example, showing great courage and stamina in the face of opposition, assaults and threats of assassination. He had many spells in prison, often in harsh conditions. He was a superb communicator, both with other civil rights leaders and with the nation at large. With his unrivalled ability as a preacher and his appeal to Christian values, above all to the redemptive power of love and forgiveness, he could capture his black (and sometimes white) audiences. With what the historian Vincent Harding called 'the audacious power of a religiously inspired human freedom movement', he confronted the Jim Crow South. With his appeal to American values, such as the belief in liberty, justice and democracy, he could inspire millions, black and white. Above all, he could sway the power brokers in the federal government and Congress. 'With his preaching background, intellectual training, and experience of life in Boston, he was a brilliant communicator to white America', according to historian Stephen Tuck. In 1963 he was *Time* magazine's 'Man of the Year', in 1964 he was awarded the Nobel Peace Prize and, in 1986, his birthday was made a national holiday in the USA.

There were other, more militant activists, such as Malcolm X, who were well known but it was King who, for more than a decade, attracted the national media. Thus, until the mid-1960s, it was the non-violence, the carefully planned confrontations, the positive role of religion, and faith in the all-important role of government that were highlighted in the press and on television.

Many African-American leaders had contacts in government. The NAACP continued, successfully, to bring cases to the Supreme Court, and its leaders, such as Roy Wilkins, regularly had access to officials in the White House and lobbied Congress. The SNCC kept in touch with the Justice Department, particularly Attorney General Robert Kennedy, in the early 1960s. But King undoubtedly had the greatest influence in Washington and, ultimately, that was crucial to the passing of the civil rights legislation of 1964–5.

The importance of grassroots campaigning: the view from below

The traditional view of the Civil Rights Movement focuses on the decade from *Brown* to the passing of the civil rights legislation in 1964–5. It underestimates the years of painstaking work by the NAACP in organizing, mobilizing support and undermining the legal foundations of segregation which culminated in the Supreme Court's *Brown* ruling in 1954.

A year later, in 1955, King was thrust to the fore in Montgomery and emerged, in the following year, as the most widely recognized civil rights leader. However, the success of the bus boycott in 1956 grew out of years of campaigning, most notably by E.D. Nixon.

SOURCE W

How does the author of Source W play down the importance of Martin Luther King Jr? What does he see as King's most significant contribution?

Excerpt from an essay by Charles Payne in *Debating the Civil Rights Movement, 1945–1968* by S. Lawson and C. Payne, published by Rowman & Littlefield, Maryland, USA, 1998, p. 113. Payne is a professor at the University of Chicago, USA, who specializes in African-American history.

What we see in Montgomery was that King was the inheritor of momentum that other people established, a pattern that was to be repeated often over the next several years. Other people constructed the stage, but once he stepped into the role of movement spokesperson, his charisma, broad appeal, and personal growth allowed him to project the message of the movement in ways that virtually no one could have predicted in 1956.

As suggested in Source W, King was a highly skilled communicator. However, he was less successful as an organizer. In the late 1950s, King's organization, the SCLC, made little progress and was overtaken by events initiated by others. The sit-ins surprised King as much as anyone else. They spread like wildfire and energized the Civil Rights Movement. They marked the beginning of a period of mass activism. The Freedom Rides, initiated by CORE, had an equally dramatic impact. Many of those, mostly young, people who had participated in sit-ins and Freedom Rides became full-time activists, especially in Mississippi. The outstanding example of grassroots organizing was to be in Mississippi.

SOURCE X

Excerpt from Scholars Online, part of The Choices Program, Brown University, USA, located at: www.choices.edu/resources/scholars_civilrights.php. Charles E. Cobb, currently professor of history at Brown University in the USA, was a SNCC activist, mostly in Mississippi, from 1962 to 1967.

The biggest misconception of the movement is that it was a movement led by charismatic leaders engaging in direct action in public spaces. The real tradition of the Civil Rights Movement has to do with community organizing …

SNCC's approach to community organizing was shaped by the influence of Ella Baker, one of the greatest women of twentieth-century political struggle. Her great lesson to us was: 'Organize from the bottom-up, not from top-down'. This was very different from more mainstream, established civil rights organizations.

What does the author of Source X see as the key characteristic of the Civil Rights Movement?

At the grassroots level many thousands risked life and limb yet remain nameless. Typical of these were the SNCC workers in Mississippi and other states. The historian Adam Fairclough wrote that, for three years, 'Mississippi became the most sustained, intensive project of the entire Civil Rights Movement.'

The breakthrough legislation of 1964–5 could not have been achieved without the work of thousands of activists campaigning at local and regional level. They constituted the critical mass, the nationwide core of support for civil rights without which King and the other leaders could not have exerted such force on the federal government.

Conclusion

The historian Clayborne Carson believes that: 'If King had never lived, the black struggle would have followed a course of development similar to the one it did.' Yet, it is hard to see the civil rights legislation being passed in 1964 and 1965 without King.

It is undeniably true that King was never in one place long enough to see that a local infrastructure was created which could then carry the struggle on with or without him. Nowhere was this more evident than in Albany. However, he was unrivalled in his ability to mobilize people, in involving large numbers of people in short-term, media-oriented events. The historian Stephen Tuck pinpoints King's crucial contribution to the Civil Rights Movement: 'King and his team played the media with the consummate skill of seasoned politicians – much to the annoyance of seasoned politicians. He presented local dramas to a national audience.'

Once King and his SCLC advisers had selected a particular campaign, they used non-violence in order to provoke violence ('creative tension', King called it). And it worked in places like Birmingham and Selma because the police subjected the demonstrators to violence. This was captured on television and shown nationally and internationally, thus forcing Kennedy and then Johnson to act.

The role of the federal government was, of course, essential. The breakthrough legislation of 1964–5 could not have been achieved without the commitment of Kennedy and, particularly, of Johnson. However, the movement would have achieved little without the involvement of hundreds of thousands of people; in other words, if it had not been a *mass* movement.

? Who, according to Source Y, made civil rights reform necessary and for what reasons?

SOURCE Y

Excerpt from an essay by Steven Lawson in *Debating the Civil Rights Movement, 1945–1968* by S. Lawson and C. Payne, published by Rowman & Littlefield, Maryland, USA, 1998, p. 42. Lawson was professor of history at Columbia University, New York, USA, and an expert on the history of the civil rights campaign.

The federal government made racial reform possible, but Blacks in the South made it necessary. Had they not mobilized their neighbors, opened their churches to stage protests and sustain the spirits of the demonstrators, and rallied the faithful to provoke a response from the federal government, far less progress would have been made. Thus, the real heroes of the civil rights struggle were the Black foot soldiers and their white allies who directly put their lives on the line in the face of often overwhelming odds against them. Federal officials were not heroes yet they proved essential for allowing the truly courageous to succeed.

TOK

Consider the loose dichotomy of Martin Luther King Jr's theories on non-violence and Malcolm X's advocacy of more militant tactics. In what ways was each approach ethical and in which ways unethical? (Ethics, Language, Logic, Faith, Intuition)

Chapter summary

The achievements of the Civil Rights Movement

President Johnson brought all his experience and political skill to bear to ensure the passing of the Civil Rights Act, which effectively ended Jim Crow in the South. Grassroots campaigning by the SNCC in Mississippi, culminating in Freedom Summer in 1964, was sustained for three years but with mixed results. The huge publicity attracted by the 1965 Selma campaign, led by Martin Luther King Jr, enabled the Civil Rights Movement to exert great pressure on president and Congress to pass the Voting Rights Act in 1965. Malcolm X highlighted the impact of racial discrimination and instilled racial pride in many urban, young blacks in the North and West. Finally, Martin Luther King Jr's role in the achievement of civil rights is undoubtedly of massive significance, yet there is a need to recognize the importance of a grassroots, mass movement in that achievement.

All in all, major civil rights victories had been achieved by 1965 but the USA had not achieved equality. Living conditions, education levels and incomes of black people would continue to lag behind those of white people for decades.

Examination advice

Interpreting visual sources

Visual sources are often included on Paper 1 examinations and can be used in any of the questions. Visual sources include cartoons, maps, graphs, charts, tables, photographs, posters and potentially many other types of graphic art. Some visual sources are easier to understand than others.

Graphs, charts and tables

Graphs, charts and tables usually convey very specific information such as economic data, how many people from a particular political party were in parliament, or how many leaders a country had over a period of time. However, these still need interpreting.

Example: table

This source is from the Gilder Lehrman Institute of American History.

SOURCE N

Table illustrating African-American voter registration.

State	1960	1966	Percentage increase
Alabama	66,000	250,000	378.79%
Arkansas	73,000	115,000	157.53%
Florida	183,000	303,000	166.57%
Georgia	180,000	300,000	166.67%
Louisiana	159,000	243,000	152.83%
Mississippi	22,000	175,000	795.45%
North Carolina	210,000	282,000	134.29%
South Carolina	58,000	191,000	329.32%
Tennessee	185,000	225,000	121.62%
Texas	227,000	400,000	176.21%
Virginia	100,000	205,000	205.00%

Quantifies the percentage increase in voter registration from 1960 to 1966.

Indicates that this data relates to eleven southern states.

Refer to the dates covered (1960 and 1966).

Source N conveys a tremendous amount of information, although it appears quite simple. On close examination of the data, we can come to a deeper understanding of how few African-Americans were registered to vote in 1960 and how this number dramatically increased over a short span of time. We can also make conclusions about which states showed the greatest increase in voter registration (Mississippi and Alabama) and which showed the least (Tennessee and North Carolina). After examining the table, we can also point out information that is missing and that might help us to better understand the dynamics of voter registration. For example, the table does not tell us why the numbers increased. After reading Chapter 3, you should be able to answer this. Source N also does not tell us the percentage of each state's population that was African-American and/or white. If we knew this, we would have a better sense of how great the changes were. In other words, did the 329 per cent increase in South Carolina mean that a significant percentage of the African-American community who could register actually did register?

Cartoons, posters and photographs

Cartoons and posters can be very similar in terms of symbolism, message and intended effect. Either can be intended to make fun of something, criticize a person or idea, try to get the viewer to agree with their point of view, or inform. They can be complex and should be treated very carefully and thoroughly.

Symbolism

First, we need to consider symbolism. The chart below gives some symbols and their potential meanings. However, these are just some of the basics and you should know that the list is almost endless.

Symbol	Represents	Symbol	Represents
Hooded and robed figures	Ku Klux Klan	White House	US president
Burning cross	Ku Klux Klan	Scales, blindfolded woman	Justice
Noose	Lynching of African-Americans	Chains, shackles, ball and chain	Slavery, apartheid
Sheriff	Southern policemen	'Net Blankes' signs	White people only
Confederate flag	Segregationists	'Europeans only' signs	White South Africans
White cross in circle	Ku Klux Klan symbol	Figure with globe as head	The world
Crossed US and Confederate flags	Citizens' Councils: white segregationists	Pass documents	Internal passports for black South Africans
Raised black fist	Black Power	Desolate lands, barbed wire	Bantustans
Lunch counter	Sit-ins	African with spear and shield	Symbol of the armed wing of the ANC
Burning bus	Freedom Rides attacked	Island prison	Robben Island, where Mandela and other African leaders were imprisoned
Capitol building	US Congress	Olive branch, dove	Peace
Turtle	Slow movement	Statue of Liberty (one arm holding torch, other holding tablet)	Democracy, USA
Black schoolchild	Quest for non-segregated schooling	Hourglass	Time
Woman or baby crying	Misery, death, destruction	Factory, smokestack	Industry

Representations of people

Additionally, significant people like Dr Martin Luther King Jr, Malcolm X, Rosa Parks, Dwight Eisenhower, Lyndon Johnson, Nelson Mandela, Chief Luthuli, Daniel Malan, Hendrik Verwoerd and others dealt with in this and other chapters in the book appear in photographs and other visual sources. In many cases, cartoon representations of people in the news tend to focus on their physical features or references to their nationality, and often have racist themes.

Captions

Captions are the labels that accompany visual sources. These are very important, often informing you of the date of creation, name of artist and perhaps country of origin. All of this information helps to determine the message of the source. Often captions include a direct message which is easy to understand, such as the message in Source K in Chapter 1 (see page 34). Read captions carefully.

Example: cartoons

Cartoons can provide insights about particular historical events and often convey a number of important ideas, both amusing and ironic. Always be sure to note the date, artist and accompanying information about the cartoon's origin. These often are helpful when analysing cartoons.

Examine Source V, the editorial cartoon by Herb Block on page 70. The cartoon originally appeared in the *Washington Post* newspaper in September 1963. This was a period of increasing civil unrest as many African-Americans protested the lack of opportunity and equal rights. If you were asked, 'What is the message of this source?' you could explain that many areas of life were restricted for black people, including housing, schools, jobs and hotels. In this cartoon, the African-American man is being pushed into the street by a white person who says that taking to the streets or demonstrating will get black people nowhere. The irony here is that the only way African-Americans can be heard and win equal rights is by doing just that, since all other avenues have been closed.

Photographs

Photographs are another visual source. Photographs can capture a specific moment. Sometimes photographs just record what the photographer saw at that particular moment, while many photographs, especially of political events, politicians and conferences, are usually ones in which everyone poses in a specific way for an intended effect.

How to answer

You may be asked to analyse one of the visual sources that appear on your Paper 1 examination in Question 13. The questions are usually very straightforward, asking you to indicate the message of the source.

Example 1

This question (in the style of Question 13b) uses Source K (page 56).

> What message is conveyed by Source K? (2 marks)

First, take note of any words. The caption clearly indicates that a mob had firebombed a bus containing Freedom Riders in Alabama. Take note of what is in the photo:

- Smoke pours out of the bus.
- Two Freedom Riders, at least one of whom is white, are sitting on the ground.
- Two others, one white and one black, are standing and face the burning bus.

Lastly, write your answer to the question.

> Source K is a photo which captures a very dramatic event in the Civil Rights Movement. The photo shows the aftermath of the firebombing of a bus in Alabama in 1961. The photo conveys two possibly dazed and injured Freedom Riders on the grass near the bus. Another two people are watching the bus burn. The photo received widespread attention because of its depiction of the violence directed at Freedom Riders, regardless of their race. The attackers hoped to disrupt the whole Freedom Ride enterprise through violence and intimidation.

> The answer indicates that the question was understood. There are at least three points made about the photo. All points are clear, supported with evidence from the photo, and accurate. Good use of analysis and deduction. Mark: 2/2.

Example 2

This question (in the style of Question 13b) uses Source K (page 93).

> What message is conveyed by Source K? (2 marks)

First, take note of any words. The caption states: Police attack demonstrators on Bloody Sunday, 7 March 1965. SNCC leader John Lewis, on the ground, sustained a broken skull.

Remember that questions for Prescribed subject 4 will be numbered 13, 14, 15 and 16 in the Paper 1 exam.

The type and origin of the source are stated in the opening of the answer.

Next, examine what is taking place in the photograph:

● White policemen with helmets, clubs and gas masks running after blacks.
● John Lewis on the ground, being clubbed.
● Disorder and chaos.

Lastly, write your answer to the question.

Source K is a photograph that was taken on 7 March, 1965. It is evidence of white policemen attacking unarmed black protestors. The policemen are chasing the black people, and in the foreground of the photo John Lewis, a SNCC leader, has his hand upraised as he is about to be clubbed by a white officer. The photo conveys a chaotic moment as the policemen chase after black demonstrators. One has even fallen to the ground in the melee.

The photo also suggests that the black people hope to escape the baton-wielding policemen who appear to show no mercy. As the caption suggests, the event was very violent because 7 March, 1965 was also known as 'Bloody Sunday.' The photo is an excellent example of unarmed black protestors meeting violent suppression by the armed southern forces of law and order.

> The answer indicates which source is being analysed, the type of source and the date.

> The caption is discussed and integrated with a discussion of the imagery.

> 'Suggests' and 'appears' and other terminology is used when making hypotheses based on elements in the photo.

> All major elements depicted in the photo are discussed and analysed, including the policemen, John Lewis, and the chaotic and violent atmosphere.

> The answer is summarized in the final sentence to make sure the meaning is clear.

> The answer indicates that the question was understood. There are at least two points made about the photograph. All points are clear, supported with evidence from the photo, and accurate. Good use of analysis and deduction. Mark: 2/2.

Examination practice

Using the examples given above, explain the message of each of the following sources:

Cartoons
Source H from Chapter 3 (page 86)

Photographs
Source D from Chapter 1 (page 24)
Source E from Chapter 1 (page 29)
Source B from Chapter 3 (page 79)

The following are exam-style questions for you to practise, using sources from the chapter. Sources can be found on the page references given.

The questions also reflect the numbering style of the exam (there are no questions 1–12; questions for Rights and protest begin at question 13).

PAPER 1 PRACTICE QUESTIONS FOR CASE STUDY 1 (USING SOURCES FROM CHAPTER 1)

See Chapters 4 and 5 for advice on answering Questions 15 and 16.

These sources and questions relate to segregation and education.
Source F: page 30
Source H: page 31
Source I: page 31
Source K: page 34

13 a) What, according to Source F, were the main problems with the doctrine of 'separate but equal? [3 marks]

13 b) What message is conveyed by Source K? [2 marks]

14 With reference to its origin, purpose and content, analyse the value and limitations of Source I for historians studying the reaction of some southern whites to the Supreme Court's *Brown* v. *Board of Education* decision. [4 marks]

15 Compare and contrast what Sources H and I suggest the Supreme Court decision will bring to the nation. [6 marks]

16 Using the sources and your own knowledge, evaluate the difficulty in desegregating schools in the southern USA from 1954 to 1957. [9 marks].

PAPER 1 PRACTICE QUESTIONS FOR CASE STUDY 1 (USING SOURCES FROM CHAPTER 3)

See Chapters 4 and 5 for advice on answering Questions 15 and 16.

These sources and question, relate to Lyndon Johnson's role and significance in promoting civil rights change.

Source B: page 79   Source V: page 107

Source D: page 80   Source Y: page 110

13 a) What, according to Source D, did President Johnson mean when he said
'... it is not enough just to open the gates of opportunity'?   [3 marks]

13 b) What message is conveyed by Source B?   [2 marks]

14 With reference to its origin, purpose and content, analyse the value and limitations of Source V for historians studying the role of leadership in the Civil Rights Movement.   [4 marks]

15 Compare and contrast what Sources V and Y indicate about who was most instrumental in pushing for change.   [6 marks]

16 Using the sources and your own knowledge, evaluate the part President Johnson played in ending segregation in the USA.   [9 marks]

 # Activities

I Many cartoonists chose to portray the Civil Rights Movement in the USA, among them 'Baldy' Clifford H. Baldowski. Many of his cartoons can be found at the Civil Rights Digital Library (http://crdl.usg.edu).

– Each student in the class could select a cartoon to analyse, with no two students selecting the same cartoon.

– Each student should then answer the question: 'What message is conveyed by your selected cartoon?' Try and make at least three points.

– Each student should present his or her analysis to another student for marking, along with the title of the cartoon. Students should mark each other's analysis out of two possible points.

– Time permitting, students could also explore the cartoons of Herblock and Bill Mauldin, and compare and contrast these to Baldy's.

2 One way to learn cartoon symbolism is to create a bingo-like game where symbols are represented on a grid pattern. Each grid card should have symbols arranged in a different order from any of the others. Someone calls out the meaning of a symbol, keeping track, of course, of which meanings and symbols have been called out. As meanings are matched with symbols, students may cross out or otherwise mark the appropriate symbol. Once a line of symbols is complete, that individual is the winner of that round. Grid patterns can contain any number of symbols, with perhaps five across and five down being the easiest to work with.

3 As a class, debate which form of propaganda presented in this chapter is the most effective. Continue the debate regarding which forms of propaganda and political advertising are the most used and most effective today. Be sure to support your ideas with evidence.

Case Study 1: Timeline

1863	Emancipation Proclamation **Dec:** 13th Amendment abolished slavery
1866	Ku Klux Klan founded
1868	**July:** 14th Amendment guaranteed 'equal protection of the law' to all citizens
1870	**March:** 15th Amendment granted black male suffrage
1881	First Jim Crow laws passed
1890	Mississippi became first state to disenfranchise blacks
1896	**May:** *Plessy* v. *Ferguson* ruled that 'separate but equal' treatment of the races was not unconstitutional
1909	NAACP formed
1941	**June:** President Roosevelt banned discrimination in war industries after Randolph threatened March on Washington
1943	Race riot in Detroit
1948	President Truman ordered desegregation in armed forces
1954	**May:** *Brown* v. *Board of Education* ruled that segregation in education was unconstitutional **July:** First White Citizens' Council formed
1955	**May:** *'Brown II'* ruling called for desegregation in education 'with all deliberate speed' **Aug:** Emmett Till murdered **Dec:** Start of Montgomery Bus Boycott

1956	**March:** Southern Manifesto **Dec:** Successful end to Montgomery Bus Boycott
1957	**Jan:** SCLC formed **Sept:** Civil Rights Act passed **Dec:** President Eisenhower sent federal troops into Little Rock, Arkansas
1959	TV programme *The Hate that Hate Produced* about Malcolm X and Nation of Islam
1960	**Feb:** Sit-ins began **April:** SNCC formed **May:** Civil Rights Act
1961	**May:** Freedom Rides began **Nov:** Albany Movement began Start of SNCC campaign in Mississippi
1962	**Sept:** 'Battle of Ole Miss'
1963	SCLC campaign in Birmingham, Alabama **June:** Kennedy's speech called civil rights a 'moral issue' and sent a civil rights bill to Congress **Aug:** March on Washington **Nov:** Assassination of President Kennedy
1964	MFDP organized **July:** Civil Rights Act passed
1965	**Feb:** Assassination of Malcolm X **March:** Selma–Montgomery march led to 'Bloody Sunday' **Aug:** Voting Rights Act passed Race riots erupted in Watts, Los Angeles

Case Study 2

Apartheid South Africa
1948–1964

CHAPTER 4

The creation of the apartheid state

This chapter considers how far South Africa already practised segregation before the National Party won its electoral victory in 1948. It examines some of the historical factors through the 1930s and 1940s that led to the National Party victory and its initial impact. It also explores the response to and protests against racism and segregation. You need to consider the following questions throughout this chapter:

★ What led to apartheid becoming law?

★ To what extent was segregation introduced before the National Party victory?

★ What was the impact of the National Party victory in the 1948 election?

★ How effectively did protesters oppose segregation in the period 1910–49?

KEY TERM

Coalition A partnership between different political parties to try to win elections together.

Apartheid Strict separation of different racial groups. It is an Afrikaans word, meaning 'separate' or 'apartness'.

Afrikaners Descendants of immigrants to South Africa mainly from the Netherlands and Germany.

> What was petty and grand apartheid?

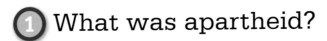

① What was apartheid?

▶ *Key question: What led to apartheid becoming law?*

In 1948 in South Africa, the National Party won 79 seats in parliament during the election. It was a close-run race; the party's rivals, a **coalition** of the United Party and South African Labour Party, gained 71 seats (see page 134). The National Party began to institute a system of **apartheid** in which the different races in South Africa were segregated as much as possible.

Apartheid in practice

The concept of apartheid was established on four principles:

● South Africa comprised four racial groups, each with its own inherent and separate culture (see page 123).

● Whites were the 'civilized' race and were entitled to absolute power over the interests of all others.

● The white race was a single entity, despite comprising **Afrikaners** (see page 123) and English speakers.

- Black **Africans** (see page 123), meanwhile, were made up different tribes. This was a particularly important concept as it implied Africans were different from each other, and indeed should be kept separate, so that each tribe could maintain its own culture. This meant that whites, a seemingly homogeneous group, could call themselves the majority.
- Because it was believed that the other races were inferior, the facilities provided for them could also be inferior. It was not necessary to provide separate but equal facilities (as would be seen in the USA in the early twentieth century). Other races would not appreciate the better facilities provided for whites.

Soon after 1948, laws were enacted which determined which race one belonged to, which in turn effectively determined one's whole expectations of life. Factors such as the thickness of one's hair were considered highly important by a growing **bureaucracy**. White South Africans benefited from apartheid as it guaranteed them the majority of the wealth of South Africa, the vast majority of the well-paid **white-collar** jobs, and pleasant, well-ordered lifestyles – while Africans suffered discrimination all their lives, and did the hard work in the mines and on the farms for little pay. Apartheid is generally referred to in two forms:

- Grand apartheid referred to the overall policy to keep the different races as separated as possible, for example by ensuring that they lived in different areas.
- Petty apartheid meant the day-to-day restrictions, such as separate facilities and restrictions – the segregation between the races.

Segregation preceded the National Party victory, but the intellectuals behind National Party policy implemented apartheid to fully legislate this segregation to protect both white superiority and survival. It developed on a scale almost unimaginable to those living in multiracial, multicultural societies today. In order to understand the significance of the National Party victory, we need to understand what went before.

South Africa: a brief history before 1948

Before European colonization, South Africa was a vast area of 470,000 square miles (1.2 million km²) inhabited over thousands of years by **Bantu** groups and tribes such as Zulu, Ndebele and Xhosa. Although Portuguese explorers were the first to land on South Africa, the first wave of Europeans, mainly employees of the **Dutch East India Trading Company**, arrived in 1652. They met the **indigenous** San and the Khoi, who rightly feared the arrival of these interlopers. More European settlers began to arrive and set up farms, employing slaves trafficked from elsewhere in Africa. The settlers began to fan out, moving north and west and meeting the more powerful Xhosa population, who equally resented their presence.

 **KEY TERM**

Africans The original black population of Africa.

Bureaucracy Members of the administration which implemented government policies.

White-collar Professional jobs such as administrators.

Dutch East India Trading Company Company established in 1602 to conduct trade with Asia. It used the Cape as a supply post for vessels *en route* to and from Asia.

Bantu An African people who speak a common group of languages. In the apartheid era, the white minority used 'Bantu' or 'native' to refer to Africans in South Africa, often in a derogatory way.

Indigenous Native to an area.

> How did the National Party come to win the election?

 KEY TERM

French Revolutionary and Napoleonic Wars A series of wars fought between France and Britain and their respective allies between 1792 and 1815.

Hinterland A remote area of a country, generally away from coastal regions.

Great Trek The movement of Boer farmers into the vast South African interior, away from British rule, which began in 1834.

Covenant Solemn oath, in this sense the agreement apparently made between God and the Boers in 1838.

Republic Country without a monarch at its head, usually led by a president.

Gold rush Migration of people to an area to find gold and become rich.

Second Boer War (South African War) between Britain and the Boers between 1899 and 1902. The Boers wanted complete independence from Britain, who wanted to expand to control the gold and diamond industries in the Transvaal.

What were the main racial groups?

 KEY TERM

Cape The southernmost province of South Africa, originally Cape Colony, part of the British Empire.

Dominion Largely self-governing country within the British Empire, recognizing the monarch as head of state.

Early European colonialization

The British arrived as a result of the **French Revolutionary and Napoleonic Wars**. The nineteenth century saw the Africans losing more and more land to settlers, and being diminished by warfare and disease.

The Afrikaners

The Afrikaners had begun to call themselves Boers (the Dutch word for farmer). The British abolished slavery within the British Empire in 1833, at which point the many Boers who kept slaves moved into the vast **hinterland**, away from British rule. This was called the **Great Trek** and had enormous ramifications in the subsequent history of South Africa. It became a sacred event for future generations of Afrikaners. On the eve of the Battle of Blood River against the Zulus in 1838, they were alleged to have made a **Covenant** with God, asking for victory. This subsequently became the basis of their belief that God had granted them the land of South Africa (see page 125).

The Boers founded two **republics**: the Transvaal and Orange Free State. As a people they were characterized by:

● hard work, mainly farming land that was often naturally infertile
● a stern puritanical Christianity: a belief in the literal truth of the Bible
● extreme racism: believing that people without white skin were inferior. Some even believed these people had been cursed by God.

The gold rush and Boer Wars

Diamonds and gold were discovered in great quantities in the Transvaal in 1867 and 1886, respectively. This led to a **gold rush** and eventually to the **Second Boer War** in 1899. When Britain emerged the victor in 1902, it eventually absorbed the two Boer republics in a new Union of South Africa in 1910. This was made up of the two predominantly Afrikaner areas, and the British-dominated **Cape** and Natal, which had been British colonies. The Union of South Africa became a self-governing **dominion** within the British Empire with a Constitution outlining the laws (see page 130).

The racial makeup of South Africa in the early twentieth century

Black Africans were overwhelmingly the largest group, but all political and economic power was essentially monopolized by the whites by 1904.

Table 4.1 The 1904 census was the first general census of all inhabitants of South Africa

Ethnic groups	Population	Percentage
Black Africans (many different tribes)	3,490,061	67.4%
Indians	122,734	2.4%
Coloured people	445,228	8.6%
Whites	1,116,804	21.6%
Total	5,174,827	100%

Africans

By far the largest group, Africans had been dispossessed of much of their land, could not vote except in the Cape, and were subject to widespread discrimination. Successive government policies not only kept them separate from whites, but tried as far as possible to keep them separate from each other – a sort of divide and rule. At the beginning of the twentieth century, over 80 per cent of Africans lived in rural areas either as sharecroppers or working their own farms. However, the whites wanted men for cheap labour, particularly in the mines, and drew up laws to force Africans off their own land so they could exploit them for labour.

Indians

Indians were descendants of 150,000 people imported by the British during the nineteenth century, originally as agricultural labourers. Many found work as administrators and founded a prosperous merchant class of traders and shopkeepers. They lived mainly in Natal and were largely seen by Afrikaners as foreign interlopers.

Coloured people

Coloured people lived overwhelmingly in the Cape area. Many owned land and could vote, and spoke Afrikaans and English.

> **A note on 'coloured'**
>
> In most countries, the use of 'coloured' to describe a black or mixed race person is old-fashioned and derogatory. In the context of South Africa, and this book, 'coloured' refers very specifically to a social categorization of people. From 1950 to 1990, under apartheid, 'coloured' was legally defined as 'a person of mixed European ("white") and African ("black") or Asian ancestry'.

Whites

Generally, whites were the only people who could vote. Elections, when they occurred, were between white political parties supported by different groups of white voters. There tended to be one and a half times as many Afrikaners as English speakers.

There were tensions between Afrikaners and English speakers. Afrikaners resented:

- the ties with Britain that dominion status brought
- South Africa's automatic entry into the **First World War** on the side of Britain; many maintained ties with Germany
- the economic domination of English speakers.

Afrikaners began to develop their own identity and institutions during the **interwar years**, which was a key driver in the National Party's eventual implementation of apartheid. This included the Afrikaner Broederbond, a secret club set up in 1918 dedicated to Afrikaners and their interests. During apartheid, from 1948 until 1994, every South African leader was a member of the Broederbond.

 **KEY TERM**

First World War
The 1914–18 war fought between the Allied Powers, notably Britain, France, Russia and from 1917, the USA, and the Central Powers dominated by Germany.

Interwar years The years between the First (1914–18) and the Second World Wars (1939–45).

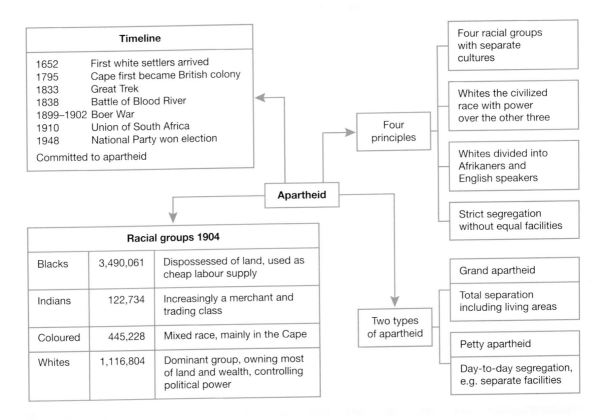

Timeline

1652	First white settlers arrived
1795	Cape first became British colony
1833	Great Trek
1838	Battle of Blood River
1899–1902	Boer War
1910	Union of South Africa
1948	National Party won election

Committed to apartheid

Four principles

- Four racial groups with separate cultures
- Whites the civilized race with power over the other three
- Whites divided into Afrikaners and English speakers
- Strict segregation without equal facilities

Apartheid

Two types of apartheid

- Grand apartheid
  - Total separation including living areas
- Petty apartheid
  - Day-to-day segregation, e.g. separate facilities

Racial groups 1904

Blacks	3,490,061	Dispossessed of land, used as cheap labour supply
Indians	122,734	Increasingly a merchant and trading class
Coloured	445,228	Mixed race, mainly in the Cape
Whites	1,116,804	Dominant group, owning most of land and wealth, controlling political power

SUMMARY DIAGRAM

What was apartheid?

② The segregation era 1910–48

▶ *Key question: To what extent was segregation introduced before the National Party victory?*

While politicians may have disagreed vehemently about respective rights of English speakers and Afrikaners, there was comparatively little disagreement about the need to exclude other groups from the political process.

Segregation in legislation

How far did legislation separate the races?

Both Afrikaners and English speakers agreed on their perception that Africans were racially inferior. Various laws were passed both to impose segregation and to reduce Africans as far as possible to the role of cheap labour, unable to compete with whites, for whom the better jobs were reserved.

A series of Acts before 1948 discriminated against the indigenous black population. These Acts highlighted the fundamental contradiction in segregation legislation: the whites tried to exclude Africans, but needed them at the same time to do the work they did not want to do. Therefore, because their labour was needed, laws such as the 1913 Native Land Act were passed in part to encourage them to leave the rural areas to work in industry, particularly the mines.

Table 4.2 Racial legislation 1910–36

1911 Mines and Works Act	• Excluded Africans from most skilled jobs in the mines, which were reserved for whites.
1911 Natives' Labour Regulation Act	• Africans were to be recruited in rural areas, fingerprinted and issued with **pass books** which gave them permission to enter their areas of work. This was one of the Acts known as the pass laws (see the box below, page 126).
1913 Natives Land Act	• Restricted African ownership of land (the reserves) to seven per cent of South Africa. The government argued that this figure was equivalent to African land holdings before the whites occupied the hinterland (see page 122).
	• Many Africans were now forced to work for white farmers – or leave to work in the temporary contracts in the mines and cities. This was necessary because the **homelands** (tribal reserves) such as Zululand and Transkei soon became overcrowded.
	• Most of the land Africans were allowed to keep was of the poorest quality – the land whites had not taken.
	• Early activists and some black farmers attempted to buy up as much land as they could before the Act was passed, leading to '**black spots**' across South Africa (these black spots were separate to the seven per cent 'given' to black Africans).
1923 Natives (Urban Areas) Act	• Africans should remain in cities only to administer to the needs of the white inhabitants, for example, as domestic servants.
	• Africans employed in industry or mining were expected to live in **townships** specially built for them on the outskirts of the cities, and to leave when their contract ended.
1924 Industrial Conciliation Act	• Restricted the right of Africans to organize themselves into trade unions and negotiate their terms of employment. They were given no rights as employees.

 **KEY TERM**

Pass books Internal passports to restrict the movement of people.

Homelands Areas laid aside for Africans to live in according to their tribal groups.

'Black spots' Areas outside the land officially designated for settlement by black Africans where they nevertheless managed to acquire land.

Townships Areas where black people lived separately from other races.

Department of Native Affairs The government department that regulated the lives of black citizens.

Pastoral environment Rural life based on small-scale agriculture or animal husbandry.

1927 Native Administration Act	• Set up the **Department of Native Affairs** (or Native Affairs Department, NAD) to control all matters relating to Africans. They were thereby separated in law from all other South Africans and had no civic rights outside this structure.
1936 Native Trust and Land Act	• Extended the amount of tribal reserves to 13.6 per cent of the total from the original seven per cent in the 1913 Native Land Act. Africans were not allowed to buy any land outside the tribal reserves.
1936 Representation of the Natives Act	• Approximately 10,000 Africans had been able to vote in the Cape on the same basis as whites (in other words, if they owned sufficient property, they could vote). This Act removed such rights. Africans were effectively disenfranchised and were treated as foreigners with no rights of permanent residence outside the designated tribal reserves. • African leaders in the Cape – about 4000 – were allowed to vote for four white representatives to the Senate. A Native Representation Council was created of six white officials, four nominated and twelve elected Africans to represent the views of Cape Africans in parliament.

Pass laws

The pass laws were developed to control the movement of Africans and manage migrant labour. They operated as a type of internal passport system to control where Africans could live, work and visit. While each South African province had its own system of pass laws, the pass laws overall were formalized and centralized by the Abolition of Passes and Co-ordination of Documents Act 1952 (see page 166).

White justification for segregation

Most whites had racist views which included Africans being lazy, untrustworthy and, if given the opportunity, dangerous. They considered black people most content in rural areas, tending to their farms and cattle, away from the temptations of urban life. These views were largely based on two factors:

● ignorance and fear of the consequences for their own position, and indeed safety, if Africans were given political or economic rights
● a need to feel reassured that segregation was in the Africans' best interests – that they were most contented in a simple **pastoral environment**.

The reserves

These factors led to a feeling that Africans were best living on tribal reserves. The reserves, of course, could not support their numbers.

SOURCE A

Excerpt from the *South and East African Yearbook and Guide for 1921*, published by Sampson, Low, Marston & Co., London, UK, 1921, p. 195.

*Although these are altered somewhat in the last present day, the social customs of the Bantus, which have always allotted to the women all work except cattle tending and hunting, still permit the man who has acquired a wife to live in almost complete idleness. It might be supposed that contact with civilised life would have early created a desire for what we are accustomed to look upon as the comforts and necessities of civilisation but although some change has taken place in recent years, the visitor to a **Kaffir kraal** cannot fail to notice how little influence the white man's mode of living still has on the natives' surroundings and how capable they are of providing for their own limited wants and comforts.*

SOURCE B

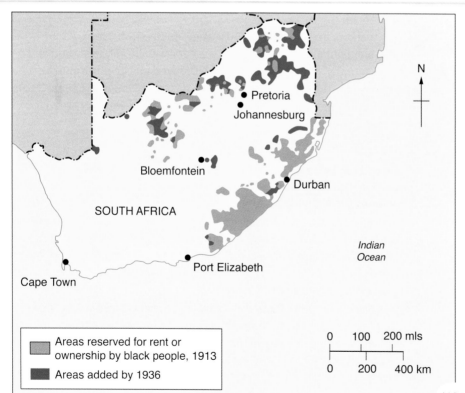

The land in South Africa reserved for Black African ownership or rent by the Natives Land Acts of 1913 and 1936.

Map legend:
- Areas reserved for rent or ownership by black people, 1913
- Areas added by 1936

KEY TERM

Kaffir Derogatory name given to black Africans.

Kraals Name given to African collections of farms where families or close members of tribal groups may live together.

What can you infer from Source A about the author's attitude towards the lives of Africans?

What does Source B indicate about land ownership in South Africa in 1913?

Transient migration and urbanization

After 1925, every African over the age of eighteen years had to pay a tax of the equivalent of £1.50 per dwelling. This opened up a system of **transient migration** whereby they had to borrow this money and then leave to find work, for example in the gold or diamond mines in the white areas, to repay the loan. In 1936, 447,000 of Africans in the 15–50 age group out of a total population of 43,410,000 were absent from the reserves. They were overwhelmingly male. During the interwar years, it is estimated that almost every African male went to work for whites at some time in his life.

KEY TERM

Transient migration
Temporary resettlement or movement, for example as guest workers. The government also called migrants temporary sojourners.

SOURCE C

Excerpt from *Travel In South Africa*, a guide book published by the authority of the general manager, South African Railways and Harbours, Johannesburg, 1937, p. 74.

Many of the Zulu men depart, in season, for the large towns of the Union, there to engage in domestic service, to work in the mines, or follow other pursuits, but sooner or later they return to their kraals, whereafter it takes them little time to shed what measure of veneer city life has given them.

? How reliable is Source C as an account of migrant labour?

Work

African workers lived in compounds: huge single-sex barracks where families were not allowed. Contracts were for usually between nine and eighteen months, but often by that time the worker's health would be broken. Usually they worked eight-hour shifts in the mines, in temperatures of over 100° Fahrenheit (38°C), for wages that could be as low as twelve pence per day – although they did receive free food.

SOURCE D

Excerpt from *Inside Africa* by John Gunther, Hamish Hamilton, 1955, pp. 545–6. Gunther was a well-respected journalist who surveyed conditions throughout the whole of Africa in this book.

*The dormitories are well built, the streets are paved with asphalt and the **accoutrements** are clean. There are big somewhat dank kitchens, laundries and lavatories. The physical circumstances of life are perhaps more attractive than in the **locations**, but the atmosphere is (no matter how well the workers are cared for) inhuman and forbidding.*

*At any given time in the **Rand** compounds there will be between 285,000 and 315,000 African workers. … Families are not allowed, workers have to be single or live apart from their wives for the duration of their contract, and 95 percent are migratory.*

? In Source D, why does Gunther says the atmosphere is inhuman and forbidding?

KEY TERM

Accoutrements Facilities.

Locations Townships reserved for Africans on the edge of urban centres.

Rand The goldmining areas in the Transvaal, known more correctly as Witwatersrand.

SOURCE E

Men leaving the reserves to work in the Kimberley diamond mines.

What impression does Source E give of migrant workers? **?**

Urbanization

The need for cheap labour always outweighed any political pressures to practise **influx control**. As early as 1900 there were 100,000 African workers in the mines. By the mid-1950s, the African population of the city of Johannesburg was 500,000 African and 450,000 white, even though Africans could not officially live in its environs except as transient workers. This rapid urbanization was largely unplanned (although there were more coloured and Indians in urban areas than Africans; see Table 4.3). Many Africans ended up living in **shanty towns**. They faced discrimination and hardship, knowing they were needed but not wanted, in a country they largely considered their own.

 **KEY TERM**

Influx control Methods used to control African migration into urban areas, such as the pass laws.

Shanty towns Areas made up of temporary, often inadequate accommodation and lacking proper facilities such as sanitation or supplies of fresh water.

Table 4.3 Proportion of each group of the population living in urban areas 1921–60

Year	All (%)	Total (thousands)	White (%)	Coloured (%)	Indian (%)	African (%)
1921	28	1933	60	52	61	16
1936	32	3106	68	57	71	21
1946	38	4384	75	61	71	23
1951	43	5398	78	65	78	27
1960	47	7473	84	68	83	32

A shanty town outside Johannesburg, South Africa, 1948.

> ?
> What does Source F indicate about the living conditions in a shanty town?

South Africa and political power

As South Africa was a British dominion, the British government appointed a governor general and a two-house legislature, the parliament, comprising the Senate and House of Assembly. The 50 senators in the Senate were appointed by either the governor general or the Regional Assemblies of the four provinces of Cape Province, Natal, Orange Free State and Transvaal. The membership of the House of Assembly was usually elected every five years. The two main parties were the United Party, dominated by English speakers who sought to maintain close ties with Britain, and the National Party, comprised mainly of Afrikaners who sought a more independent path, with the ultimate goal of a republic. Any legislation to change the **1910 Constitution** needed a two-thirds majority in a joint sitting of both legislative houses to pass.

> **How was South Africa governed before 1948?**

Political parties before the Second World War

There were many political parties vying for power in South Africa. All were comprised almost exclusively of white men, and white men constituted the majority of voters (white women did not gain suffrage until 1930):

 **KEY TERM**

1910 Constitution
The key document which set out how South Africa was to be governed and what powers it possessed as a dominion within the British Empire.

- *South African Party (SAP) and United Party (UP)*. Broadly speaking, the South African Party (led by Jan Smuts) and United Party both favoured a link with Britain, although they still supported a system of segregation and white supremacy.
- *South African Labour Party (SALP)*. English-speaking; favoured improvements in working and living conditions for working-class whites.
- *Dominion Party*. Established in late October 1934 by the merger of the South African Party and National Party.
- *National Party*. Mainly comprised of Afrikaners; keen on promoting Afrikaner identity and values; intent on imposing apartheid, white supremacy and independence from Britain.
- *Purified National Party (GNP) and Reunited National Party (HNP)*. In 1934, D.F. Malan had founded the Purified National Party in Transvaal in opposition to the merger of the National Party and South African Party. Dissidents from the United Party (see page 130), including Prime Minister Herzog, later joined with the Purified National Party to form the Reunited National Party (HNP).
- *Afrikaner Party*. Formed from members of the United Party split; entered into a coalition with the National Party to win power in the 1948 elections and was absorbed into the National Party in 1951.

D.F. Malan

Daniel François Malan was born in 1874 in Riebeeck West, Cape Province. Extremely intelligent, he attended Stellenbosch University, where he studied philosophy and theology. Although he did not fight in the Boer Wars he hated the British and their influence, and sought greater Afrikaner autonomy. He was a minister for the **Dutch Reformed Church** until 1915 when, concerned about the extent of British influence, he changed career and began to edit the Afrikaner newspaper *Die Burger* (*The Citizen*). By 1918 Malan had entered politics. He rose quickly in Hertzog's administrations, serving as minister of the interior, education and health through the 1920s until 1933 when he split from Hertzog.

Hertzog had merged the National Party with Smuts' South African Party to win the 1933 election. In protest, Malan formed the Purified National Party, which was to pursue an agenda of apartheid and anti-British policies.

However, the outbreak of the Second World War was to have a large impact on South Africa and the way in which it was governed.

Political allegiance in South Africa after the Second World War

The outbreak of the **Second World War** further divided the whites in South Africa. Many Afrikaners felt affinity with **Nazi Germany**. English speakers were more likely to support the **Allies**.

 **KEY TERM**

Dutch Reformed Church Afrikaner Church which supported apartheid.

Second World War Fought from 1939 and 1945 between the Allies, primarily the USA, the UK, France and the USSR (Union of Soviet Socialist Republics, or the Soviet Union), and Nazi Germany, Japan and their allies.

Nazi Germany The German regime under Adolf Hitler.

Allies The USA, the UK, France, the USSR and other countries who supported them during the Second World War.

Malan's Purified National Party increasingly attracted the allegiance of Afrikaners. It associated itself with the resurgence in Afrikaner identity and looked to the **fascist dictatorships** in Europe. Hendrik Verwoerd, future prime minister (see page 154), became the editor of *Die Transvaler* (*The Transvaler*). This was the newspaper of the National Party, which became notorious not only for its pro-Nazi stance but also for its anti-Semitism.

Hertzog wanted neutrality, whereas the pro-British Smuts sought to join the Allies. The United Party favoured joining the war, and so Smuts became prime minister. Many Afrikaners were particularly incensed when Smuts declared South Africa's entry into war on Germany on 4 September 1939. While half the white South African male population (180,000) volunteered to join the Allied forces in 1939, some Afrikaners actively worked for a Nazi victory, for example by broadcasting and publishing pro-Nazi material. Many joined the openly pro-fascist Greyshirt movement and even committed acts of sabotage against their own government.

Hertzog subsequently joined Malan in a new Reunited National Party (HNP). In the 1943 elections they achieved 43 seats, but were organizing at local levels to prepare for a post-war strategy to achieve power.

How significant were the economic effects of the Second World War in South Africa?

Economic effects of the Second World War

Clearly, those whites who had volunteered to fight needed to be replaced. Hence, the laws against African labour were relaxed: of the 125,000 extra workers employed in manufacturing and construction industries during the war years, just 25 per cent were white. However, the growth in production was uneven – as low as 0.5 per cent during the war years, compared with 2.5 per cent from 1938 to 1939. The reason for this was that many industries became more labour intensive as machinery and equipment from abroad became scarcer. This made it possible to employ more Africans. Indeed, one pre-war trend, caused by the increasing availability of machinery, had been the need for fewer skilled workers in industry. Factory work for Africans typically involved them minding machines, while white workers did the more skilled engineering work. This was reflected in wages: in 1935: the average wages for white and African workers in industry were £240 and £42 a year, respectively.

The government, influenced by Deputy Prime Minister Jan Hofmeyr, appeared to be formulating a new, more moderate racial policy. Hofmeyr encouraged African education so that Africans could eventually provide a more skilled workforce, and relaxed the pass laws in 1942 to facilitate employment in urban areas. In a speech to the moderate Institute of Race Relations in Cape Town in January 1942, Smuts had even argued that the policy of racial segregation had been a failure for Africans, citing statistics of African poverty and infant mortality as examples. In 1946, a commission to investigate the possibility of a National Health Service even recommended a non-discriminatory healthcare system – although this was not taken any further.

Laws affecting Africans		
Year	Title	Aim
1911	Mines and Works Act	Excluded from skilled jobs in mines
1911	Native Regulations Act	Control through compulsory pass books
1913	Native Land Act	Land ownership limited to tribal reserves: 7% of total land in South Africa
1923	Urban Areas Act	Must live in townships in white areas
1924	Industry Concentration Act	No rights as employees
1927	Native Administration Act	Native Affairs Department set up to run African affairs
1936	Representation of Natives Act	Africans disenfranchised in the Cape
1936	Native Trusts and Lands Act	Tribal reserves could be extended to 13.6% of total land area of South Africa

Aims

For Africans to stay on reserves except when required for cheap labour

For families and dependants as far as possible to stay on the reserves while men worked as migrant labour

Types of work

Working on white farms, mining, industry, domestic labour

SUMMARY DIAGRAM

The segregation era 1910–48

3 The 1948 election and its effects

▶ **Key question:** *What was the impact of the National Party victory in the 1948 election?*

The 1948 election was fought between the HNP, in coalition with the Afrikaner Party, and the United Party, in coalition with the South African Labour Party.

SOURCE G

Excerpt from *The Rise of the South African Reich* by Brian Bunting, published by Penguin, Harmondsworth, UK, 1964. Bunting was a journalist and member of the South African Communist Party who opposed the South African government.

The only alternatives before the country, the special commission of the Nationalist Party had reported, were apartheid or complete equality. The United Party was following the latter course. Only apartheid could save the country from the ultimate disaster of miscegenation.

It [apartheid] envisages the maintenance and protection of the indigenous racial groups as separate ethnological groups with possibilities to develop in their own territories into self-reliant national units … National policy must be framed in

How useful is Source G in explaining the policy differences between the two main political parties during the 1948 election?

?

such a way that it promotes the ideal of eventual total apartheid in a natural way.

On 14 July 1947, Strijdom [minister of agriculture and irrigation and future prime minister] told the Nasionale Jeugbond *(the Nationalist Youth Association) at Bloemfontein: 'The only alternative is the policy of the Nationalist Party of separation and apartheid in the sense that the natives must stay in their own territories and should come to the cities only temporarily as workers.'*

Integration or apartheid – that was the issue put to the voters in the 1948 elections. Nobody could be quite sure as yet what apartheid meant, but at least everybody was quite clear what it did not mean. It did not mean equality; it did not mean race mixing; it did not mean integration and the extension of rights to the non-Whites. Fundamentally the Nationalist Party stood for **baaskap***, and everybody knew what* baaskap *meant.*

After its victory, the HNP renamed itself the National Party and the Afrikaner Party was absorbed within it. Even though the National Party did not win the popular vote – the United Party gained 524,230 votes over the National Party's 401,834 – they gained more MPs (see Table 4.4).

Table 4.4 Election results showing number of seats 1948

Reunited National Party (HNP)/Afrikaner Party coalition	United Party (UP)/South African Labour Party coalition	Prime minister
79 seats	71 seats	D.F. Malan

Why did the National Party win the 1948 general election?

Reasons for the National Party victory

Various reasons have been offered for the National Party's victory:

- Smuts, the leader of the United Party, was old and tired
- the United Party was poorly organized
- the unfair tactics (see below) which led National Party candidates to accuse their opponents, particularly Jan Hofmeyr, of supporting racial integration.

SOURCE H

Why, according to Source H, are the nationalists attacking Hofmeyr?

Excerpt from 'South African Elections – From Our Own Correspondent', *The Times*, 26 May 1948. *The Times* is a British newspaper.

The Nationalists have been … assiduous in exploiting against the Government every little discomfort, every possible cause of fear … they are even trying to proselytise [seek to convert people to your own point of view] English speaking voters on the plea that they were temporarily putting their republicanism into cold storage in order to secure the collaboration of both European groups in solving the native problem for all time.

This then is the theme of their electioneering, and the main target of their attack is Mr J.H. Hofmeyr, the deputy prime minister. Mr Hofmeyr is a Liberal … he

has repeatedly said … that discrimination on grounds of race alone is morally wrong …

The Nationalists argue that Mr Hofmeyr will advocate a policy of economic and political equality for all races which must lead to social equality, intermarriage and the end of white race and white civilisation in South Africa. The overtones and undertones of this argument are calculated to give the ignorant and prejudiced the impression that almost as soon as Mr Hofmeyr comes to power, natives will be asking for their sister's hand in marriage.

In his campaign, Malan criticized Smuts for allowing the influx of black and coloured people into white areas seen during the war years. He acknowledged, however, that they could continue to work in white areas, albeit having to live in strictly segregated and regulated communities.

The difference between the main parties was apparent. One seemed imprecise beyond continuing as before; the other offered what appeared to be a radical alternative – but was in fact only a continuation of the policies of segregation which had been carried out during the previous 40 years. Most white people argued that the races should be segregated as far as humanly possible. However, they also recognized two further points: that there was a need for cheap African labour, and that the country should be strictly governed in the interests of the white minority. They felt therefore that, given these complications, there should be a radical, rigorous, well-planned scheme for the implementation of segregation. The era of apartheid had begun.

SOURCE I

Pamphlet issued by the National Party head office in late 1947 ahead of the May 1948 general election, located at: www.politicsweb.co.za/ politicsweb/view/politicsweb/en/page71619?oid=298016&sn=Detail.

Race relations policy of the National Party

Introduction

There are two distinct guiding principles determining the South African policy affecting the non-Whites. One line of thought favours a policy of integration, conferring equal rights – including the franchise as the non-whites progressively become used to democratic institutions – on all civilised and educated citizens within the same political structure.

Opposed to this is the policy of apartheid, a concept historically derived from the experience of the established White population of the country, and in harmony with such Christian principles as justice and equity. It is a policy which sets itself the task of preserving and safeguarding the racial identity of the White population of the country; of likewise preserving and safeguarding the identity of the indigenous peoples as separate racial groups, with opportunities to develop into self-governing national units; of fostering the inculcation of national consciousness, self-esteem and mutual regard among the various races of the country.

Compare and contrast the views about apartheid expressed in Sources I and J (page 136).

The choice before us is one of these two divergent courses: either that of integration, which would in the long run amount to national suicide on the part of the Whites: or that of apartheid[,] which professes to preserve the identity and safeguard the future of every race, with complete scope for everyone to develop within its own sphere while maintaining its distinctive national character, in such a way that there will be no encroachment on the rights of others, and without a sense of being frustrated by the existence and development of others.

SOURCE J

Excerpt from *Long Walk to Freedom* by Nelson Mandela, published by Abacus, London, UK, 2013, pp. 126–7. Nelson Mandela became the first president of a democratic South Africa in 1994, after being imprisoned for years due to his anti-apartheid views and actions.

Malan's platform was known as Apartheid. Apartheid was a new term but an old idea. It literally means apartness, and it represents the codification in one oppressive system of all the laws and regulations that had kept Africans in an inferior position to whites for centuries. … The often haphazard segregation of the past three hundred years was to be consolidated into a monolithic system that was diabolical in detail, inescapable in its reach and overwhelming in its power. The premise of Apartheid was that whites were superior to Africans, Coloureds and Indians, and the function of it was to entrench white supremacy forever … Their platform rested on the term baaskap*, literally 'boss-ship', a loaded word that stood for white supremacy in all its harshness. The policy was supported by the Dutch Reformed Church, which furnished Apartheid with its religious underpinnings by suggesting that Afrikaners were God's chosen people and that blacks were a subservient species. In the Afrikaners' world view, apartheid and the church went hand in hand.*

The National Party Government 1948–53

In May 1948, on the National Party's victory, Malan said, 'Today South Africa belongs to us once more. South Africa is our own for the first time since Union, and may God grant that it will always remain our own.' Some called the 1948 election the final Afrikaner victory of the Boer War. The new government had two overarching aims:

- To impose white supremacy through an all-embracing system of apartheid.
- To end political ties with Britain and form a republic.

The National Party was to win every election until the demise of apartheid in 1994, and its support grew over the period 1948–64 (see Table 4.5, opposite). In 1953 it won a majority on its own for the first time; in the two subsequent elections it had a majority of almost 50 seats.

Table 4.5 Election results showing number of seats 1948–64

Year	National Party	United Party	South African Labour Party	Progressive Party	National Union	Prime minister
1953	94	57	5	–	–	D.F. Malan retired 1954, then J.G. Strijdom
1958	103	53	–	–	––	J.G. Strijdom died 1958, then H. Verwoerd
1961	105	49	–	1	1	H. Verwoerd

SOURCE K

Children sit on a bench along the waterfront in Durban, a large, modern city on the Indian Ocean, 27 May 1960.

What can you infer from Source K about the effects of apartheid?

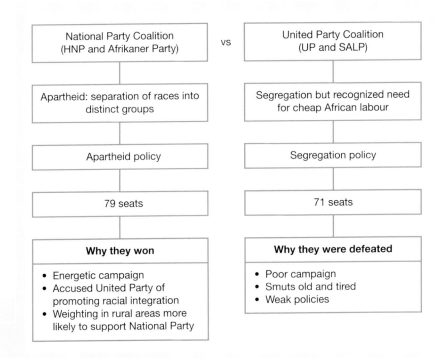

National Party Coalition (HNP and Afrikaner Party) vs United Party Coalition (UP and SALP)

National Party Coalition (HNP and Afrikaner Party)	United Party Coalition (UP and SALP)
Apartheid: separation of races into distinct groups	Segregation but recognized need for cheap African labour
Apartheid policy	Segregation policy
79 seats	71 seats

Why they won
- Energetic campaign
- Accused United Party of promoting racial integration
- Weighting in rural areas more likely to support National Party

Why they were defeated
- Poor campaign
- Smuts old and tired
- Weak policies

SUMMARY DIAGRAM

The 1948 election and its effects

4 Growth of resistance

▶ *Key question: How effectively did protest groups oppose segregation in the period 1910–49?*

This section considers the activities of the following groups prior to 1948:

- African National Congress (ANC)
- Labour organizations
- Communist Party of South Africa (CPSA)
- South African Indian Congress (SAIC).

African National Congress (ANC)

How effective was the ANC between 1910 and 1948?

KEY TERM

Polyglot Someone fluent in different languages.

There was a small but vociferous African elite who had remained loyal to Britain during the Boer War, and had hoped for political rights in the ensuing settlement. Solomon Plaatje was one of these elite, a **polyglot** who spoke seven languages. He had worked as a court interpreter in Mafeking and aided British intelligence during the Boer War.

Plaatje met other educated middle-class African elites in Bloemfontein in the Orange Free State in January 1912. The meeting at Bloemfontein saw the creation of the South African Native National Congress (SANNC), which became the African National Congress (ANC) in 1923. Plaatje was its first secretary. Its first president, John L. Dube, a Christian minister who had been educated in the USA, was greatly influenced by Booker T. Washington, an African-American leader who advocated that his people needed help from whites to elevate themselves.

SOURCE L

Excerpt from the Constitution of the SANNC, drawn up at Bloemfontein on 8 January 1912, quoted in *A History of the ANC* by Francis Meli, published by James Currey, Woodbridge, UK, 1989, p. 52.

To encourage mutual understanding and to bring together into common action as one political people all tribes and clans of various tribes or races and by means of combined effort and united political organisation to defend their freedom, rights and privileges … and to enlist the sympathy and support of Europeans; to educate African people on their rights, duties and obligations to the state and to themselves and to promote mutual help …

According to Source L, what does the ANC see as important to achieve its aims?

Appeals to Britain and the Peace Conference at Versailles

One early issue among the SANNC leadership was its willingness to look to Britain as the former colonial authority for support. It looked for international help in the context of international events rather than concentrating inwardly on what was happening in South Africa. Hence, in 1914, after the Governor General Lord Gladstone had refused to meet SANNC members in May 1913, a delegation was sent to London to see the colonial secretary about their plight in South Africa. When they finally arrived in London in May 1914, they had to wait for weeks before Lord Harcourt, the colonial secretary, would meet them, only to be told it was a matter for the government of South Africa, not that of Britain.

In 1918, the ANC **petitioned** King George V with 7000 signatures to protest continued racism, despite 17,000 Africans volunteering to fight against German troops in East Africa and 25,000 serving on the Western Front. They received no response.

 **KEY TERM**

Petitioned Presented an appeal bearing the signatures of as many supporters as possible.

> **Paris Peace Conference 1919**
>
> An ANC delegation even went to the Paris Peace Conference, where those involved spoke of self-determination for all people. However, as the main victor nations, including Britain, France, Italy and the USA, had their own empires, issues such as decolonization or racial equality were not on the agenda. The ANC delegation was denied entrance.

The ANC in the interwar period

Historians have often seen the interwar period as an unsuccessful one for the ANC. Its middle-class leadership was alleged to be out of touch with the day-to-day realities of life for Africans. The ANC produced newspapers and pamphlets in voluminous quantities but the vast majority of Africans were illiterate and had no understanding of concepts such as nationhood, in which all black Africans were considered members of the same race who belonged to the same country. Most still saw themselves primarily as members of distinct tribes who had comparatively little in common with each other – which is, of course, how the white rulers wanted them to perceive their identity. This view is being re-examined, however. Historian Peter Lamb, writing in 2013, insisted that despite setbacks, the ANC leadership never wavered in its commitment to improving the lot of African workers. Lamb saw the ANC as very much involved in local and regional disputes and far more active than one might suppose.

Clearly, the ANC leadership faced severe problems in trying to galvanize African support:

- One of the main principles of segregation (and later apartheid) was to maintain tribal diversity, rather than group unity, through, for example, the pass system's restrictions on movement. This made it difficult for Africans to communicate with each other, let alone organize together.
- Among Africans there were several different languages, and the high illiteracy level made it impossible to communicate effectively via the written word.
- It was also difficult to find common ground. The concerns of rural dwellers were different from those who worked in the mines or factories.

One should not forget, however, the determination of the government, which simply refused to open up any meaningful dialogue and was quick to fight action with repression.

The leadership of the ANC was eminently respectable and middle class, and its main policies of persuasion, argument and respectful discourse were simply inappropriate for the period. When a more radical president, J.T. Gumede, was elected in 1927, he found little support for his willingness to work with the **Communist Party of South Africa (CPSA)** (see below), and was defeated in the 1930 election for ANC president.

Greater radicalism in the 1940s

From 1940, under the leadership of Alfred Xuma, the ANC began to work with other organizations such as the South African Indian Congress (see below) to develop a **policy of non-cooperation** and also to link the struggle in South Africa with that of other oppressed people in the world. Interestingly, Prime Minister Jan Smuts was instrumental in formulating the 1945 **Charter of the United Nations**, which spoke of equal human rights and liberty. Smuts subsequently assured National Party leader D.F. Malan that he did not mean this for Africans.

Nelson Mandela

Nelson Mandela was the most famous of the leaders within the ANC and went on to become the first democratically elected president of a unified South Africa in May 1994. He was born in July 1918 in the tribal reserve of

KEY TERM

Communist Party of South Africa (CPSA)
Communist Party believing in ideas such as state ownership of industry and equality for everyone.

Policy of non-cooperation Civil disobedience, for example leaving pass books at home or entering white-only facilities.

Charter of the United Nations Document outlining the aims and organization of the United Nations, including racial equality and social and economic justice for all. The United Nations was formed in 1945 to promote cooperation among nations worldwide.

Transkei. After his father, a senior tribal official, died when he was nine years old, he was adopted by the chief of the Thembo people. Mandela was subsequently educated in mission schools and attended Fort Hare University, where he studied law. It was at Fort Hare where he became involved in his first political protest. He refused to serve on the Student Representative Council because the vast majority of students had boycotted the election (in a protest against the quality of the food provided to them). The principal gave him an ultimatum: either to serve or be expelled. This, coupled with the prospect of an arranged marriage to a girl whom he knew loved someone else, persuaded him to flee to Johannesburg in 1941. Here, he worked in various jobs as a clerk while studying part-time for a law degree at the University of Witwatersrand. He also joined the ANC. His anti-apartheid activities caused many to call him by his clan name, Madiba, loosely meaning 'father'.

The ANC Youth League (ANCYL)

The frustrations over ANC demands being ignored by successive governments led to more radical movements within the organization. In 1943, Walter Sisulu formed the ANC Youth League, which featured a new generation of leaders such as Mandela, Oliver Tambo and Robert Sobukwe (see pages 203–5). Its first president, Anton Lembede, asserted that South Africa belonged to black Africans: 'Look at my skin, it is black, black like the soil of Mother Africa. We must believe that we are inferior to no other race. We must develop race pride.'

> #### Oliver Tambo
>
> Tambo was a leading activist in the ANC, serving as its president in exile in 1967 following the death of Chief Luthuli (see page 187). He was born in 1917, and educated at the University of Fort Hare, where he met Nelson Mandela (see page 140). Tambo initially became a teacher, joined the ANC, and with Mandela and others was instrumental in forming the ANC Youth League to engender more radicalism into the movement (see page 186). He shared in all the ANC activities of the late 1940s and 1950s, and was chosen to lead the ANC from abroad after it was made illegal in April 1960 (see page 209). Tambo returned to South Africa to great acclaim in 1990 during its transition to democracy, and died in 1993.

The ANCYL sought a broader organization with mass support and emphasized the community-based culture of Africans, as opposed to the individualism of whites. It asserted, therefore, that Africans must work together in unity and looked to promote mass action within South Africa. Some leaders, such as Lembede, felt that Africans should do this themselves without help from either whites or other groups such as Indians. This policy was known as **Africanism** and became very significant as the anti-apartheid movements developed in the 1950s (see for example pages 203–4). It was,

 **KEY TERM**

Africanism The policy of black Africans fighting for civil and political rights without help from whites or other racial groups.

however, contentious even among Lembede's own colleagues. Much debate has been generated over how far the ANC was Africanist, both from the period of its inception in 1912 and following its more radical stance in the 1940s. It may be helpful to read the extracts from the following two key policy documents (Sources M, below, and N, opposite) within this context.

SOURCE M

What does Source M indicate about the ANCYL's attitudes towards white people?

Excerpt from the ANCYL manifesto, 1944, located at: www.anc.org.za/show.php?id=4439

South Africa has a complex problem. Stated briefly it is: The contact of the White race with the Black has resulted in the emergence of a set of conflicting living conditions and outlooks on life which seriously hamper South Africa's progress to nationhood.

The White race, possessing superior military strength and at present having superior organising skill has arrogated to itself the ownership of the land and invested itself with authority and the right to regard South Africa as a White man's country. This has meant that the African, who owned the land before the advent of the Whites, has been deprived of all security which may guarantee him an independent pursuit of destiny or ensure his leading a free and unhampered life. He has been defeated in the field of battle but refuses to accept this as meaning that he must be oppressed, just to enable the White man to further dominate him.

The African regards Civilisation as the common heritage of all Mankind and claims as full a right to make his contribution to its advancement and to live free as any White South African: further, he claims the right to all sources and agencies to enjoy rights and fulfill duties which will place him on a footing of equality with every other South African racial group.

The majority of White men regard it as the destiny of the White race to dominate the man of colour. The harshness of their domination, however, is rousing in the African feelings of hatred of everything that bars his way to full and free citizenship and these feelings can no longer be suppressed.

The ANC increasingly saw the struggle for justice within the context of other colonial fights for independence, for example in India and other African countries. By 1948, the ANCYL was becoming frustrated by the lack of progress using tactics of petition and **delegations**. It began to speak of the need for **direct action** or peaceful, non-violent but assertive protests such as marches, demonstrations and non-cooperation.

In 1948, partially as a response to the election of the National Government with its apartheid agenda, the ANCYL created the Basic Policy. This proposed uniting Africans so they no longer saw themselves simply in tribal terms, and creating the conditions in which Africans could be successful in South Africa. It should be emphasized that the Basic Policy represented a position in their thinking, rather than a formal programme. However, it asserted that Africans

KEY TERM

Delegations Groups meeting those in authority to make specific requests.

Direct action Action to protest something, for example a march or demonstration.

had a fundamental right to the wealth and prosperity of Africa, and the struggle to achieve this should be led by Africans themselves – although they were prepared to accept help from other groups, as evidenced by the Three Doctors' Pact of 1947 (see page 147). Nor was it anywhere asserted that they would refuse help from sympathetic whites, even though they felt the voice of such people was negligible. Nevertheless, the very willingness to accept help from other groups would lead to significant disagreements with the Africanists in the following decade.

SOURCE N

Excerpt from the Basic Policy of the ANCYL, 2 August 1948, located at: www.anc.org.za/show.php?id=4448

Europeans: The majority of Europeans share the spoils of white domination in this country. They have a vested interest in the exploitative caste society of South Africa. A few of them love Justice and condemn racial oppression, but their voice is negligible, and in the last analysis counts for nothing. In their struggle for freedom the Africans will be wasting their time and deflecting their forces if they look up to the Europeans either for inspiration or for help in their political struggle.

Indians: Although, like the Africans, the Indians are oppressed as a group, yet they differ from the Africans in their historical and cultural background among other things. They have their mother-country, India, but thousands of them made South Africa and Africa their home. They, however, did not come as conquerors and exploiters, but as the exploited. As long as they do not undermine or impede out liberation struggle we should not regard them as intruders or enemies.

Coloured: Like the Indians they differ from the Africans, they are a distinct group, suffering group oppression. But their oppression differs in degree from that of the Africans. The Coloureds have no motherland to look up to and, but for historic accidents, they might be nearer to the Africans than are the Indians, seeing they descend in part at least from the aboriginal Hottentots who with Africans and Bushmen are original children of Black Africa. Coloureds, like the Indians, will never win their national freedom unless they organise a Coloured People's National Organisation to lead in the struggle of the National Freedom of the Coloureds. The National Organisations of the Africans, Indians and Coloureds may co-operate on common issues.

Explain what Source N says about the role of non-black African groups in the ANC's struggle for political and civil rights in South Africa.

In 1949, the ANCYL's Basic Policy was formalized into a Programme of Action which stressed:

- the rejection of white domination
- a pro-African policy which meant support for **African Nationalism** both in South Africa and throughout the continent
- an assertion of pride in being an African to counter the racist theories of white supremacy and African inferiority and worthlessness
- a demand for mass and direct action.

 **KEY TERM**

African Nationalism
The movement within Africa for independence from colonial powers such as Britain and for civil and political rights in South Africa.

How useful is Source O in explaining the aims and strategies of the ANC?

Excerpt from the ANC Programme of Action, 17 December 1949, located at: www.anc.org.za/show.php?id=4472

The fundamental principles of the Programme of Action of the African National Congress are inspired by the desire to achieve national freedom. By national freedom we mean freedom from White domination and the attainment of political independence. This implies the rejection of the conception of segregation, apartheid, trusteeship, or white leadership which are all, in one way or another, motivated by the idea of white domination or domination of the white over the Blacks. Like all other people the African people claim the right of self-determination. With this object in view, in the light of these principles we claim and will continue to fight for the political rights tabulated on page 8 of our Bill of Rights, such as:

1. The right of direct representation in all the governing bodies of the country – national, provincial and local – and we resolve to work for the abolition of all differential institutions or bodies specially created for Africans, viz. representative councils, present form of parliamentary representation.

2. To achieve these objectives the following Programme of Action is suggested:

a) the creation of a national fund to finance the struggle for national liberation.

b) the appointment of a committee to organise an appeal for funds and to devise ways and means therefor.

c) the regular use of propaganda material through:

i) the usual press, newsletter or other means of disseminating our ideas in order to raise the standard of political consciousness;

ii) establishment of a national press.

3. Appointment of a council of action whose function should be to carry into effect, vigorously and with the utmost determination, the Programme of Action. It should be competent for the council of action to implement our resolve to work for:

a) the abolition of all differential political institutions, the boycotting of which we accept, and to undertake a campaign to educate our people on this issue and, in addition, to employ the following weapons: immediate and active boycott, strike, civil disobedience, non-co-operation and such other means as may bring about the accomplishment and realisation of our aspirations.

b) preparations and making of plans for a national stoppage of work for one day as a mark of protest against the reactionary policy of the government.

The ANC annual conference accepted the Basic Policy as official policy in December 1949. ANCYL leaders increasingly began to shape and direct ANC policy into the next decade and beyond.

Direct action and labour organizations

Whichever party was in power, there were no disagreements about the subservient place of Africans. Effective dialogue with white influential politicians was unlikely – although this was a lesson which African leaders had to learn in the face of growing tensions. However, direct action relating to specific grievances did take place on numerous occasions, with varying degrees of success:

- In August 1943, a nine-day boycott of buses began in Alexandra, Johannesburg, when the Putco bus company tried to raise the daily fare from 2 to 3 pence. In a boycott which was replicated in 1957 (see page 180), thousands walked rather than pay the increased fares. Their efforts paid off when the company withdrew the price increase.
- In 1944, squatters on the outskirts of Johannesburg set up their own system of local government under James Mpanza, leader of the Sofasonke ('We Shall Die Together') movement.
- Although strikes were outlawed during the Second World War there were over 300 stoppages. By 1946 the **Council of Non-European Trade Unions (CNETU)**, formed in 1941, claimed a membership 158,000 workers in 119 unions. The African Mineworkers' Union (AMWU) claimed a membership of 21,000. These were mainly migrant workers, traditionally difficult to organize because they were on temporary contracts. In 1946, the AMWU led 100,000 African miners to strike for higher wages. Strikes were usually ended by violence on the part of the authorities. The 1946 mineworkers' strike left twelve dead. The authorities were always prepared to fire guns into crowds of African workers.

Industrial and Commercial Workers' Union (ICU)

The Industrial and Commercial Workers' Union (ICU) was founded by Clements Kadalie, a migrant worker from Malawi, among dockworkers in Cape Town. In 1918, sanitation workers in Johannesburg and mineworkers in the Rand went on strike for higher wages, while in 1919 location workers in Bloemfontein struck for a minimum wage. None of these strikes was successful but they did stimulate a desire for union organization which was met in part by the formation of the ICU. By the late 1920s it claimed a membership of 100,000. The authorities always responded to ICU industrial action with repression; when the union called out workers in Port Elizabeth, they responded with gunfire in which 24 strikers were killed.

In 1920, the ICU called a miners' strike where 70,000 workers walked out. Although workers were forced back at gunpoint and eleven of them were killed, the strike worried the authorities. The Transvaal Chamber of Commerce noted that the strike was organized on European lines and feared **Communist** influence; they were unable to believe Africans could have organized this themselves. Ironically, the ICU was anti-Communist, feeling

To what extent was African industrial action effective?

 KEY TERM

Council of Non-European Trade Unions (CNETU) African trade union formed in 1941.

Communist A person who believes that the planning and control of the economy should be by the state and people should be rewarded according to the value of their contribution.

that Communists had their own revolutionary agenda and were simply exploiting Africans to achieve this. In 1927, Kadalie expelled Communists from the ICU.

In his history of the ANC, the writer Francis Meli accuses the ICU of corruption and maladministration. The collapse of the ICU by the 1930s marks the beginning of a widespread conflation of Communist influence with African protest, which was to influence the thinking and fears behind the movement throughout the apartheid era. It also, to an extent, explained the readiness of the authorities to use a level of force disproportionate to the protest. It was not only that they feared any African successes might stimulate their overthrow – many in authority doubted Africans were capable of successful organization – but they feared they could be led by Communists to effect revolution, purely because of their great numbers.

Why did other groups not trust the CPSA?

Communist Party of South Africa (CPSA)

The Communist Party of South Africa (CPSA), founded in 1921, sought to organize Africans into trade unions and unite with white trade unionists on the basis of class rather than race.

🔑 KEY TERM

Soviet Union The leading Communist country from 1922 to 1991.

Taking its orders from the **Soviet Union**, the CPSA was tasked with the formation of a multiracial republic governed by Africans as the majority group before moving on to Communism. This meant it would be possible to work with groups such as the ANC to achieve the republic, although the ANC and other groups knew that they did not necessarily share the same goals as the CPSA.

The interwar relationship with the ANC was more ambivalent. Gumede (see page 140) was more amenable to cooperation. In February 1927, he accompanied CPSA delegates to a Communist-run League Against Imperialism Conference held in Brussels, where he made two speeches and praised the Communist ideal:

? What can you infer from Source P about Gumede's attitude to Communism?

SOURCE P

From a speech by Josiah T. Gumede, president of the ANC, at the League Against Imperialism in Brussels, February 1927, quoted in A History of the ANC by Francis Meli, published by James Currey, Woodbridge, UK, 1989, p. 75.

I am happy to say there are Communists in South Africa. I myself am not one, but it is my experience that the Communist Party is the only party that stands behind us and from which we can expect something. We know that there are now two powers at work: imperialism and the worker's republic in Russia. We hear little about the latter, although we would like to know more about it.

However, following Gumede's defeat in the 1930 ANC presidential election, the relationship cooled. The CPSA itself became riven with dissent. Gumede's successors disliked the idea of cooperation with the CPSA because they feared they were being used, but also because many of them were religious and totally opposed to the atheism of the CPSA.

The relationship between the ANC and CPSA remained consistent, in the sense that the ANC from the 1940s was always prepared to work with the Communists (see page 224). After it was banned in 1950 (see page 184), the CPSA continued operating and meeting illegally and changed its name to the South African Communist Party (SACP).

South African Indian Congress (SAIC)

How effective was the SAIC?

Like other groups, Indians had protested against segregation and unfair treatment since the days of British rule. The South African Indian Congress (SAIC) itself was not founded until 1919, although during his time as a lawyer in South Africa (1893–1914), the future Indian leader Mohandas Gandhi had been instrumental in forming Indian organizations in Natal and the Transvaal.

In the same way as the ANC, the SAIC became more radical in the 1940s with the leadership of Dr G.M. Naicker and Dr Yusuf M. Dadoo. They advocated **passive resistance** and saw the need to work with the ANC and indeed coloured groups in a common front. To this end, an alliance was made with the ANC in March 1947: the so-called 'Three Doctors' Pact', as the president of the ANC, A.B. Xuma, was also a doctor.

 **KEY TERM**

Passive resistance
Non-violent opposition.

Cooperation between groups

By the mid-1930s, all protest groups saw the need to cooperate in joint campaigns but because of the restrictions on travel caused by the pass laws, simple communication was difficult enough, let alone joint action. Yet, many people were members of more than one group: Clements Kadalie, for example, was an ANC official and Charlotte Maxeke, who organized the Women's League of the ANC, was also involved in the ICU. However, little effective joint action took place. In December 1935, 400 delegates met in Bloemfontein to establish the All-African Convention (AAC), which emphasized both loyalty to South Africa and its opposition to segregation. Delegates demanded full participation in government and politics but disagreed on methods, with many seeing that petitions and attempts at discussion were having little effect. By the late 1940s, the scene was set for more radical and direct action campaigns, particularly in response to grand apartheid.

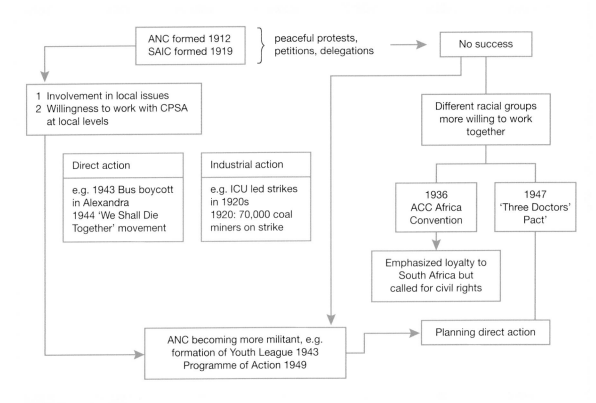

Growth of resistance

The creation of the apartheid state

Political differences between the white electorate during the period 1910–48 mainly centred on rivalries between Afrikaners and English-speaking whites and the nature of the relationship with Britain. There was little real difference about the treatment of other racial groups. For this reason, the basics of apartheid were already in place before the National Party took power in March 1948. Non-white groups such as the ANC had opposed racial legislation from its inception although their chosen methods, petitions and delegations, had enjoyed no success. Nevertheless, there was evidence of direct action, for example in local disputes, on which to build. The ANC itself became more radical in the 1940s, particularly through the influence of the Youth League. While non-white groups protested segregation legislation and demanded equal rights, various factors had worked against them, not least the difficulty of finding common ground, the problems of working together when the authorities ensured it was very difficult for them to communicate with each other and the intransigence of successive governments. This was to lead to greater radicalism and a commitment to more direct action.

✓ Examination advice

Paper 1 Question 15: comparing and contrasting sources

Question 15 on the IB History Diploma examination requires you to compare and contrast two sources. This means you will discuss the similarities and differences between the two sources. The most commonly used form of the question will ask you to compare and contrast two sources and how they view a certain historical event, document or person. Usually the similarities and differences are fairly clear and can be easily answered in a few minutes. Question 15 requires no actual knowledge of history, just the ability to read and understand the sources. It is possible that one of the sources will have been used in Question 13 or 14. If this is the case, read/analyse the source again anyway.

Question 15 is worth 6 marks out of the 24 total for Paper 1. This means it is worth 25 per cent of the overall mark. Answering Question 15 should take approximately fifteen minutes or less of your examination time.

> Remember that questions for Prescribed subject 4 will be numbered 13, 14, 15 and 16 in the Paper 1 exam.

How to answer

You will obviously need to read Question 15 carefully. Determine which sources you need to read and what exactly you are being asked to compare and contrast. You will be asked to compare and contrast not just the two sources, but the two sources' view on something specific. Do not discuss the origins or purpose of the sources; focus only on the demands of the question. You should make notes on your paper from the source regarding the question's focus. Do this for both sources. There is no need to record or use any information which does not specifically address the question. This will waste precious time and will not earn you any extra marks. Once you have completed answering your question, you should draw a line through any notes you made so they will not be reviewed by the examiner.

When you start your answer, be sure to write a paragraph that explains how the sources *compare*, or are similar, on whatever is being asked in the question. Your second paragraph should be on how they *contrast* or how they are different. You should not treat each source separately, but integrate them in the same sentences as much as possible. Using quotes from the sources to strengthen your answer is an excellent idea and will help you to obtain more marks, but do keep in mind that a good historian also knows when to paraphrase and summarize.

Remember, the total mark available for this question is 6. A general rule to follow would be to have at least three points of comparison and three for contrast. This is not always possible, so in certain circumstances it may be possible to have four compares, or contrasts, and two of the other. Again, this is a general rule and it is always better to have as many of each as possible, making sure that all points are completely relevant and focused on the question. There may be minor similarities and differences between the sources. Do not let these take the place of the more significant points.

Example

This question uses Sources I (page 135) and J (page 136).

> Compare and contrast the views expressed in Sources I and J regarding the race relations policies of the National Party of Daniel Malan. (6 marks)

Immediately start making notes on Sources I and J on your paper, perhaps organizing a chart to more easily compare and contrast the sources. Your notes may appear something like this:

Source I	Source J
Focus: National Party race policies	Focus: Mandela's interpretation of National Party policies
• Apartheid is based on Christian ideas • Policy derived from historical experience of whites • Preserves white identity • Preserves indigenous identities • Integration equals white suicide • Apartheid lets everyone develop separately • Everyone's rights will be respected	• Apartheid supported by Dutch Reformed Church • Apartheid is an old idea • Apartheid means 'apartness' • Apartheid unites all elements of oppressive system • Premise is that whites are superior to all others
Compare: • Both sources suggest apartheid has religious roots • Both indicate that it has long historical roots • Both suggest term means separate identity and development of the races	Contrast: • Source J states that apartheid equals oppression, Source I that races will be able to enjoy separate development • Source I suggests that apartheid is best for all while Source J states it is designed to make blacks inferior • Source I claims that everyone's rights will be respected unlike Source J which states that white supremacy will be enshrined in law

Your answer to this question could look like:

Sources I and J share a number of views regarding the race relations policies of the National Party. Source J suggests that the policy of apartheid was based on Christian ideas. Nelson Mandela sees apartheid as having roots in the Dutch Reformed Church, an Afrikaner Christian institution. Similarly, both sources recognize that apartheid had deep historical roots in South Africa. Source I states that it was 'a concept historically derived from the experience of the established White population.' Source J concurs, as Mandela portrayed the racial policies of which apartheid was the latest version as having kept blacks in 'in an inferior position to whites for centuries'. One further idea that is similar is that both sources agree that the National Party policies meant white and black people had separate identities and that each would develop separately. Source I details this by claiming that the policy 'professes to preserve the identity and safeguard the future of every race'. Source J supports this notion of separateness because apartheid stressed that 'Afrikaners were God's chosen people and that blacks were a subservient species.'

However, the two sources do contain significant differences. Source J strongly makes the case that the policies equalled oppression and were designed to keep black people inferior. Source I takes a different view when it states that there will be 'opportunities to develop into self-governing national units'. On a similar note, Source I clearly claims that apartheid was a policy that was in the best interests of all South Africans while Source J disputes this by describing how Africans, as well as Indians and coloureds, would forever be in an inferior position. Finally, Source I makes the point that everyone's 'rights' will be respected in a South Africa led by the National Party whereas Source J takes a very different view and asserts that 'white supremacy' would be enshrined in law.

| There is running comparison in both paragraphs. |
| There is an appropriate use of a quotation as supporting evidence. |
| Comparisons and contrasts have been separated into two paragraphs. |
| The comparisons and contrasts are the most significant ones. Minor points have not been used, keeping the paragraphs focused and strong. |
| There is an appropriate use of language, especially in connecting sources or points. Examples of words that help to build linkage include 'both', 'whereas', 'while' and 'however'. |

The answer indicates that the question was understood. There are three strong comparisons and three contrasts between the two sources. There is running comparison and contrast in each paragraph with both sources often treated in the same sentence. An appropriate quotation is used from a source to reinforce the answer. The answer addresses all criteria. Mark: 6/6.

Examination practice

The following are exam-style questions for you to practise, using sources from this chapter. Sources can be found on the page references given:

Source G: page 133
Source H: page 134
Source I: page 135

Source L: page 139
Source M: page 142
Source O: page 144

1 Compare and contrast the views expressed in Sources G and H about the major issues facing voters in the 1948 elections.

2 Compare and contrast the views expressed in Sources I and M about white and black relations.

3 Compare and contrast the views expressed in Sources L and O about the goals of the SANNC and the ANC.

 Activities

1 Search for newspaper or magazine accounts of the 1948 elections and then compare and contrast them in terms of their biases, points of view and the information they convey to the reader. You can extend this activity by trying to suggest why each article takes a specific viewpoint.

2 Investigate the political platforms of the South African Communist Party and the South African Indian Congress in the 1940s. What goals did they share? How did the parties differ?

3 Locate the British Pathé short film *The Opening of Parliament in Cape Town* (1948) on YouTube. What strikes you about the pomp and circumstance of the event? What might a white South African have felt at the time after viewing the film? And a black South African?

CHAPTER 5

The development of apartheid 1948–64

This chapter considers the legislation that imposed grand apartheid on South Africa. It goes on to examine the opposition, showing that two developments took place: a greater willingness of different groups to work together and a greater militancy. It shows how the authorities responded with more acts of repression and considers the extent of protest in rural areas. You need to consider the following questions throughout this chapter:

★ How important was the Department of Native Affairs in implementing apartheid?

★ How far did apartheid legislation affect lives?

★ How far was the National Party electoral victory in 1948 a turning point in South Africa's history?

★ How effective was the opposition to apartheid during the 1950s?

★ How extensive was rural unrest?

 # The Department of Native Affairs

▶ *Key question: How important was the Department of Native Affairs in implementing apartheid?*

After the National Party came to power in May 1948, race relations dominated the governance of South Africa. Much of the government's decision-making was made through the prism of race. It developed a bureaucracy and security service that was primarily concerned with implementing apartheid measures and fighting opposition to them. At the heart of the bureaucracy, in terms of implementing racial policies, was the Department of Native Affairs or the Native Affairs Department (NAD).

Department of Native Affairs

The Department of Native Affairs had a comparatively low profile before 1950. Even when Malan's National Party came to power, its first head as minister for native affairs, E.G. Jansen, was not particularly effective. In 1949 he even suggested the property-owning rights of black people should be improved, in order to bind them more closely to the regime of apartheid, to emphasize the common interest in keeping the National Party government secure. In October 1950, Jansen became governor general. His successor as

How significant was the Department of Native Affairs?

Ideologue Someone completely committed to a certain belief, in this case, apartheid.

minister, Hendrik Verwoerd, was an **ideologue**, absolutely committed to the apartheid project and determined that the Department of Native Affairs would expand to implement it efficiently through centralization and control.

Hendrik Verwoerd

Verwoerd was born in the Netherlands in 1902 and moved to South Africa two years later. He may have seen himself as something of an outsider, and may have wanted to prove himself as the epitome of Afrikaner values. His father was a building contractor who became a missionary. Much of Verwoerd's early life was spent among English speakers, first in the Cape and then in the British colony of Rhodesia, now Zimbabwe, where he was marked out for his Afrikaner accent. Verwoerd became professor of applied psychology at the University of Stellenbosch and editor of the newspaper *Die Transvaler*. As minister of native affairs, he worked closely with the department secretary, Werner Eiselen. Eiselen was an anthropologist, an expert on native affairs, fluent in several African languages, and author of many tracts which advocated apartheid. He thought it was important to protect Africans from Western influence, which seemingly always harmed them. He felt Africans should not attempt to develop along Western lines, but rise within their own cultures. This was one reason given for the need for grand apartheid: to protect the Africans.

The work of the bureaucracy

Historian Ivan Evans has studied the work of the Department of Native Affairs. He explores the question of whether apartheid grew from bureaucratic processes as much as from forces of oppression. He argues that it became 'a state within a state', a vast monolith which not only governed through a vast bureaucracy, but was also able to normalize apartheid to such an extent that many Africans accepted it. This had the important effect of weakening their opposition during the 1950s. In particular, the department gained the support of many tribal chieftains (see page 165) and urban tenants who were moved to better accommodation in newly built 'locations' (see page 165).

Staff

Table 5.1 Budget of Department of Native Affairs 1936–60

Year	Budget
1936	£570,158
1946	£3,087,000
1950	£3,460,000
1960	£7,205,250

As apartheid developed, the Department of Native Affairs grew significantly. New staff were often Afrikaners, who were increasingly promoted after the National Party victory in 1948. One reason why apartheid was maintained so tenaciously in the ensuing decades was that so many people relied on it for their livelihoods including those who worked at NAD. Although the number of staff grew from 3479 to 3914 between 1947 and 1951, in that year there were 384 vacancies. As its role expanded, the number of vacancies rose to 549 by 1953, although the total number of staff had risen to 4053. The department budget increased significantly by 1960 (see Table 5.1).

Between 1950 and 1960, 40 per cent of total expenditures went on wages. The number of staff had also increased: in 1962, 5675 were employed by the department, of whom 2989 were African, mainly in lowly positions.

Main responsibilities

The department implemented apartheid through the legislation it introduced and, in particular, had three key areas of responsibility:

- The Labour Bureaux. These were introduced in 1952 and were designed to allocate African workers to specific jobs in specific locations, thus controlling their mobility.
- The segregated 'locations' or townships on the edge of urban centres where Africans were forced to live. The department made it a priority in the early 1950s to address the estimated shortage of 170,000 housing units. One could say that in providing cheap, mass-produced yet adequate housing, the department helped to deflate African opposition to apartheid (see page 165). Another is the misery caused by **forced removals** to soulless, fenced-off locations with limited facilities where African workers were forced to live. The location at Orlando, for example, was next to the main power station for all Johannesburg, yet residents of Orlando had only candles, paraffin lamps and coal for warmth and light.
- The control of Bantustans. This was the name give to the homelands reserved for Africans of particular tribes. They were eventually designated as separate nations within South Africa, and instrumental in the policy of separate development (see page 220).

There were also **think tanks** which promoted ideas on how best to promote and implement apartheid. One example is the South African Bureau of Racial Affairs (SABRA), set up at the University of Stellenbosch, which published the influential *Journal of Racial Affairs* and had close ties with the racist organisation the **Broerderbund**. Its recommendations, usually to strengthen grand apartheid and educate Afrikaner youth to desire racial separation and white supremacy, were sometimes accepted, sometimes rejected. Apartheid was a complex project into which academics, politicians, journalists, administrators and other members of the professional classes all fed ideas, although the main method of enforcement was via the Department of Native Affairs.

 **KEY TERM**

Forced removals Where black, coloured or Indian people were removed from areas designated 'whites only' and forced to live in locations or townships, usually on the edge of urban areas.

Think tanks Groups of experts formed to give advice on issues.

Broerderbund
An influential Afrikaner organization promoting apartheid. Most key Afrikaner figures in politics, industry and civic life belonged to it.

How useful is Source A to a historian studying the implementation of apartheid?

SOURCE A

Excerpt from Oxford University scholar John Lazar, 'The Role of the South African Bureau of Racial Affairs (Sabra) in the Formulation of Apartheid Ideology, 1948–1961' in *Collected Seminar Papers on Societies of South Africa in the 19th and 20th Centuries*, volume 14, published by the Institute of Commonwealth Studies, 1971.

The findings of the 1951 Congress – the main theme of which was the role of Africans in South Africa's industries – seem to have been influential in a number of ways. The resolutions passed at the Congress included calls on the Government to set up a system of labour bureaux, to make employers responsible for part of the cost of housing urban Africans, to train black building craftsmen, to ensure that only African labour should be used in the building of African housing in the urban areas, and to refuse recognition to black trade unions in white areas. Clearly, it would be simplistic to suggest that apartheid legislation and ordinances of the next few years were principally the result of SABRA's research and pressure. At the same time, however, the organization seems to have had a marked effect on the formulation of many of the basic planks of Verwoerdt's departmental policy after 1950.

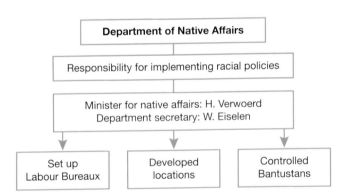

SUMMARY DIAGRAM

The Department of Native Affairs

② Implementation of apartheid

▶ *Key question: How far did apartheid legislation affect lives?*

The key to government policy was divide and rule. The intention was to keep the different races as far apart as possible, and keep Africans separated into distinct tribal units which were to become the basis of Bantustans. Different African tribes were regarded as separate embryonic nations. Townships were divided in tribal areas; homelands were exclusive for members of different tribal groups. Any unity as Africans, as opposed to say Zulu or Xhosa, was frowned on. The idea of Africanism (see page 141) was **anathema**. If Africans were separate delineated nations, whites would no longer be numerically a minority group in South Africa. Of course, the same principle held for coloureds and Indians (see page 147).

Population Registration Act 1950

This Act designated the racial category of everyone in South Africa and insisted the different groups be kept strictly separate. Husbands and wives in interracial (mixed) marriages were expected, or were forced, to split up. Everyone was registered according to their racial group and issued with an identity card with their racial group appended. Later amendments to the Act in 1964 and 1967 placed greater stress on appearance and genealogy to prevent light-skinned members of other groups passing themselves off as white. Children who appeared darker or lighter than their parents were classified differently and, in many cases, families were torn apart.

The difficulties in defining race can be illustrated from the text of the Act itself:

SOURCE B

Excerpt from the Population Registration Act, July 1950, quoted in *Atlas of Changing South Africa* by A.J. Francis, published by Taylor & Francis, 2002, p. 100.

'White person' means a person who in appearance obviously is, or who is generally accepted as a white person, but does not include a person who, although in appearance obviously a white person, is generally accepted as a coloured person.

Source C shows further ways the **Race Classification Board** tried to define the categories.

SOURCE C

Excerpt from 'What's In a Name? Racial Categorisations under Apartheid and their Afterlife' by Deborah Posel, *Transformations*, volume 47, 2001, pp. 50–74. Posel is describing the criteria different officials deployed to determine a person's racial classification.

Dress and deportment were also racially coded, typically in the view that well-dressed individuals were placed higher on the racial ladder than those more shabbily clad; likewise for the type and standard of a person's furnishing, if this entered into the ambit of discussion about his other race, as well as modes of leisure activity. The Cape Times *revealed that according to 'methods reported in Johannesburg as being used by the Race Classification Board to determine whether a man was native or Coloured: a soccer player is a native, a rugby player is a Coloured. A high bed is Coloured, a low bed native. The kinds of food eaten and alcohol drunk were also invested with racial significance. Consuming large amounts of what was then called 'kaffirbeer' became a sign of being 'native' and, obversely, having bought 'European liquor' could signify whiteness.*

How far was the Population Registration Act central to the development of apartheid?

 **KEY TERM**

Anathema Complete hostility to something.

Race Classification Board Board charged with deciding which race a person belonged to.

How useful is Source B to a historian investigating the impact of the Population Registration Act?

How scientific are the criteria mentioned in Source C to determine racial classification?

This Act also facilitated the development of a vast civil service, and a middle-class career for many Afrikaners, who thereby had a vested interest in its continuation.

? According to Spink in Source D, how fundamental to apartheid was the Population Registration Act?

SOURCE D

Excerpt from *Black Sash: The Beginning of a Bridge in South Africa* by **Kathryn Spink, published by Methuen, UK, 1991 p. 266. Spink, a journalist, was writing about the women's anti-apartheid group Black Sash (see page 179) at a time when South Africa was on the cusp of democratic change.**

*The 1950 Population Registration Act (Race Classification) which demanded everyone resident in South Africa must be classified according to their race, still dictated a person's entire existence – the state hospital or clinic in which he could be born, where he could grow up, where he could go to school, where he could live and where he could be buried. Without it all the other legislation dealing with parliamentary government, homeland and local authorities, **Regional Service Councils**, health, education, welfare, pensions, housing, Group Areas [see below], influx control, even the constitution itself, would be rendered inoperable.*

KEY TERM

Regional Service Councils Groups of local councils which shared certain functions.

What was the impact of these two Acts?

Prohibition of Mixed Marriages 1949 and Immorality Act 1950

Unsurprisingly, mixed marriages were rare but perhaps more surprisingly, they were not illegal. Nor were sexual relations between members of different racial groups, although these tended to take place in rural areas between white male employers and female servants or farmworkers, and were more an assertion of power and authority than affection. Nevertheless, in 1949 and 1950, respectively, mixed marriages and sexual relations between members of different racial groups were made illegal. Whites could be imprisoned for disobeying the latter, although their punishment was not usually as severe as for members of other groups, including their sexual partners, whether consensual or not.

What was the significance of the Group Areas Act?

Group Areas Act 1950

The Group Areas Act required registration of all land ownership, and authorized the government to designate a particular area as available for occupation by any one group, and the forced eviction of members of other groups. It was responsible for the forced removal of as many as 3.5 million Africans between 1960 and 1983, with over 1 million of these being moved from urban areas back to the homelands.

One of the main results of the 1950 Group Areas Act was the destruction of the mixed race suburb of Sophiatown, in Johannesburg.

Sophiatown

Sophiatown was one of three mixed race areas which, with Martindale and Newclare, made up the South Western Townships in Johannesburg. These had been designated as African areas, as more Africans migrated to Johannesburg during the First World War. Sophiatown was a 'black spot' (see page 125). Its population also included Indians, coloured people and some whites who had lived there before its designation as an African area, so it was a truly multiracial area. Situated in 260 acres (105 hectares), four-and-half miles (7.25 km) away from the city centre, it had been founded by a builder, Hermann Tobiansky, and named after his wife. As Johannesburg grew in population, the nearby sewage works and rubbish tip made the houses in Sophiatown uncongenial to whites – only 88 moved in. Reluctantly, Tobiansky began to sell them to other racial groups. This was before the 1923 Native Urban Areas Act banned such activities (see page 125). The British priest Father Trevor Huddleston, who served in Sophiatown from 1943 until its demise in 1955, likened it from a distance to an Italian village.

However, Sophiatown grew dramatically during the war years. In 1923 it had a population of about 10,000; by 1953 this had extended officially to 39,186, although some estimates place it as high as 60,000. Population density may have been as much as 150 people per acre (60 people per hectare); often, many families lived in one room. Over 70 per cent of the dwellings in Sophiatown could be classed as slums. This was because as more and more people moved in, attracted to its vibrant life and proximity to the city centre of Johannesburg, residents began to build sheds – sometimes called stands – in any available space on their properties. Some landlords exploited their tenants; few of the sheds had facilities such as heating and none had sanitation.

Despite these issues, Sophiatown had a distinct culture based in part on jazz and throbbing **mbaqanga music**. It was home to many South African writers, artists and musicians. It was likened to cities such as Chicago in the 1940s and 1950s because it had a high crime rate, with gangs often named after American film stars, and plenty of **shebeens**, which police often raided. It was an edgy place, often dangerous to outsiders, with great poverty and considerable crime – but with a vivacity, an overwhelming sense of community and pride in its multiracial composition.

 **KEY TERM**

Mbaqanga music
Throbbing African jazz-type music with Zulu roots.

Shebeens Often African women earned an income by brewing and selling beer in these illegal drinking dens. The government deemed them illegal because they ran and profited from official beer halls (where only weak beer with an alcoholic content of two per cent was sold), and because they feared that drunken Africans might rampage.

SOURCE E

Excerpt from *Naught for Your Comfort* by Trevor Huddleston, published by Collins, Glasgow, UK, 1987, p. 102. Huddleston was an Anglian priest who worked in Sophiatown.

The truth is that Sophiatown is a community; a living organism which has grown up through the years and which has struck its roots deep in this particular place and in this particular soil … And in my opinion the place is cosmopolitan in a real sense and has about it that sense which belongs to cosmopolitan towns the world over. It is in that sense unique. The most unlikely and unexpected things can happen here and not appear at all unlikely or incongruous.

What impression does Huddleston give about Sophiatown in Source E? ?

Although some historians have hinted that Sophiatown represented what the ideal, multiracial African city could be like – with its tolerance and warmth and sense of community – it was not without its problems. Apart from the housing situation, whites had been complaining for years about Sophiatown, particularly as their own suburbs such as Westdene and Newlands encroached upon it.

Forced removals

The 1950 Group Areas Act gave the government control over relocations. Under this Act, it was now deemed a 'white' area. In 1953, the government began building houses in an area they called Meadowlands (near **Soweto**). The Natives Resettlement Act a year later enabled the government to specifically move Africans from anywhere in and next to Johannesburg to any other area. Thus, the stage was set: notices were given for the eviction and removal of the first of Sophiatown's residents, from the now 'white' Sophiatown to the 'black' Soweto. The authorities had originally named 13 February as removal day but they arrived before dawn on 10 February to pre-empt any unrest. Although their actual numbers are disputed, there is no dispute that the enforcement officers were armed, many carrying machine guns. Their sense of intimidation was overwhelming as they caught people by surprise, sometimes kicking down doors. They brought trucks to carry people's possessions but the process of removal was so quick and ruthless that much got left behind.

Many have argued that resistance to the removals was hopeless in the face of the force the authorities were prepared to use.

KEY TERM

Soweto Acronym for South Western Townships, the African townships on the edge of Johannesburg.

?

How useful is Source F in showing the impact of the Sophiatown removals?

SOURCE F

Excerpt from *Naught for Your Comfort* by Trevor Huddleston, published by Collins, Glasgow, UK, 1987, p. 134. Huddleston (see above) was a witness to the removals in a yard near the bus station at Sophiatown.

In the yard, military lorries were drawn up. Already they were piled high with the pathetic possessions which had come from the row of rooms in the background. A rusty kitchen stove: a few blackened pots and pans; a wicker chair: mattresses belching out their coir-stuffing: bundles of heaven knows what and people, soaked, all soaked to the skin by the drenching rain. Above this strange and depressing crowd, perched on top of the van of a police truck, were more cameras filming the scene below. I deliberately put my arm around Robert Resha's shoulders [Resha was one of the residents being moved] and looked up at the camera. 'Move away there … you've no right here … get out I'm telling you … clear out of this yard.' One officer was in furious temper. Perhaps it was the rain but I think it was the sight of me, with my arm around an African's shoulder.

SOURCE G

Families on the street outside slum houses, being herded into trucks to new homes, 1955.

How well does Source G illustrate the scale of the Sophiatown removals?

Resistance to forced removals

The ANC (see pages 138–41) and **Transvaal Indian Congress** had been working together to organize resistance since June 1953, when 1200 people crowded into the Odin cinema to begin the campaign against the Group Areas Act. There were twice-weekly rallies and public meetings throughout 1954 and into 1955, which the authorities largely ignored because they were mainly peaceful. Meanwhile, local gangs were arming themselves and there were common slogans among the resistance, 'Over Our Dead Bodies' and 'We Will Not Move'. Ultimately, on the night before the removals were about to start in June 1955, Joe Modine, the local ANC leader, called off resistance. This was because it was known the security forces were preparing to cordon off the area and had introduced possibly as many as 4000 troops to keep order during the dispersals – so they knew resistance would be ineffective and costly in terms of arrests and injury. Ultimately, the ANC knew the local population would suffer in any confrontation with the security forces. British journalist Anthony Sampson, then the editor of the magazine *Drum*, aimed at an African audience, disputed the numbers of officers present, but wrote that they were removing furniture from people's homes while the owners looked on. The amount of force the state was prepared to use was simply too great for people to resist. Nelson Mandela, writing in 1994, argued that resistance failed in Sophiatown because of government resolve.

 **KEY TERM**

Transvaal Indian Congress Branch of the South African Indian Congress (SAIC) based in Transvaal.

SOURCE H

How useful is Source H in explaining the futility of resistance to the Sophiatown removals?

Excerpt from *Long Walk to Freedom* by Nelson Mandela, published by Abacus, London, UK, 2013, pp. 193–4. Nelson Mandela became the first president of a democratic South Africa in 1994.

We never provided the people with an alternative to moving to Meadowlands. When the people in Sophiatown realized we could neither stop the government not provide them with housing elsewhere, their own resistance waned and the flow of people to Meadowlands increased. Many tenants moved willingly, for they found they would have more space and cleaner housing in Meadowlands. We did not take into account the different situations of landlords and tenants. While the landlords had reasons to stay, many tenants had an incentive to leave. The ANC was criticized by a number of Africanist members who accused the leadership of protecting the interests of the landlords at the expense of the tenants.

The lesson I took away from the campaign was that in the end, we had no alternative to armed and violent resistance. Over and over again, we had used all the nonviolent weapons in our arsenal – speeches, deputations, threats, marches, strikes, stay-aways, voluntary imprisonment – to no avail, for whatever we did was met by an iron hand. A freedom fighter learns the hard way that it is the oppressor who defines the nature of the struggle, and the oppressed is often left no recourse but to use methods that mirror those of the oppressor. At a certain point, one can only fight fire with fire.

Reasons for the removals

The government gave various reasons for the forced removal of mixed areas, notably that the different races were not able to live together peacefully, and that they needed to clear the slums. Undoubtedly much of Sophiatown and indeed many other black or coloured areas were slums because little was ever invested in their infrastructure. There was no evidence to suggest the races could not get along together in Sophiatown – indeed, it may be the very reason that because they did seem to live harmoniously together, Sophiatown became such a crushing issue for the authorities. Ultimately, the prime motive for its destruction was to keep black and coloured people in certain areas and, particularly for Africans, in 'locations' or townships where transience was emphasized. These locations were places offering temporary accommodation, while their occupants worked on largely temporary contracts. The true *homes* of Africans were meant to be in the tribal homelands.

SOURCE I

How far does Source J (page 163) support the view expressed in Source I about the 'locations'?

Excerpt from *Naught for Your Comfort* by Trevor Huddleston, published by Collins, Glasgow, UK, 1987, pp. 94–5.

… in a location you have row upon row of small box like houses of almost identical shape and size. Such variation as there is marks the end of one housing contract and the beginning of another, or the start perhaps of some new

*experiment in **pre-fab construction**. It is never variety for its own sake. It is a 'location' – not a village you must remember. As such it is unnecessary for streets to be named. You simply number the houses from one to two or ten thousand and leave it at that … The great advantage of the location is that it can be controlled. People who come to visit their friends for the weekend must have permits before they can set foot on the arid, municipal turf.*

KEY TERM

Pre-fab construction
Houses made from prefabricated parts.

SOURCE J

Meadowlands, the new township outside Johannesburg.

The townships had to be separated from white suburbs by at least 500 yards (460 m) of non-residential areas – possibly industrial estates, roads, or just scrubland. Older ones had fences and gates. They were out of bounds to white people and indeed any non-residents. They lacked basic facilities such as electricity and plumbing. Even if the houses were well built, they were merely intended as dormitories where Africans slept between work shifts. No one would willingly have called them 'home'.

Triomf

After the first removals, Sophiatown was gradually emptied as new quarters were made ready in Meadowlands. Although the final residents were not removed until 1959, Sophiatown remained largely a wasteland for years during and after the removals. Its name was removed from maps, and in 1962 it became an all-white suburb called Triomph or Triomf, Afrikaans for 'triumph'– the name seemingly an insult and a powerful assertion of the government's resolve.

How have commentators interpreted the removals from Sophiatown?

The impact of the forced removals

Although thousands of Africans were relocated by force throughout South Africa, Sophiatown is the example which caught the public imagination. Commentators continue to debate its significance.

Culture

Some commentators perceive Sophiatown's significance in the sense of its vibrant culture. In this context its destruction has been dramatized in two significant plays: Todd Matshikiza's *King Kong* in 1959 and Malcolm Purkey's *Sophiatown* in 1986. It has also featured in novels by writers such as Nadine Gordimer. Many literary critics cite the impassioned prose of novelist Bloke Modisane's 1963 autobiography, *Blame Me on History*.

? How reliable is Source K in explaining a resident's reaction to the destruction of Sophiatown?

SOURCE K

Excerpt from *Blame Me on History* by Bloke Modisane, first published in 1963, located at: www.legacy-project.org/index.php?page=lit_detail&litID=86.

Something in me died, a piece of me died, with the dying of Sophiatown; it was in the winter of 1958, the sky was a cold blue veil which had been immersed in a bleaching solution and then spread out against a concave, the blue filtering through, and tinted by, a powder screen of grey; the sun, like the moon of the day, gave off more light than heat, mocking me with its promise of warmth – a fixture against the grey-blue sky – a mirror deflecting the heat and concentrating upon me in my Sophiatown only a reflection.

In the name of slum clearance they had brought the bulldozers and gored into her body, and for a brief moment, looking down Good Street, Sophiatown was like one of its own many victims; a man gored by the knives of Sophiatown, lying in the open gutters, a raisin in the smelling drains, dying of multiple stab wounds, gaping wells gushing forth blood; the look of shock and bewilderment, of horror and incredulity, on the face of the dying man.

Some writers go beyond this to argue that Sophiatown was destroyed *because* of the vibrant culture, because it showed a community completely incompatible with the government's vision. Writing in 1956, Huddleston hints at this when he argues that a living mixed race community with a sense of permanence was anathema to the architects of apartheid. They needed to reinforce the sense of a transient population, whose real home was in the tribal homelands but could dwell temporarily in soulless, government-built 'locations'.

The resolve of the government and the shift to violent resistance

Mandela asserts that one significance of the Sophiatown removals was that it taught him that only violence and an armed struggle would work against such intransigence. This view was reinforced by Daniel R. Magaziner in 2012, who argues that the Sophiatown removals radicalized a new generation of young people who had seen how ineffective previous peaceful protests and rallies had been.

Landlords and tenants

Historian Steve Lebelo, writing in 1991, took a somewhat different approach to the Sophiatown removals. He argued that many Sophiatown residents were in fact comparative newcomers. He estimates that up to 82 per cent of those living there were subtenants or people living in sheds on residents' property. These were mainly single, had moved fairly recently and were transient in the same way that single migrant workers were in other African townships. They had more to gain from moving to Meadowlands, where they would be placed on the waiting list for houses, than remaining in Sophiatown, where they lived in squalor. As a result, they did not generally share in the opposition to the removals. Interestingly, Mandela appeared to support this point when he said 'while landlords had reasons to stay, tenants had reasons to leave' (see Source H, page 162).

Bantu Authorities Act 1951

> **What was the impact of the Bantu Authorities Act?**

This Act reiterated the assertion that the only places Africans were entitled to live were their 'tribal reserves' set out in the 1911 and 1936 legislation. As Africans were technically foreigners in South Africa, the Native Representative Council (see page 126) was abolished. The tribal reserves were to be governed by tribal leaders designated by the government. However, these leaders could be deposed if uncooperative (see page 195). Many chose to comply because it allowed them to maintain some authority, and the alternative might be worse. Tribal leaders were ostensibly responsible for allocation of land, development programmes and welfare policies. Yet, the problem remained that the homelands were never going to be self-sufficient. The government set up the Tomlinson Commission (1956) to report on how the homelands might be developed. This report reasserted:

- that homelands could never support more than two-thirds of their populations and advised more land be allocated
- that policies of **betterment** should be developed to combat problems such as soil erosion, and bring in experts to teach techniques such as contour ploughing; it was estimated that the cost of this would be at least £100 million
- that the agricultural workforce be reduced and industrial concerns be moved to just outside the borders, with urban centres developed just within, so homeland residents could travel to them for employment.

 **KEY TERM**

Betterment First used in the Betterment Proclamation of 1939 to describe government-driven improvements in agriculture and living conditions in the homelands.

The government broadly accepted the Tomlinson Commission's findings, although it had no intention of providing more land, and disliked the recommendations concerning industrial developments because by the use of cheap labour such ventures would undercut white-staffed competitors.

According to Source L, who does Verwoerd blame for the failings in the tribal territories?

SOURCE L

Excerpt from *Verwoerd Speaks: Speeches 1948–1966* edited by A.N. Pelzer, published by APB Publishers, Johannesburg, South Africa, 1966.

For the present these territories cannot provide the desired opportunities for living and development to their inhabitants and their children, let alone to more people. Due to neglect of their soil and overpopulation by man and cattle, large numbers are even now being continuously forced to go and seek a living under the protection of the European and his industries. In these circumstances it cannot be expected that the Bantu community will so provide for itself and so progress as to allow ambitious and developed young people in their own national service out of their own funds … Our first aim as a Government is, therefore, to lay the foundations of a prosperous producing community through soil reclamation and conservation methods and through the systematic establishment in the native territories of Bantu farming on an economic basis.

The idea was that Africans in the homelands could develop at their own pace. Verwoerd and his supporters argued that the Bantu Authorities Act was a protective measure, to avoid white exploitation of Africans. For example, whites were forbidden to invest in the homelands. However, whatever the intentions and however honestly they were intended, the Bantustans were never viable.

The Bantu Authorities Act provided the lynchpin for grand apartheid. The ambitious policy of Bantustans as separate and independent countries developed from this Act (see page 220).

How significant was the Native Laws Amendment Act to the idea of grand apartheid?

Native Laws Amendment Act 1952

This Act was also known as the Abolition of Passes and Co-ordination of Documents Act. It regularized the use of passes by Africans throughout South Africa, by officially abolishing existing passes and replacing them with standardized reference books. In the past, the precise details of what information Africans needed to carry with their passes varied from province to province. The Act now stated specifically:

- All Africans had to carry reference books, which contained a photograph, employment record and personal details such as marital status, at all times.
- Neither African men nor women could remain in urban areas longer than 70 hours after their permits had expired.
- No African could live permanently in an urban area unless he or she had been born there, lived there for over fifteen years, or been with the same employer for over ten years.
- It was a criminal offence not to carry these reference books.

The Act's purpose was to standardize the use of passes throughout South Africa. The abolition of passes and their replacement with reference books was simply a matter of form. The use of passes in practice became even more rigorously enforced and most people still called them passes rather than reference books.

Some historians, for example William Beinart, have seen this Act as particularly important in the control of Africans. While other groups had to carry identity cards, Africans needed this complex and bulky document with them at all times. As the journalist Kathryn Spink later wrote, 'In reality, far from abolishing [this] old style system, the 1952 Act simply gathered the previous assortment of papers between the cover of a single reference book and extended and intensified it. The men were worse off than they used to be.'

One legal expert, Professor Julius Lewin of Witwatersrand University, reported that the pass system was so complex that no African could obey it even if he had wanted to. If any African was stopped by a police officer pedantic enough, the officer would inevitably be able to discover some infringement. This was particularly the case when one considers that many Africans were at best semi-illiterate and unable to read much of the information in their passes. In the early 1950s, there were 968,593 arrests for violations of the pass laws with 861,269 convictions.

Separate Representation of Voters Act 1951: a constitutional crisis in the 1950s

> **Why did this Act lead to a constitutional crisis?**

Malan's government decided to remove the vote from coloured people because they believed only whites should be allowed to participate in elections. The problem was that coloured people's right to vote was protected by the 1910 Constitution (see page 130), which meant the measure to abolish it required a two-thirds majority in a joint sitting of both houses. Against the rules of the court, the National Party introduced their Separate Representation of Voters Bill separately into each house instead.

Although the Act received the required majority, the United Party contested its legality. Its protest was upheld by the Court of Appeal, saying it must go to a joint sitting. The government responded with a new law that introduced a new body, a High Court of Parliament, which could repeal any Appeal Court judgment. This was boycotted by the United Party.

The National Party insisted that the 1910 Constitution had been forced on them by Britain and was unjust because it constrained South African sovereignty. English-speaking white voters began to worry about the extent of National Party control and whether or not they intended a dictatorship. The ensuing argument was therefore about the relationship between the British state and South Africa, and the right of South Africa to run its own affairs (rather than about the rights of coloured voters).

The 1953 general election

In the event, voters on the general roll comprised coloured voters in Natal and the Cape Province, and white voters from South-West Africa and the entire Union. (Three white MPs known as native representative members (NRM) represented all black voters.) Even with all the opposition to the Act, the National Party won the majority of seats, 94 over the United Party's 57 (see Table 4.5, page 137). After their victory, the government introduced the bill into a joint parliamentary sitting but failed to get the required majority. The result was a decision to enlarge the senate from 48 to 89 members (the Senate Act 1955) and ensure the National Party had the required majority. By doing this, the measure became law, with the coloured voters disenfranchised in February 1956.

Protests against the Act

As well as the political opposition to the Act, a number of protest groups sprang up against it.

Torch Commando

The anti-fascist organization which fought the proposals, the Torch Commando, was made up largely of Second World War veterans, yet still precluded the membership of coloured veterans.

Black Sash

While the Torch Commando had made little impact, another white protest group did become a significant force in South African politics. The Women's Defence of the Constitution League, otherwise known as the Black Sash, comprised mainly disaffected middle-class women whose tactics included mass rallies and silent vigils. They wore distinctive black sashes to symbolize their mourning for the loss of democracy.

KEY TERM

Anti-pass protests
Protests against the requirement to carry passes which proliferated during the 1950s, especially when the government tried to force African women to carry them.

While the Black Sash too did not welcome black or coloured people joining its organization, the experience of its vigils and protests politicized them and they learned the value of publicity. More importantly, they turned their attention to civil rights, initially in supporting the **anti-pass protests** of African women. One member recalled being shocked by an African woman who explained why she, and hundreds of other African women, always had their babies with them: if they left their breastfeeding babies with child-minders, and if the police found any problems with their pass, they could be arrested, deported to a homeland, and their baby left behind. In the late 1950s the Black Sash became part of the opposition to apartheid (see page 179), which may not have been the intention of the original leaders.

Franchise Action Council (FRAC)

This largely informal group, born out of opposition to the Act, was supported by white and non-white protesters, and led to a huge demonstration of over 50,000 people in a march to Cape Town in 1951. However, FRAC diminished with the collapse of the Defiance Campaign (see pages 186–7).

Reservation of Separate Amenities Act 1953

How important was this Act?

This legislation was born out of a legal challenge. While petty apartheid (see page 121) had been in operation for some time, it was not universal. There were anomalies, particularly in the Cape. For example, segregation was enforced on the mainline trains but not at stations or on local trains. In the face of Afrikaner protest at this, Africans were excluded from concourses in stations in Cape Town, and all ticket offices were segregated. When the ANC launched a protest to the Court of Appeal, this was upheld on the grounds that separate facilities were legal so long as they did not result in racial inequality – in other words, the separate but equal principle which was meant to operate in the southern states of the USA (and was shortly to be overturned by the US Supreme Court). The government responded with the Reservation of Separate Amenities Act, which asserted that separate facilities in South Africa did not have to be equal: African expectations and standards were lower than those of whites, so they would be happy with less.

This law led to a huge growth in petty apartheid, with segregation notices springing up seemingly everywhere, on park benches, public toilets and beaches, in libraries and cinemas, in restaurants and public offices. Of course, many of these had been in operation for years, in ways such as how Africans usually had to go around the back of white-run restaurants to order food to take away. However, they were now given legal status.

Native Labour Act 1953

What was the effect of this Act?

Africans were not allowed to join trade unions or take part in strikes. This Act led to '**stayaway**' protests to circumvent the ban on strikes (see page 184).

Bantu Education Act 1953

Why was education so important to the architects of apartheid?

The government realized the education was crucial in the imposition of apartheid, in that it must prepare Africans for their allotted role and no more. It was important therefore for the government to gain control of education in both schools and universities.

The Bantu Education Act was one of the most important Acts in implementing apartheid. It was largely the brainchild of minister for native affairs, Verwoerd, and the Eiselen Commission he appointed in 1949 to investigate African education.

Education before the National Party victory

The vast majority of education for Africans was provided by Church-run **mission schools**. In 1945, there were 4360 mission schools and 230 government-run ones. These mission schools largely taught a Western-style curriculum, based on such subjects as English and Maths. Many were excellent and often produced future African leaders both in areas such as homeland administration and business, and in organizations such as the

 **KEY TERM**

Stayaway Where workers protested by staying at home rather than actually going on strike.

Mission schools Schools run by various Churches to educate African children.

ANC (Mandela, for example, was educated in one). The mission schools were largely subsidized by the state, although the state spent sixteen times as much on education for white children as on Africans.

By 1948, the system was breaking down. With poor funding, often dilapidated buildings and scarce resources, the schools were coming under increasing pressure to maintain their standards. The rise in African populations and urbanization meant they were vastly overcrowded and regularly had to turn prospective pupils away. The reality was that less than 33 per cent of African children attended school at all. Of those who did, less than four per cent stayed on to take the leaving exam at Standard Six (eleven to twelve years old). Everyone agreed that reform was necessary and the state needed to take more responsibility, hence the appointment of Eiselen's Commission.

Education was compulsory for whites but not Africans. People of all races feared the great numbers of African children and young people who were adrift on the streets of urban locations during the daytime. With parents necessarily at work, many had no supervision and inevitably drifted into antisocial behaviour and crime. They were commonly called *tsotsi*, which became a euphemism for hooligan or gangster, and were widely blamed for the high crime rates both in the locations and in the towns and cities themselves.

Youth crime

Many disaffected youngsters joined gangs both to afford themselves protection and to acquire money from theft and other crimes. These gangs were often named after Hollywood film stars, although one of the most notorious was simply called 'The Russians'. Crime was a serious problem in South Africa. In the Witwatersrand area, for example, there were 186 murders in 1945 and 472 by 1951. Incidents of serious crime in this one area rose from 69,036 to a staggering 158,513 during the same period. White people feared African street gangs as much as Africans did; they were often the victims of muggings and burglary. The authorities inevitably perhaps took more notice of African-on-white crime than of African-on-African.

> **Impact of gangs on ordinary people**
> Priest Trevor Huddleston, who also testified to the random nature of violence and murder in the locations, reported in the early 1950s that 'The Russians' gang in Johannesburg were so notorious that they actually drove people out of their homes to squat on an empty space known as Reno Square. Soon there were 1500 people living in desperately overcrowded conditions and minimal facilities there, and in another space known as Charles Phillips Square. The squatters were eventually evicted as part of the forced removals to Meadowlands (see page 163) but little was done about 'The Russians', the perpetrators.

The Eiselen Report

Eiselen personally believed Africans needed to be 'protected' from Western culture (see page 154). This idea to a large extent was reflected in his report, which suggested:

- education should ideally be based in the homelands
- it should be taught in tribal languages
- it should reflect the needs of Africans.

In other words, he wanted to offer Africans a curriculum based on the limited skills they needed to function as a reservoir of cheap labour.

Eiselen's experts studied for two years, and wrote a dense, double-columned 200-page report, without speaking to any Africans or representatives of the mission schools. The liberal-minded African Institute of Race Relations was quick to criticize it, through the contradiction which acknowledged that Africans were perfectly capable of benefiting from education, thereby belying the idea of their intellectual inferiority to whites. The Commission reported that there was no reason why Africans could not intellectually benefit from an academic curriculum, but it was best if they did not receive one. Ultimately, it was a question of control. The government could not control what mission schools taught and it was feared, with some justification, that their education was producing a disaffected educated African elite who may one day rise up against them.

The Bantu Education Act:

- moved control of African education from the Ministry of Education to the Ministry for Native Affairs
- removed state subsidies from mission schools, so most were forced to close
- expanded the government-run system and set a limited vocational-based curriculum.
- The work of the Department of Native Affairs grew significantly; the Act, for example, gave them management of 26,000 African teachers. In 1958, a separate Department of Bantu Education was created to meet this increased workload.

As Verwoerd most famously said, 'What is the purpose of teaching a Bantu child mathematics?' He meant that it was harmful to give Africans ideas above their station; to do this would be to merely breed discontent.

SOURCE M

Excerpt from Verwoerd's speech to the Senate on 7 June 1954, quoted in *Verwoerd Speaks, Speeches 1948–1966* edited by A.N. Pelzer, published by APB Publishers, Johannesburg, South Africa, 1966, p. 83.

It is the policy of my department that education should have its roots entirely in the Native areas and in the Native environment and Native Community … The Bantu must be guided to serve his own community in all respects. There is

Why, according to Source M, is it important for South African blacks to have their own separate system of education?

no place for him in the European community above the level of certain forms of labour ... For that reason it is of no avail to him to receive a training which has as its aim absorption in the European community while he cannot and will not be absorbed there. Up till now he has been subjected to a school system which drew him away from his own community and practically misled him by showing him the green pasture of the European but still did not allow him to graze there.

The impact of the Act

While everyone agreed that education needed to be reformed, few were satisfied with this solution. ANC leader Professor Z.K. Matthews of Fort Hare University (see page 190) said, 'Education for ignorance and inferiority in Verwoerd's schools is worse than no education at all.'

All Churches, with the exception of the Dutch Reformed Church, opposed the Bantu Education Act. Nevertheless, the government insisted on the Act, saying that mission schools must be handed over to the government by December 1954. The alternative was to accept decreasing subsidies until they ceased altogether and the schools became fully independent. The vast majority of mission schools closed, although the Roman Catholic Church, **Seventh Day Adventists** and some Jewish groups kept theirs open. Some Africans began to operate their own unofficial schools in garages and living rooms. When the government passed a law to outlaw unofficial education for Africans, they were renamed 'cultural clubs' to avoid being illegal, but lack of funds forced most of them to close.

Most Churches complied with the terms of the Act and handed over their schools because they wanted to keep African children off the streets (see page 170). However, the Bishop of Johannesburg, Ambrose Reeves, refused and reopened Anglican schools as private institutions, charging fees of 50 pence per month. However, although many parents could not afford even this, those who could faced long waiting lists before their children could be admitted.

Protests against the Act

Many Africans had no wish to send their children to schools where they would be taught white superiority and the limited role of the African. The ANC lacked the resources to provide alternative education for all but a few. Nevertheless, the annual ANC conference at Durban in December 1954 voted for an indefinite boycott of the new government-run schools. Verwoerd said in return that all schools affected by a boycott would be closed on the grounds that if children did not want to attend, the schools were unnecessary. Any children boycotting schools would not be readmitted. As a result, the boycott was only partially successful. In the East Rand in Johannesburg, where ANC support was particularly strong, thousands stayed home and **pickets** forced those who wanted to go to school to leave. In most areas, however, the schools continued as normal. The potential consequences

KEY TERM

Seventh Day Adventists
Religious group who see Saturday as the Sabbath.

Pickets A method of protest whereby groups of people gather to stop people from going into an institution or a location.

of a boycott, for example, the closure of affected schools or children never being able to attend school in the future, were too severe.

As the boycott fizzled out, the government relented and allowed those who wanted to, to attend their schools. In the long term, they may have unwittingly politicized many children by the frustrations generated by the poor-quality education on offer and the resultant lack of opportunities. Most African children and their parents realized their education was inferior to that of whites, and was being used as a weapon to limit their opportunities for advancement.

The Extension of Universities Act 1959

There were four English-language universities, four Afrikaner universities and another, Fort Hare, in South Africa during the 1950s. At Fort Hare, coloured, Indians and African students studied in an integrated environment under lecturers of all races; its non-discriminatory principal was highly valued and defended. Three of the English-speaking universities also took African, coloured or Indian students and indeed employed some of these groups as lecturers; in 1954, Robert Sobukwe (see pages 203–4) was employed to teach African studies at the University of Witwatersrand. All universities were dependent on government subsidies. Unsurprisingly, the National Government remained unhappy about Africans in particular studying to degree level and beyond. Therefore, in 1959, the Extension of Universities Act was passed to ban the English-language universities from accepting African students. By way of recompense, three new strictly segregated colleges were opened for coloured, Indian and Zulu students, and another for Africans in the Transvaal. Fort Hare remained under a new and more conciliatory principal for Xhosa-speaking students only.

> What point is being made in Source N?

SOURCE N

A cartoon from *Nelson Mandela: A Life in Cartoons* edited by Harry Dugmore, Stephen Francis and Rico Schacherl, published by David Philip Publishers, Claremont, South Africa, 1999. Francis and Schacherl produce the daily South African comic strip 'Madam & Eve', which Dugmore founded. The artist, J.H. Jackson, was a well-known South African cartoonist. This cartoon dates from 1958. The man pictured is Dr Verwoerd.

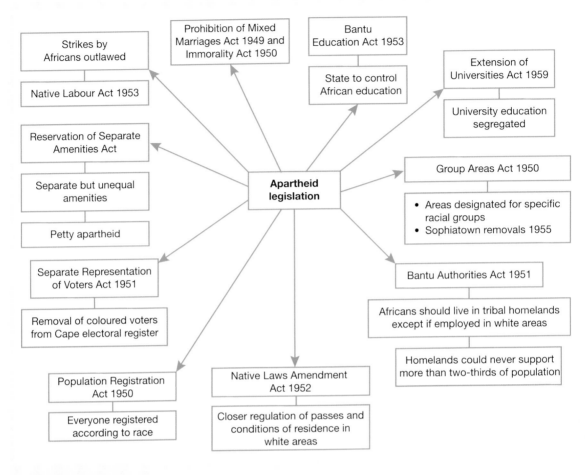

The implementation of apartheid

 Key debate

▸ *Key question: How far was the National Party electoral victory in 1948 a turning point in South Africa's history?*

Many believed that the National Party victory in 1948 was a significant development in South Africa's racial history. By 1948, policies of segregation were already well developed and white supremacy was already in force. While the National Party may have developed these factors under apartheid, particularly during the 1950s and 1960s, commentators tend to disagree about how far this was taken during the early years of National Party rule.

Continuity

Some historians are more inclined to stress the continuity rather than change in Malan's government. Ivan Evans, for example, writing in 1997, has argued that the central themes were already in place and there was no grand plan, just a series of developments from which grand apartheid emerged at the end of the 1950s. While grand apartheid may have been the ultimate goal, as exemplified in the 1948 election campaign, it was by no means completely thought out beforehand, particularly in terms of the detail. Such views tend to acknowledge that National Party policy built on existing principles.

Journalist Allister Sparkes argued that the National Party simply codified and formalized the existing system in law. Historian Anthony Butler, writing in 2009, wondered whether in reality the United Party would have done the same. Its policies were similar to the National Party's, if less carefully thought out; it was equally committed to white supremacy and the issues to which it responded would have been the same, particularly African migration to urban areas (see Table 4.3, page 129). These arguments go on to suggest that as apartheid was consolidated, and particularly during the premiership of Hendrik Verwoerd (see page 154) from 1958, apartheid entered a second, more all-embracing and coherent phase, especially with the development of the Bantustans as independent countries. Technically, black Africans were simply guest workers or illegal immigrants in South Africa.

Political constraints

One school of thought emphasizes the constraints on the National Party in 1948, with its small majority leading it to move with caution until growing confidence, as exemplified by large electoral victories in the 1950s, accelerated the process of apartheid. *The Times'* correspondent suggested the new government would have to proceed with caution.

SOURCE O

Excerpt from 'South African Government's Defeat – From Our Own Correspondent', *The Times*, 29 May 1948. *The Times* is a British newspaper.

If the nationalists were immediately to attempt to apply their policy of Apartheid (total segregation) in native affairs there might well be turmoil in the country. But this policy cannot be carried out without legislation and legislation affecting native political rights as profoundly as this requires a two-thirds majority of both Houses of parliament, sitting together – which Dr Malan cannot on present figures command …

It is expected that the new government will feel its way and that its native and constitutional outlook will be apparent in the beginning at any rate, only in altered administration emphasis in European privilege and South African domestic interests respectively.

According to Source O, what does the National Party need to do to implement apartheid?

The balanced view

Historian G.H.L. Lemay, writing in 1969, attempted a balanced view. On the one hand, he asserted that the National Party argued that their predecessors had effectively practised apartheid and the difference in their policies was only a question of degree. He did recognize, however, that the 1948 election victory marked a decisive change based on three factors:

- that race became a central concern
- that international conditions altered, in particular with India condemning South Africa in the United Nations (see page 213)
- that the demands of Africans grew more radical.

In 1991, William Beinart identified one fundamental difference between the Nationalists and their predecessors in that they were more prepared to stretch the Constitution to achieve their objectives and their racism was more entrenched. Having said this, Beinart acknowledges that there was no complete blueprint in 1948 and the apartheid system evolved over the ensuing years. This point was reiterated by Saul Dubow, writing in 2014, who emphasized the lack of a master plan and also asserted that the victory was unexpected, with the result that the party was to some extent unprepared for governance.

African responses to the National Party victory

Lemay's final point about the radicalization of the opposition was developed by Mandela, writing in 1994. While Africans were shocked by the National Party victory, they expected little from the United Party and felt that 'our land would henceforth be a place of tension and strife'. For the first time in South African history, an exclusively Afrikaner party led the government. At least, according to ANC activist Oliver Tambo, Africans now knew where they stood. It was indeed this, according to Mandela, that led the ANC to become more radical.

SOURCE P

How well does Source P exemplify the response of the ANC leadership to the National Party victory?

Excerpt from _Long Walk to Freedom_ by Nelson Mandela, published by Abacus, London, UK, 2013, p. 128.

The victory came as a shock. The United Party and General Smuts had beaten the Nazis and surely they would defeat the National Party. On election day, I attended a meeting in Johannesburg with Oliver Tambo and several others. We barely discussed the question of Nationalist government because we did not expect one. The meeting went on all night, and we emerged at dawn and found a newspaper stall selling the Rand Daily Mail: _the Nationalists had triumphed. I was stunned and dismayed, but Oliver took a more considered line. 'I like this', he said, 'I like this.' I could not imagine why. He explained. 'Now we will know exactly who our enemies are and where we stand.'_

Even General Smuts realized the dangers of this harsh ideology, decrying apartheid as 'a crazy concept born of prejudice and fear'.

It may be seen that on a spectrum of continuity and change, many historians and contemporary commentators seem to veer towards the former, while African leaders themselves at the time understood the consequences of the National Party victory. If the National Party moved cautiously to apartheid in their early period of office, building on existing structures, it is evident that the policy then developed and grew more ambitious in successive years, to make grand apartheid as far as possible a reality.

T O K

Can a case be made that the language used by the National Party in 1948 represents something new in South African race relations? (Language)

Opposition and repression

▶ **Key question**: *How effective was the opposition to apartheid during the 1950s?*

As the 1950s progressed, the government passed successive legislation to stifle dissent, including the power to detain anyone without charge. As the government grew more extreme, so did the opposition to it. The largest developments among opposition groups during the 1950s were:

- a growth in boycotts against apartheid legislation
- an increased readiness for the different ethnic groups to work together
- a growing militancy and acknowledgement that tactics such as petitions and delegations did not work.

Opposition groups: boycotts

How effective were boycotts?

Opposition groups organized a plethora of boycotts during the 1950s, with varying degrees of success. Often these were targeted at companies which relied on African labour, and were concerned with improvements in working conditions and pay.

Women's pass protest 1956

The Federation of South African Women (FSAW), formed in April 1954, organized a significant women's protest movement against women having to register for passes and carry passbooks, a new amendment to the pass laws (see page 166). Anti-apartheid activists such as the president of the ANC Women's League, Lilian Ngoyi, organized and led mass demonstrations.

On 9 August 1956, now known as Women's Day in South Africa, 20,000 women from all over South Africa marched on Pretoria with a petition bearing 100,000 signatures, as seen in Source Q, overleaf. The government buildings were largely empty; they were received by the Prime Minister Johannes Gerhardus Strijdom's secretary.

How far is Source Q reliable to a historian studying women's protest movements?

Radima Moosa Lilian Ngoyi, Helen Joseph and Sophie Williams, leaders of the FSAW, deliver their petition to the office of the prime minister in Pretoria in 1956.

SOURCE R

What does Source R indicate about the FSAW?

Excerpt from *Side by Side* by Helen Joseph, published by Zed Books, London, 1987. In her autobiography, anti-apartheid activist Joseph gives her account of the march on Pretoria.

Four women had been chosen as leaders for the day: Lilian Ngoyi, the African; Rahima Moosa, the Indian; Sophie Williams, the Coloured; and I, the white. We took the piles of protests and left them outside ministers' offices when our knocking brought no response: 'We have not come here to please but to ask for what is our right as mothers, as women and as citizens of this country …'. Lilian Ngoyi asked them all to stand in silent protest. As she raised her arm in the Congress [the ANC] salute, 20,000 arms went up and stayed there those endless minutes. We knew that all over South Africa women in cities and towns were gathered in protest …

At the end of half an hour Lilian began to sing, softly at first 'Nkosi Sikelel' iAfrika'. For the blacks, it has become their anthem and the voices rose, louder and louder. Then I heard a new song, composed especially for the protest 'Wathint' a bafazi, wa uthint' imbolodo uso kufa.' ['You have struck a rock, you have tampered with the women, you shall be destroyed.']

The protests continued: 1000 women protested in Lichtenburg in the Western Transvaal when officials tried to register them, and the police fired into the crowd, killing two women. At Nelspruit in eastern Transvaal, a group of women attacked the official charged with their registration. Five were arrested, and 300 marched on the local police station to demand their release – the police response again was brutal.

By March 1960, 3,020,281 African women (75 per cent of the total African female population) had been issued with passes, but the fact of accepting them did not end their protests.

Black Sash

One effect of the women's protest against passes was the radicalization of the white protest group the Black Sash (see page 168), who supported this action and also began to open advice centres for black women. They also arranged bail for arrested women who otherwise would not be allowed to return home to look after their children. The group built up a pool of lawyers who would represent African women for minimal fees. Gradually, the group built up trust among Africans who previously had been universally wary of white people offering to help them.

SOURCE S

Excerpt from Amy Thornton's testimony, quoted in *Black Sash: The Building of a Bridge in South Africa* by K. Spink, published by Methuen, London, UK, 1991, pp. 62–3. Thornton was an activist in the ANC organization.

In those days there was no contact. Very few whites were actively involved in the Congress [the ANC]. The Black Sash were this group of rather prim and proper upper middle class ladies with their gloves and their sashes. Everybody took it for granted that the blacks carried passes and sometimes there was a raid and the police came and knocked your 'boy' up to ask him for his pass, but of course nobody knew that in the townships the police would come knocking people up at 3 or 4 am, breaking doors down and asking for their passes. They didn't know that when the authorities were short of money they would have a raid on passes and reap in the fines. They didn't know what those bits of paper really meant.

How far does Source T bear out the evidence of Source S about the Black Sash?

SOURCE T

Black Sash members demonstrate against arbitrary government arrests in 1962.

White opposition parties

Some white political parties opposed apartheid, although they had limited influence:

- The non-racial Communist Party (see page 146) included many white members, and the Progressive and Liberal parties both fought for racial equality.
- The Progressive Party, formed in 1959, had only one MP, Helen Suzman; nevertheless, it fought tirelessly against key apartheid issues such as the pass laws, detention without trial and influx control.
- The Liberal Party had begun during the 1950s to try to educate whites against apartheid and, like the Communists, accepted a multiracial membership. In the 1960s it became more radical in its quest for a non-racial South Africa. Some members formed the African Resistance Movement (see page 227), while between March 1961 and April 1966, 41 leading members faced banning orders (see page 184).

The Alexandra bus boycott, January to June 1957

One successful boycott was against the Putco bus service in Alexandra when, in January 1957, it raised fares from 2 to 3 pence. The company said it had to do so to remain economically viable in the absence of government subsidies. In protest, thousands of commuters walked to work, some as many as twenty miles (32 km) per day. The boycott spread to other cities, notably Pretoria. Only in June was it called off when, in the face of local companies losing business through an erratic attendance by the workforce, Johannesburg City Council agreed to subsidize the company. This boycott was seen as one of the most successful protests of the 1950s.

SOURCE U

How useful is Source U to a historian studying the Alexandra bus boycott of 1957?

Excerpt from 'The Bus Boycott' by Ruth First, published in *African South*, volume 1, number 4, pp. 55–64, 1957. First was an anti-apartheid activist married to Communist leader Joe Slovo. She was arrested and rearrested under the 90-day law before escaping to Britain. She was assassinated, probably by South African security forces, in 1982.

'The tiger has fallen', the people cheered. The streets were strangely quiet. First the great lumbering green buses of the largest transport organization for Africans in the country travelled empty along the route; later they were withdrawn altogether. But for five and six hours every day endless streams of walkers filled the pavements. Over the rise that obscures Alexandra Township from the main road came the eruption of workers in the dawn hours when mists and brazier fires mingle indistinguishably together. End to end the road was filled with shadowy, hurrying figures. Then the forms thinned out as the younger men with the firmest, sprightly step drew away from the older people, the women, the lame … in the late afternoons and early evenings, the same crowds turned their backs

on the city and again took to the roads. Down the hill the footsloggers found it easier (though by the tenth and eleventh weeks of the boycott many shoes were worn to pitiful remnants), the spindly-legged youngsters trotted now and then to keep up, the progress of the weary women was slower still, here a large Monday washing bundle carried on the head, there a paraffin tin, or the baby tied securely to the back. In the pelting rain, through the sudden fierce storms of the Johannesburg summer, running the gauntlet of police patrols, the boycotters walked on. They gave the cities of the boycott a new air. Here was no protest by Africans hidden among the dusty squares of the segregated locations, but an army of protesters, voting with their feet, it has been said, before the eyes of White Johannesburg and the Reef.

The potato boycott 1957/1959

The ANC agreed to this boycott at is annual conference in 1957. The Ministry of Justice had been using unemployed African workers together with those convicted of petty crimes to work on farms. The farmers paid the authorities 4.5 pence per day for the use of such labour, and normally gave the workers nothing beyond basic food and shelter. Often they were locked in at night, in poor-quality accommodation. Elsewhere, adults and children were forced to dig potatoes with their bare hands. Articles by sympathetic journalists and activists, such as Ruth First (see page 180) and the priest Michael Scott, had drawn attention to these conditions throughout the 1950s, but only in May 1959 did the boycott begin. It was successful because potatoes rot quickly, and as people refused to buy them they piled up in the fields. Many fish and chip shops even sold only fish. By August 1959, farmers began to improve conditions for their workers and the boycott was hailed as a success.

Shebeen protests

Many African women in the townships made a living brewing and selling beer in shebeens (see page 159). Cato Manor was an overcrowded area near Durban, with 50,000 people living in about 6000 houses. In 1959, it was redesignated a white-only area and the African residents were expected to move. This led to widespread protests which soon focused on the shebeens. After continued police raids, angry shebeen owners took their revenge by attacking some government-run establishments. The next day, the security forces responded brutally to their actions: Cato Manor was torn down and its residents were forcibly removed.

While boycotts and protests may sometimes have resulted in victories, it is important to note that they did not address the long-term goals of overthrowing the system of apartheid. They tended to be localized and short term. The government tended to respond to every major protest with new laws of repression. Its intransigent commitment to apartheid never diminished.

? What does Source V suggest
about police tactics against
protesters?

**At Cato Manor, 1959, police respond brutally to shebeen owners
marching in protest against the police raids.**

How effectively did
different ethnic
groups work
together?

Opposition groups: cooperation and mass action

The common aims – to win civil rights, and defeat white supremacy and
apartheid – of various groups far outweighed the differences between them.
Nevertheless, the road to cooperation was not smooth. For example, some
within the ANC were always wary that Communists were using them for
their own purposes. At a local level there were often conflicts between
different groups, particularly Africans and Indians.

Durban riots, January 1949

The cause of these riots, which resulted in the deaths of 142 people
(including 87 Africans and 50 Indians), has been attributed to the Africans
accusing Indian shopkeepers of exploiting them by charging high prices for
food. The Natal Indian Council argued that wholesale prices kept rising
– tea, for example, had been 5 pence per pound in the pre-war era, and was
now 20 pence. In the disturbances, 58 stores, mainly belonging to Indians,
were destroyed.

Some people have argued that the real cause of the riots was the shocking
conditions in which Africans were forced to live. Indians just happened to be
the unlucky victims of their anger because they lived in proximity to them.
A May 1949 editorial in the magazine *The People's Forum* by a journalist,
R.S. Nowbath, asserted that the authorities did little to prevent or stop the
rioting, so long as it did not affect white areas. Indeed, in an official inquiry
into the unrest, no witnesses were cross-examined. The inquiry

acknowledged that living conditions in African areas were dreadful but stated that Africans, with their low standards and expectations, were happy to live in them. If it apportioned blame to anyone it did so to young Indians who, it asserted, often treated Africans as their racial inferiors.

SOURCE W

Excerpt from *The People's Forum*, 29 January 1949, located at: www.sahistory.org.za/archive/70-durban-riots-1949. Journalist R.S. Nowbath was a former editor of the *Forum*, which was aimed at a largely Indian readership.

> How useful is Source W in explaining how the Durban riots were interpreted at the time?

But at midday on Friday a veritable human cyclone hit the Indian business area. Hordes of Africans, armed with a varied assortment of improvised weapons, swooped down on the Indian people and destroyed both property and persons in their wake. Looting followed and the whole grim episode took on a positive aspect – the African had something material to gain. The convulsion had taken on a sinister aspect for, despite the efforts of the police, and egged on by many Europeans (who subsequently joined in the looting), the Africans discovered that their reign of terror could have a positive enriching value. They set to it with barbarous determination.

The forces of law and order stood by, almost helplessly it seemed, as the Africans swept forward in their savage march, and the terror immediately spread to the peri-urban areas where the outburst of the previous evening became an orgy of murder, arson, rape and looting which did not seem altogether without aim, purpose and direction.

The storm burst with unbridled fury on people who, in the main, lived almost under the same conditions as the Africans who attacked them.

The Ilanga Lase Natal, Natal's leading African newspaper, has blamed the Indian bitterly, for it says 'the whole grim business was logical, simply inevitable'. It then advances the following reasons for the convulsions: black-marketeering by Indians, Indian opposition to the economic expansion of the African, 'shacketeering' by Indian landlords, social and racial humiliation of Africans by Indians and the differential treatment of Indians by Europeans which gives the Indians 'not only better rights, but a sense of snobbishness and superiority over the Africans'.

Unity under non-violent protest

The ANC and SAIC in particular were influenced by the tactics of Gandhi in his quest for independence in India. The idea of non-violence was crucial, that protests would be peaceful and there would be no retaliation whatever the provocation from the authorities. The theory was that most authorities cannot win their case by using violence against protesters who do not retaliate: it merely makes them look like brutal oppressors. Gandhi's principle of non-violence was almost sacred within the SAIC, in which his son, Manilal, was an influential figure – although the SAIC did become more radical, and joined in with the armed struggle in the early 1960s (see pages 225–7).

For the ANC, non-violence was more of a tactic. It was prepared to adopt it so long as it seemed to have a chance of success. If, however, the authorities kept responding to peaceful protest with violence, the ANC was prepared to rethink the policy.

Despite conflicts and differences between the opposition groups, there were determined efforts to cooperate, such as the Day of Protest in 1950.

May Stayaway 1950

Many African leaders such as Mandela welcomed the pact with the SAIC of 1947 (see page 147). The SAIC was to organize a boycott called the May Stayaway which was subsequently joined by the **African People's Organisation (APO)**, comprising coloured South Africans. The cooperation over the 'stayaway' acted as a basis for future cooperation – although, despite fierce internal disagreements, the ANC pulled out of a campaign to extend the vote to all black, coloured and Indian people (as it felt at the time it should only be involved in campaigns it actually led).

In March 1950, the APO, ANC, TIC and the CPSA (Johannesburg branch) came together to organize a 'Defend Free Speech' convention. They resolved to hold a one-day general strike or 'stayaway' on 1 May to protest against apartheid legislation. In the event, the strike was co-ordinated by the SAIC and SACP, and the ANC did not give its official support because it was not leading it. With the authorities notified of the protest, the actual day was only a partial success. There were reports of employers locking their workforce in overnight to ensure they could not take part, or the security forces escorting people to work under duress so that they could not attend the protest. Nevertheless, up to 66 per cent of Africans stayed at home or attended protest meetings. At one such meeting in Orlando, the police charged into the crowd, killing eighteen Africans.

Government repression: Suppression of Communism Act 1950

The government, always prepared to blame African protest on Communist agitation, prepared this Act soon after the May strike. It defined Communism as any scheme aimed 'at bringing about any political and social and economic change within the Union by the promotion of disturbance and disorder'. Communism was therefore a euphemism for any form of unrest, and this Act could be used to imprison anyone for more or less anything the authorities deemed subversive. It could also ban organizations and indeed individuals from contacting others for periods of up to five years by the use of **banning orders**. For many, this meant house arrest. The British Lord Chancellor Lord Gardiner summed the Act up succinctly when he reported that anyone was a Communist if the South African minister of justice said so. It must also be said that the fear of Communism in South Africa mirrored that in the USA, where witch-hunts of suspected Communist sympathizers were taking place during the Cold War.

KEY TERM

African People's Organisation (APO) An organization for coloured South Africans opposing apartheid.

Banning orders Orders by which individuals or groups were banned from certain areas or from contacting others, or forced to live in specific areas.

SOURCE X

Excerpt from 'Watch on Communists in South Africa – From Our Own Correspondent', *The Times*, 17 September 1954.

Allegations that arms were being smuggled to South African Natives from Portuguese territories were made to Congress by Mr H.E. Martins MP. He said the Government should be congratulated for its actions against Communism and against the subversive activities among Natives. He was glad the Government was taking actions against natives who obtained arms in the Union's eastern border area. Mr Martins was speaking in support of a resolution asking the Government to ban celebrations such as those on May Day that had a Communistic colour.

How well does Source X explain the fear of Communism among South Africa's ruling classes?

The Communist Party after the Suppression of Communism Act

The CPSA dissolved itself after the Suppression of Communism Act (see page 184) and became an illegal organization, the South African Communist Party (SACP). Some white members also formed the Congress of Democrats. The SACP's policy, that Communism could not come about in South Africa until apartheid had been overcome and there was a non-racial state, continued. Some influential Communist leaders were also members of the ANC, while many members of the ANC had sympathy with Communist ideas. Many Communists worked closely with ANC activists throughout the years of apartheid and there was particularly close cooperation in the armed struggle of the early 1960s (see page 224).

Day of Protest 1950

The ANC called for an emergency conference in Johannesburg to plan a campaign in response to banning orders. It was at this conference that the future ANC leader Oliver Tambo made the influential speech: 'Today it is the Communist Party. Tomorrow it will be the trade unions, our Indian congress, our APO, our African National Congress'. The SAIC, ANC, APO and the SACP called together for a Day of Protest on 26 June 1950, in homage to the deaths at Orlando and to protest the Act which would make the SACP an illegal organization. Many urban Africans did refuse to go to work and there was a large protest of 5000 people in the location of Bethal, in the Transvaal. It was the first truly cooperative protest between all the opposition groups.

The M Plan

It was partly as a response to the Suppression of Communism Act that Nelson Mandela designed the M Plan. Fearing that the ANC would also be banned, the M Plan was how leaders could communicate effectively using an underground network of cells of supporters. Mandela also told local and regional leaders that if they could not hold meetings openly, then they must develop their own secret means of communicating with each other. This plan was implemented in part when Mandela and other leaders went underground after the ANC was banned in 1960.

Why did the
opposition groups
become increasingly
militant?

Growing militancy

As the 1950s progressed, the opposition groups moved from mainly non-violent protests to an increasingly militant stance. They co-ordinated various campaigns to protest against apartheid. This period also saw the rise to prominence of the most celebrated opposition leader, Nelson Mandela.

The ANC Youth League (ANCYL)

In 1944, Mandela was one of the founders of the ANCYL, with the aim of turning the ANC into a mass movement based on direct action. Lembede (see page 141) was the major founder and first president of the ANCYL. It was more radical in scope than the ANC and drove a more militant agenda. It was born out of the frustration that peaceful parliamentary protest did not work (see page 140). Mandela and others apparently went to see ANC president Dr Xuma in November 1949 to present their case for more direct action. When Xuma refused to countenance new policies he was ousted in the December 1949 annual conference and replaced by James Moroko. Leaders of the ANCYL took influential positions: Walter Sisulu, for example, became the first full-time ANC secretary. In 1950, as Lembede had died in 1947 of a medical condition, Mandela was elected to become the national president of the ANCYL.

Defiance Campaign 1952

The Defiance Campaign was preceded by a letter from the ANC to Prime Minister Malan demanding the complete repeal of apartheid laws and the Suppression of Communism Act by the end of February 1952. Malan's private secretary replied that whites had to protect themselves and any disturbances would be severely dealt with. It was decided that the Defiance Campaign would be non-violent and divided into two stages:

- an initial stage of local protest in which participants would break the law by not carrying passes or by staying in urban areas after the African curfew and inviting themselves for arrest – the intention being that the numbers arrested would overwhelm the prisons and the authorities' ability to cope, and also demonstrate the weight of opposition
- a second stage based on mass defiance which would extend the campaign by strikes and mass protests throughout the country.

At its inauguration event in Durban, over 10,000 people listened to Nelson Mandela, who had been instrumental in organizing the campaign, tell them that this would be the biggest action ever undertaken against apartheid. The size of the crowd showed that the ANC was reaching a wide audience. Indeed, its membership rose from an estimated 4000 to over 100,000 after the campaign.

SOURCE Y

Excerpt from *Long Walk to Freedom* by Nelson Mandela, published by Abacus, London, UK, 2013, p. 148.

I had never addressed such a great crowd before and it was an exhilarating experience. One cannot speak to a mass of people as one addresses an audience of two dozen. Yet I have always tried to take the same care to explain matters to great audiences as to small ones. I told the people that they would make history and focus the attention of the world on the racist policies of South Africa. I emphasised the unity among the black people – Africans, Coloureds and Indians – in South Africa had at least become a reality.

What does Source Y suggest about Mandela as a leader?

Results of the campaign

Any significant, organized protest rattled the government. In the six months of the campaign, 8500 participants were arrested for various acts of defiance – but the vast majority of the 8 million Africans did not become involved. While those arrested were treated lightly, with penalties rarely exceeding the equivalent of £10 (although this was a lot of money to most Africans), the government subsequently passed a raft of measures to make civil disobedience a crime (see page 189). The government also:

- used crude propaganda to limit support for the protest, saying opposition leaders were living easy lives while the ordinary members were imprisoned
- tried to infiltrate anti-apartheid groups with spies, often African policemen working undercover
- tried to blame violence in Port Elizabeth and East London on the campaign, although the actual causes of these disturbances had nothing to do with the campaign.

The campaign organizers, including Mandela, were inevitably arrested. The president of the ANC, Moroka, pleaded guilty alone among the defendants and admitted he had been wrong in becoming involved. After this plea, Chief Albert Luthuli replaced him as leader.

Chief Albert Luthuli

Luthuli's grandfather had been chief of the Zulu tribe which lived in Groutville in Natal, but his father became a missionary, serving the Matabele tribe in Rhodesia (now Zimbabwe) where Albert was born. Luthuli grew up to become a teacher, working for years at the prestigious Adams College, where he was one of only a few African staff. He was committed to a broad-based academic curriculum for African children available to all. By 1933, he was president of the African Teachers' Association and recognized as one of the most important African educators in South Africa. In 1936, however, he agreed to become the chief of the tribe around Groutville, where he spent the rest of his life.

Luthuli was instrumental during the ANC's Defiance Campaign, encouraging volunteers and addressing rallies, particularly in the East Rand. The government gave him an ultimatum: resign from the ANC or from his chieftainship. They clearly saw the two roles as incompatible: chiefs were meant to be compliant with the government, not defiant opponents of apartheid. When Luthuli chose neither option, he was dismissed from his chieftain's role and spent most of the 1950s under banning orders. Inevitably, this led to problems with his role as ANC president. For example, he was not present when the Freedom Charter (see pages 189–92) was signed because he was in exile. Colleagues often found it difficult to get in touch with him as a result of the banning orders, particularly when it was necessary to do so quickly.

The Road to Freedom is the Cross

Luthuli remained a devout Christian all his life, and this was to lead many to doubt his commitment to an armed struggle (see page 225). On his dismissal as chief in November 1952, he produced a key policy document, *The Road to Freedom is the Cross*. This outlined many of his ideas, advocating non-violent protest and recognizing that, almost like Christ, some had to lead and suffer for freedom, in this sense the end of apartheid, to be achieved.

SOURCE Z

How useful is Source Z in explaining the position of Chief Luthuli in supporting the Defiance Campaign and refusing to resign from the ANC?

Excerpt from *The Road to Freedom is the Cross*, a public statement by Chief Luthuli in November 1952. The authorities had dismissed him from his position as chief when he refused to leave the ANC. Located at: www.sahistory.org.za/archive/road-freedom-cross-1952.

In so far as gaining citizenship rights and opportunities for the unfettered development of the African people, who will deny that thirty years of my life have been spent knocking in vain, patiently, moderately and modestly at a closed and barred door?

What have been the fruits of my many years of moderation? Has there been any reciprocal tolerance or moderation from the Government, be it Nationalist or United Party? No! On the contrary, the past thirty years have seen the greatest number of laws restricting our rights and progress until today we have reached a stage where we have almost no rights at all: no adequate land for our occupation, our only asset, cattle, dwindling, no security of homes, no decent and remunerative employment, more restriction to freedom of movement through passes, curfew regulations, influx control measures; in short we have witnessed in these years an intensification of our subjection to ensure and protect white supremacy.

New spirit of the people
It is with this background and with a full sense of responsibility that, under the auspices of the African National Congress (Natal), I have joined my people in the new spirit that moves them today, the spirit that revolts openly and boldly against injustice and expresses itself in a determined and non-violent manner. Because of my association with the African National Congress in this new spirit

which has found an effective and legitimate way of expression in the non-violent Passive Resistance Campaign, I was given a two-week limit ultimatum by the Secretary for Native Affairs calling upon me to choose between the African National Congress and the chieftainship of the Groutville Mission Reserve. He alleged that my association with Congress in its non-violent Passive Resistance Campaign was an act of disloyalty to the State. I did not, and do not, agree with this view.

The end of the campaign

The ANC leadership disagreed among themselves as to when to call off the campaign. Dr Xuma, still influential, asserted that it had lost momentum. Mandela felt, with hindsight, it had gone on too long. Certainly, it never moved to the second stage beyond one mass protest in the Eastern Cape, and there was little participation in rural areas. The campaign formally ended in January 1953, having lasted for six months.

One could argue that the campaign had only limited success, yet, by its end, the ANC:

- had become a mass organization led by committed and experienced activists
- had maintained the policy of non-violence
- realized it could embarrass the government by tactics of protest and non-participation, but not topple it – campaigns such as Defiance would not be successful in themselves if their goal was to abolish apartheid, no matter how many people participated in them.

Government repression: further measures of repression and control

In 1953, the government announced its right to suspend all laws if necessary and shift the burden of proof from the state to the accused. If people were arrested and charged, they were now assumed to be guilty unless they could prove their innocence, which was often difficult to do while languishing in a jail cell. Other acts of repression followed:

- 1953 Public Safety Act: allowed the government to call a state of emergency for up to twelve months in the first instance, with the power to renew it indefinitely.
- 1953 Criminal Law Amendment Act: said that anyone accompanying a person found guilty of a crime would automatically be presumed guilty also and have to prove their innocence.
- 1956 Riotous Assemblies Act: passed as a response to the mass meeting at Kliptown (see page 190). Any open-air meetings could be banned if the minister of justice felt they endangered peace or fomented hostility between white and African groups.

Creation of a Freedom Charter

The ANC and other protest organizations held meetings nationwide in the early 1950s to hear people's demands and grievances. These included a key meeting in 1954, where it was decided to create a charter of universal rights, based on what the African people wanted. Volunteers travelled the country to listen to the people.

? What does Source AA suggest about the people of South Africa who wanted change?

SOURCE AA

Excerpt from an interview with Wolfie Kodesh, quoted in *New Africa History* by N. Frick, S. Janari, G. Weldon, A. Proctor and D. Wray, published by New Africa Books, Cape Town, South Africa, 2006, p. 176. Kodesh was an anti-apartheid and SACP activist who later worked with Ruth First and helped to hide Mandela from the authorities seeking to capture him.

We went right into the countryside to all the places we'd known before – a whole network. We got resolutions from women, farm workers … We even got resolutions written on the back of Cavalla cigarette boxes … It was a very difficult task because people were not used to expressing themselves … [The volunteers] had to go out and explain to the people carefully, 'Look here, I'm not telling you what to say, you tell me what you want' … [The demand] varies from being able to get a uniform at work, for instance, for the wives to be able to live with their husbands and not be separated, to much more comprehensive political ideas such as a vote for all …

With so many protest leaders caught up in trials and banning orders, the creation of the Freedom Charter took a long time. The Freedom Charter was presented to a People's Congress at Kliptown, near Johannesburg, between 25 and 26 June 1955. The congress was attended by 3000 representatives of all the opposition groups.

Z.K. Matthews and Lionel Bernstein

Bernstein was the son of Jewish immigrants in South Africa. Born in Durban, He grew to join and become secretary of the SACP (Johannesburg District). When the SACP was banned in 1950, he helped to form the Congress of Democrats. He played a leading role on the committee to organize the People's Congress, helped by Z.K. Matthews, head of Fort Hare's Department of African Studies. Both Matthews and Bernstein were among those arrested at the Treason Trial.

The different groups came together and began to call themselves the Congress Alliance, although some in the ANC did not want to be part of it. This was the beginning of the split in the ANC between those who believed in the Freedom Charter and the more Africanist members who did not. Some, including Sobukwe, felt the ANC had betrayed its principles by cooperating with other racial groups.

The Congress Alliance ratified the Freedom Charter. The crowd was broken up by the police, who announced that they suspected treason was being committed and took the name of everyone attending before they could leave. Many were subsequently arrested. As Mandela was under banning orders at the time, he watched the events in secret and disguised himself in order to escape police detection.

The significance of the Freedom Charter

The Freedom Charter was a statement of ideals and aims rather than strategy. Much of its significance was in its preamble.

SOURCE BB

Excerpt from the preamble to the Freedom Charter, quoted in *A History of the ANC* by Francis Meli, published by James Currey, Woodbridge, UK, 1989, p. 210.

We, the people of South Africa, declare for all our country and the world to know:

- *That South Africa belongs to all who live in it, black and white, and that no government can justly claim authority unless it is based on the will of the people;*
- *That our people have been robbed of their birthright to land, liberty and peace by a form of government founded on injustice and inequality;*
- *That our country will never be prosperous or free until all our people live in brotherhood, enjoying equal rights and opportunities;*
- *That only a democratic state, based on the will of all the people, can secure to all their birthright without distinction of colour, race, sex or belief;*
- *And therefore we, the people of South Africa, black and white together – equals, countrymen and brothers – adopt this Freedom Charter. And we pledge ourselves to strive together, sparing neither strength nor courage, until the democratic changes here set out have been won.*

What can you infer from Source BB about the aims of the Freedom Charter?

The Freedom Charter went on to demand:

- equal political rights for all
- an end to discrimination and apartheid
- equality before the law
- human rights
- freedom to join trade unions
- fair employment practices
- equality of educational opportunity
- decent housing conditions
- peaceful foreign relations.

Critics, however, latched on to the clauses that seemed to suggest equalization of wealth.

According to Source CC, what is the reason for wanting an equal share of wealth?

SOURCE CC

Excerpt from the Freedom Charter, quoted in *A History of the ANC* by Francis Meli, published by James Currey, Woodbridge, UK, 1989, p. 211.

The people shall share in the country's wealth!

The national wealth of our country, the heritage of all South Africans shall be restored to the people.

The mineral wealth beneath the soil, the banks and monopoly industry shall be transferred to the ownership of the people as a whole …

The land shall be shared among those who work it!

Restrictions of land ownership on a racial basis shall be ended and all the land re-divided among those who work it, to banish famine and land hunger.

These clauses, some argued, suggested that the authors of the Freedom Charter represented Communist organizations. However, this was hotly disputed by members of the Congress Alliance, who argued that they merely sought a fair distribution of income and an end to monopolistic practices, for example in the mines, where competition was stifled. They argued that there was nothing in the Freedom Charter that attacked fair competition or the rights of people to make profits in private industry.

In Source DD, how convincingly does Mandela refute the allegations of Communism in Source CC?

SOURCE DD

Excerpt from *Long Walk to Freedom* by Nelson Mandela, published by Abacus, London, UK, 2013, pp. 205–6.

The charter guaranteed that when freedom came, Africans would have the opportunity to own their own businesses in their own names, to own their own houses and property: in short, to prosper as capitalists and entrepreneurs. The charter does not speak about the eradication of classes and private property, or public ownership of the means of production, or promulgate any of the tenets of scientific socialism. The cause discussing the possible nationalisation of the mines, the banks and monopoly industries was an action that needed to be taken if the economy was not to be solely owned and operated by white businessmen.

The Treason Trial

Eighteen months after the ratification of the Freedom Charter, on 5 December 1956, the authorities arrested 156 of those who had attended the Kliptown meeting and charged them with high treason. They included the entire leadership of the ANC and most of the other opposition groups. After five months, they were accused of conspiring to overthrow the government and replace it with a Communist regime.

From 1957 onwards, some defendants were released for lack of evidence and indictments were withdrawn against 73 defendants. The trial against the remaining 30 defendants finally began in August 1959. Mandela had founded the first African law firm in Johannesburg with Oliver Tambo in 1952 – this effectively went out of business during the trial. Luthuli joined colleagues in the dock during the Treason Trial; his banning order had been revoked to enable him to do so. However, in 1958 a third banning order was imposed which stated that he was not allowed to publish anything for five years, or move outside a fifteen-mile (24-km) radius of Groutville. Although he remained leader of the ANC until his death in 1967 (see page 214), these restrictions limited his effectiveness.

When, in March 1961, the trial finally came to an end, with the acquittal of all the defendants, there was little cause for rejoicing. Not only had the years taken their toll on the livelihoods of the defendants, but South Africa itself had changed. The government was becoming more ambitious in its apartheid programme and was prepared to use even more oppression to enforce it. There were increasing concerns within the anti-apartheid groups about the efficacy of the ANC cooperating with other ethnic groups, and in April 1959 the **Pan Africanist Congress (PAC)**, with an Africanist agenda, was to split away; its first campaign resulted in the hugely significant massacre at Sharpeville (see pages 206–14). Fearing further arrests, Tambo went into exile to lead the ANC from abroad. Mandela went underground and was subsequently to lead the military wing of the ANC. By the early 1960s, the fight against apartheid had become more protracted and more violent. Peaceful protest was largely at an end.

KEY TERM

Pan Africanist Congress (PAC) Black African organization that set up an Africanist agenda, in which the government of South Africa should comprise only black Africans.

SOURCE EE

A montage of those accused in the Treason Trial, 1956.

What can you infer from Source EE about the scale of the Treason Trial?

The Treason Trial's 'star witness'

The trial itself had elements of farce. During preliminary hearings in 1957, the state produced Professor Andrew Murray as an expert in Communism to give evidence that the defendants were preparing a Communist revolution in South Africa. To test his credentials, the defence lawyers read to Murray a variety of sources and asked him if they represented Communist views. He said yes. The quotations were subsequently shown to have been authored by former US presidents Abraham Lincoln and Woodrow Wilson, and in a final irony, one written by Murray himself.

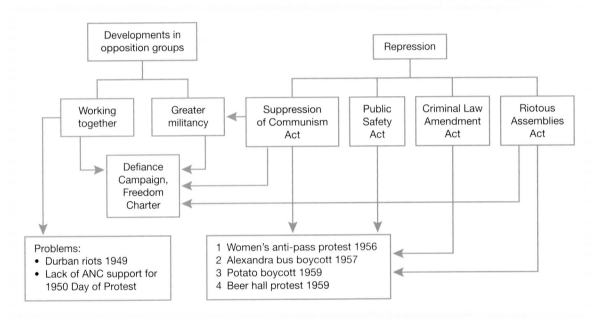

Opposition and repression

⑤ Rural unrest

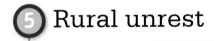

▶ **Key question:** *How extensive was rural unrest?*

The ANC admitted that it had more support in urban than in rural areas. However, there were numerous cases of unrest in rural areas during the 1950s. These often concerned the white governmental authorities trying to dictate matters when the tribal leaders were ostensibly in charge. Uprisings against the government in rural areas appeared more spontaneous and unplanned, but this made them more unpredictable, and difficult to both to anticipate and suppress.

Zeerust uprising 1957

This uprising was precipitated by the imposition of passes for women living in the Zeerust area in western Transvaal. When, in 1957, Chief Abraham Moiloa was ordered to compel women in his jurisdiction to accept passes, he refused. Women boycotted the premises of the white shopkeeper from where the passes were to be issued. At a public meeting convened by the local white Native Commissioner in April to explain the need for passes, Moiloa was dismissed from his office. The result was protest. Men and women from Zeerust, currently living in Johannesburg, chartered buses to return to join in these protests. On 14 April, one such meeting condemned officials in their absence to death: over 100 male supporters were arrested on their return journey and five were accused of attempted murder. Meanwhile women burned their passes and boycotted the schools where teachers had accepted passes. Subsequently, a special police squad was appointed to force women to accept passes.

While women had eventually to accept the use of passes in Zeerust, as elsewhere, the authorities blamed outside agitators for the disturbances – specifically the protesters who came from Johannesburg – and were incandescent when the vast majority of those arrested were acquitted.

Although the Zeerust uprising was significant, most of the unrest throughout the rural areas was mainly about the power of the local chieftains.

Why was unrest centred on Zeerust?

East Pondoland

In East Pondoland, Chief Botha Sigcau sided with the authorities in disputes about land. He and his councillors were also accused of corruption in selling off mineral rights, and land to railway companies. His councillors were attacked and the government sent in the security forces to keep order. Violent clashes took place between residents and police, for example at Ngqindile, near the town of Flagstaff, after the police were tipped off about a mass meeting there in November 1960. When their demands that Sigcau and his supporters be replaced were ignored, residents began a boycott of white-owned stores. A state of emergency was declared and a home guard was established by the chief to help enforce order. Eventually, the rebellion was suppressed, with the boycott ending in January 1961.

The Promotion of Self-Government Act of 1959 (see page 221) was to turn the local chieftains into government agents rather than representatives of the people. Government officials gained the right to attend all meetings and, if necessary, to dismiss the African officials. The policy was developing into the idea of grand apartheid in which these tribal areas would become Bantustans, ostensibly independent but under close supervision from Pretoria. As the 1950s came to a close, apartheid was entering a new phase in terms of both its extent and the nature of its opposition.

What were the causes of the uprising in East Pondoland?

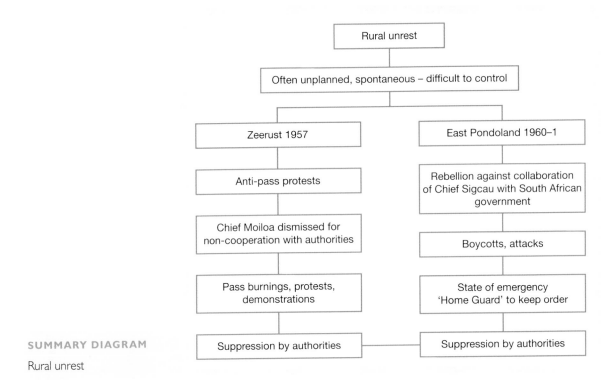

```
                          ┌─────────────────┐
                          │  Rural unrest   │
                          └─────────────────┘
                                  │
          ┌───────────────────────────────────────────────────┐
          │  Often unplanned, spontaneous – difficult to control │
          └───────────────────────────────────────────────────┘
                                  │
          ┌───────────────────────┴───────────────────────┐
  ┌───────────────────┐                         ┌───────────────────────┐
  │   Zeerust 1957    │                         │  East Pondoland 1960–1 │
  └───────────────────┘                         └───────────────────────┘
          │                                               │
  ┌───────────────────┐                         ┌───────────────────────┐
  │ Anti-pass protests│                         │ Rebellion against      │
  └───────────────────┘                         │ collaboration of Chief │
          │                                     │ Sigcau with South      │
  ┌───────────────────────────┐                 │ African government     │
  │ Chief Moiloa dismissed for│                 └───────────────────────┘
  │ non-cooperation with      │                             │
  │ authorities               │                 ┌───────────────────────┐
  └───────────────────────────┘                 │   Boycotts, attacks   │
          │                                     └───────────────────────┘
  ┌───────────────────────────┐                             │
  │ Pass burnings, protests,  │                 ┌───────────────────────┐
  │ demonstrations            │                 │  State of emergency   │
  └───────────────────────────┘                 │ 'Home Guard' to keep   │
          │                                     │ order                  │
  ┌───────────────────────────┐                 └───────────────────────┘
  │ Suppression by authorities│─────────────────│ Suppression by         │
  └───────────────────────────┘                 │ authorities            │
                                                 └───────────────────────┘
```

SUMMARY DIAGRAM

Rural unrest

Chapter summary

The development of apartheid 1948–64

The government was to develop a complex machinery to implement apartheid with the Department of Native Affairs at its heart. Laws were passed to control the movement and activities of non-whites through both the pass system and where they could live. The Group Areas Act, for example, involved the forced removal of up to 3.5 million people. The destruction of Sophiatown is often cited as an example. Increasingly, however, opponents were prepared to take direct action. The 1950s was characterized by both increasing militancy and a growing tendency for different ethnic groups to work together, as exemplified by the Defiance Campaign and the production of the Freedom Charter. Many leaders, however, were tied up in a Treason Trial which lasted for four-and-a-half years. Meanwhile, protests against specific issues went on apace, for example against women having to carry passes. Protests also spread to rural areas, where some places such as East Pondoland seemed increasingly ungovernable. The authorities always responded with determination and brutality. Opponents such as Ruth First asserted that boycotts politicized Africans and became a focus for their determination. By the end of the 1950s, apartheid was firmly enforced and protesters' anger and action were growing.

Examination advice

Paper I Question 16: how to integrate sources and write a good essay

Question 16 is always an essay question. It requires you to write what you know while integrating the sources provided. The sources are there to support your own knowledge. Therefore, it is important that you prepare yourself for this type of question by knowing and understanding the major topics that are presented in this book.

Question 16 is always worth 9 marks. This means it is worth over 37.5 per cent of the overall possible mark. You should spend 30–35 minutes answering this question, using the first five to eight minutes of this time to summarize the sources and outline your response.

Remember that questions for Prescribed subject 4 will be numbered 13, 14, 15 and 16 in the Paper 1 exam.

How to answer
Summarize the sources and outline your essay
It is best to first list and summarize your sources to focus your thoughts. This should be done in about five minutes and should be in the form of short bullet points. Once you have summarized the sources, briefly outline your essay's structure. This outline should include some sort of introduction to your essay and a concluding answer to the question. Write your outline down on your examination paper, but put a single line through everything that you do not want the examiner to mark.

Writing the essay
When you write your essay, make sure you follow your outline and use all the sources. This should take the remainder of your time, which should be at least 25 minutes.

You need to start with a good introduction to focus your essay and which defines anything that might be open to interpretation. Your introduction should conclude a definite answer to the question. This should further serve to focus your essay. Usually you can introduce one or more of your sources in the introduction to support what you are going to cover.

All sources must be used at least once, but use them multiple times if they will help your essay. Remember: the sources should support your essay.

Finally, under no circumstances are you to actually just list the five sources and a couple of bullet points beneath each in a sort of preamble to a real essay. Sources should be integrated and quoted to support your essay.

Your concluding paragraph should clearly answer the essay question, summarizing your main arguments. For example, if the question asks you 'to what extent', answer the question:

- 'to a great extent'
- 'to some extent' or
- 'to no extent'.

Your conclusion will then include a summary of your main points.

Example

Source A: see page 156
Source L: see page 166
Source M: see page 171
Source N: see page 173

This question uses Sources A, L, M and N found in this chapter:

> Using Sources A, L, M and N, and your own knowledge, evaluate the impact that South African apartheid laws had on black–white relations. (9 marks)

First, very briefly summarize the sources just for your own information in five minutes or less.

Source A: SABRA (1951): keep black and white people separate; don't allow black trade unions in white areas.

Source L: Verwoerd speech: make 'native territories of Bantu farming' better so they won't seek protection of Europeans (white people).

Source M: Verwoerd speech (1954): education should be in Native Areas; Bantus must be 'guided'; no place for the South African black people in European community.

Source N: Jackson cartoon (1958): Verwoerd passing laws which meant loss of human rights; process well under way.

Own knowledge: Among the points you could raise are: Department of Native Affairs grew after 1948 elections; 1950 Group Areas Act led to forced removals; 1951 Bantu Authorities Act forced many black people to live in 'homelands'; 1953 Bantu Education Act saw growth of government control.

Second, briefly outline in bullet points the main parts of your essay in five minutes or less.

Introduction: impact of policies on race relations
- Goal was separation not unification
- Affected all aspects of daily life: education, work
- Policies did not develop South African black people, economically or socially
- Deeper divisions were created

Paragraph 2: 1948 elections and government and govt's goals
- *Verwoerd and National Party take control*
- *Govt justification for separation (Sources I and J)*
- *SABRA (A)*

Paragraph 3: Implementing apartheid
- *Dept of Native Affairs*
- *1951 Bantu Authorities Act*
- *Forced removals – Sophiatown*

Paragraph 4: Role of education
- *1953 Bantu Education Act*
- *Education in Native Areas (J)*
- *Impact on mission schools*

Paragraph 5: Laws and human rights
- *1950 Suppression of Communism Act*
- *Step-by-step legislative process meant steady erosion of human rights (K).*

Paragraph 6: Conclusion

Third, write an answer to the question.

The rise to power of the National Party in 1948 ushered in a government that pushed for a comprehensive set of laws which were designed to separate the races. Apartheid, as the general policy was known, affected all aspects of daily life for black and white people in South Africa, including education, housing and work. While the government claimed that these legislative measures were designed to help each and every ethnic community develop, the evidence in the four sources, as well as other knowledge, suggests otherwise. The apartheid policies held back South African blacks socially and economically and created deeper divisions in white–black relations.

The National Party had promised far-reaching changes if elected, and it was true to its word. Hendrik Verwoerd, known as the 'architect of apartheid,' began to make serious changes in black–white relations, first as head of the Department of Native Affairs, and then as prime minister.

> Thesis about impact of apartheid on black–white relations clearly stated.

Relevant sources and own knowledge used to provide evaluation of the impact of government plans to separate the races.

Government policy was clearly expressed in Source L, when Verwoerd stated that the poor conditions found in the 'native territories' would need to be improved in order to stem the tide of black Africans seeking the protection and help of the 'European.' He further elaborates in Source M, explaining that the black people needed separate educational opportunities because they could not be absorbed by the white neighbourhoods or even be allowed to live among white people. A leading think-tank at the time, the South African Bureau of Racial Affairs (SABRA), provided research which the government used to support its racial policies. In Source A, specific programmes are suggested that would further divide the races. Among these were the call to forbid black trade unions in white areas and the need to train 'black building craftsmen, to ensure that only African labour should be used in the building of African housing in the urban areas.' The implication here is that white and black people should have as little to do with one another as possible.

Appropriate use of sources as supporting evidence, as well as significant own knowledge to expand on the points raised in the analysis of the sources.

In order to move the process along, the government expanded the powers of the Department of Native Affairs, giving it greater control over the lives of the blacks. In 1951, the Bantu Authorities Act was passed and this asserted that the only places Africans were entitled to live were their 'tribal reserves' that had been created earlier. While these reserves could never be economically self-sufficient, they did absorb many black people and provided the physical location of separate areas reserved for black people. The government promised to improve conditions in the reserves greatly, as shown in Sources L and M. Legally, black people now were not citizens of South Africa but of their reserves or 'Bantustans'. However, there were hundreds of thousands of black people who did live in racially mixed urban areas. The government moved to empty the inhabitants out of these neighbourhoods because they ran counter to separate development. Sophiatown was the most famous example of these forced removals. One of the justifications for these was that idea that people of different races would not live together peacefully so they had to be separated.

Another significant policy set into law was the 1953 Bantu Education Act. To educate the African in 'useful' activities instead of ill-suited European ones, a large bureaucracy was created to take control of the educational system, in this case from the Ministry of Education to the Ministry for Native Affairs. As Verwoerd said in Source M, 'It is the policy of my department that education should have its roots entirely in the Native areas and in the Native environment.' What he did not say was that, prior to 1948, most 'Native' or African children had been educated in Church-run mission schools. These, for the most part, were forced to close once they no longer received government subsidies. The government system focused on a limited vocational-based system which was meant to teach basic skills and nothing more. What had once been a wide gap between the education that black and white children received was now enormous.

The government took every opportunity to alter dramatically the racial landscape. In 1950, the Suppression of Communism Act was passed. Because Communists in South Africa were colour blind, accepting both black and white people into their party, they were viewed as a threat by the authorities. By crushing the Communist political party, the government also closed off yet another area where blacks and whites cooperated, so deep was its zeal to separate whites and blacks. Source N, a cartoon by the South African J.H. Jackson, clearly illustrates how Verwoerd was enacting laws step-by-step and what the results of his actions were. By drawing the shades marked 'LAWS,' he was putting South Africa into darkness while the sunshine of human rights would no longer be seen. The loss of human rights was felt most keenly by the South African black people, but white South Africans too were punished because they could not mix with the majority of the population.

The impact of South Africa's racial policies after the 1948 elections was profound. White and black people could no longer socialize, work or live in close proximity. The systematic application of apartheid legislation created the divided nation envisioned by the National Party.

The conclusion stresses the main points argued in the essay and supports the main thesis.

This is a response that would achieve the upper mark band used to mark Paper 1 Question 16 because:

- The response is clearly focused on the question.
- There are references to all four sources and they support the essay as evidence.
- Accurate, relevant knowledge of the topic is provided and there is a synthesis of own or outside knowledge and material from the sources.

Examination practice

The following are exam-style questions for you to practise, using sources from Chapters 4, 5 and 6. Sources can be found on the page references given.

Chapter 4

Source K: page 137

Source N: page 143

Chapter 5

Source C: page 157

Source D: page 158

1 Using these sources from Chapter 4, Chapter 5 and your own knowledge, evaluate the human costs of 'petty' and 'grand' apartheid.

Chapter 5

Source B: page 157

Source C: page 157

Source D: page 158

Source E: page 159

2 Using these sources from Chapter 5 and your own knowledge, explain how South African blacks responded to forced removals.

Chapter 6

Source D: page 207

Source E: page 208

Source F: page 209

Source G: page 209

3 Using these sources from Chapter 6 and your own knowledge, discuss why people lost their lives at Sharpeville.

Activities

1 The Defiance Campaign of 1952 was a watershed event in the anti-apartheid campaign. In groups of two or three, create a bibliography and filmography of the campaign. Try to include sources that are both primary and secondary, South African and non-South African. What sources offer the most complete explanation of the campaign? What differences do you notice between South African and non-South African sources?

2 Create an illustrated timeline of the events in this chapter that demonstrate resistance to apartheid laws.

3 The 1955 ANC Freedom Charter was a strong call for racial equality. Read the complete charter (see http://www.anc.org.za/show.php?id=72) and discuss what problem or concern each article was addressing.

CHAPTER 6

Protests and action up to 1964

This chapter examines opposition to apartheid and the response from the authorities, initially by exploring the Sharpeville massacre. It also looks at the nature of government repression before going on to examine why the opposition groups adopted a policy of armed struggle and how successful this was. The chapter goes on to investigate the Rivonia Trial, its impact, and how deeply apartheid was entrenched by 1964. You need to consider the following questions throughout this chapter:

★ How significant was the Sharpeville massacre?

★ How has the Sharpeville massacre been interpreted?

★ What was the impact of the main government policies against opposition groups?

★ Why did opposition groups engage in an armed struggle?

★ How effectively did the authorities react to violent protest?

★ How effectively was apartheid entrenched by 1964?

 # The significance of the Sharpeville massacre 1960

▶ *Key question: How significant was the Sharpeville massacre?*

The Sharpeville massacre in 1960 was one of the defining events in the history of apartheid in South Africa. The explanation for it is hotly debated to this day, often polarized between those who argue that it was a case of premeditated murder against protesters, and others who see it as vastly outnumbered policemen trying to defend themselves from a hostile crowd.

The Pan Africanist Congress (PAC)

The Pan Africanist Congress (PAC), formed in 1958, was borne out of dissatisfaction with the **integrationalist** approach of the ANC, and possibly because so many ANC leaders were either in prison or tied up with the Treason Trial (see pages 192–3). Its most charismatic leader was Robert Sobukwe.

Robert Sobukwe

Robert Sobukwe was born in December 1924 in Cape Province, the youngest of six children. His parents were unskilled: his father was a labourer and mother variously a cleaner, or cook, in a local hospital. Sobukwe was highly intelligent and studied at Fort Hare University, where his fine oratorical skills

> **What was the PAC's role in the Sharpeville massacre?**

 KEY TERM

Integrationalist Made up of different groups, in this case of all races in South Africa.

were evident during his tenure as president of the Student Representative Council. He also edited an African journal called *Beware* which advocated protest and non-cooperation. Sobukwe joined the ANC Youth League (ANCYL) but was always more attracted to the Africanist wing and was particularly influenced by Anton Lembede (see page 141). A teacher and academic, he was appointed to the University of Witwatersrand in 1954 where he taught African Studies. In 1957 he became the editor of *The Africanist*, a periodical intended for an African readership which promoted Africanist ideas.

It was perhaps inevitable that Sobukwe would be attracted to a movement which blamed the apparent lack of success of the ANC on its willingness to work with other ethnic groups, which it felt exploited them for their own purposes. The PAC greatly opposed the Freedom Charter, which it felt contradicted the 1949 Programme of Action (see page 144). It felt that the ANC had betrayed its principles by cooperating with other racial groups and this helped to explain its comparative lack of success.

Why, according to Source A, has the PAC come to 'a parting of the ways' with the ANC?

SOURCE A

Excerpt from a speech in 1958 on the reasons for the formation of the PAC by Robert Sobukwe, located at: www.sahistory.org.za/people/robert-mangaliso-sobukwe.

In 1955 the Kliptown Charter was adopted, which according to us, is irreconcilable conflict with the 1949 Programme seeing that it claims land no longer Africa, but is auctioned for sale to all who live in this country. We have come to the parting of the ways and we are here and now giving notice that we are disassociating ourselves from the ANC as it is constituted at present in the Transvaal.

 **KEY TERM**

Proportional representation
The concept that the government of a country must be proportionally represented. In this sense Sobukwe meant that Africans, as the overwhelming racial majority, should govern South Africa.

The PAC philosophy

The embryonic PAC was particularly opposed to Communism, and associated itself with movements for independence throughout Africa. Sobukwe was not anti-white as such, unlike other members of the PAC who saw whites as the enemy and spoke of driving them into the sea. He did, however, feel that Africans had to be responsible for their own destiny; people who knew him well, like Mandela, often asserted that Sobukwe was far more moderate than many of his supporters.

Explain Sobukwe's arguments in Source B.

SOURCE B

Excerpt from Sobukwe's inaugural speech on the formation of the PAC in April 1959, located at: http://v1.sahistory.org.za/pages/governance-projects/organisations/pac/origins.htm.

*... Further, multi-racialism is in fact a pandering to European bigotry and arrogance. It is a method of safeguarding white interests, implying as it does, **proportional representation** irrespective of population figures. In that sense it is a complete negation of democracy.*

To us the term 'multi-racialism' implies that there are such basic insuperable differences between the various national groups here that the best course is to keep them permanently distinctive in a kind of democratic apartheid. That to us is racialism multiplied, which probably is what the term truly connotes. We aim, politically, at government of the Africans by the Africans, for the Africans, with everybody who owes his only loyalty to Afrika [sic] and who is prepared to accept the democratic rule of an African majority being regarded as an African.

We guarantee no minority rights, because we think in terms of individuals, not groups.

The formation of the PAC in April 1959 did not take the ANC by surprise – it had already expelled one of its founders, Potlako Lobello, for his Africanist views – but the ANC disagreed profoundly with its philosophy. As the ANC understood it, the PAC saw the liberation of South Africa from apartheid in the same context as anti-colonial movements throughout Africa. Africa belonged to black Africans, who must fight alone for their liberation. The ANC had no problem with this view in relation to countries such as Ghana and Kenya, which were fighting for independence from colonial masters. They felt, however, that it was inappropriate for South Africa, where 'Africans' were not exclusively black. Extremists in the PAC argued that there was no place in Africa for whites or Indians, whereas the ANC embraced all groups who would support their struggle whatever their ethnicity, and also recognized that all the inhabitants of South Africa should have equal rights. The ANC was opposed to the apartheid regime rather than to any specific group of people.

SOURCE C

Excerpt from Walter Sisulu in *Africa South*, volume 3, number 4, 1959, p. 34, quoted in *A History of the ANC* by Francis Meli, published by James Currey, Woodbridge, UK, 1989, p. 139.

… in a country like South Africa, where the whites dominate everything and where ruthless laws are ruthlessly administered and enforced, the natural tendency is one of growing hostility to Europeans. In fact most Africans come into political activity because of their indignation against the Whites, and it is only through their education in Congress and their experience of genuine comradeship in the struggle of such organisations as the [all white] Congress of Democrats that they rise to the broad non-racial humanism of our Congress movement.

What can you infer from Source C about Sisulu's feelings towards white people in 1959?

The PAC and anti-pass law protests

The ANC had called for a series of anti-pass protests for 31 March 1960; the PAC, in the first test of its strength, decided to pre-empt the ANC and announced one for 21 March. The campaign was poorly organized. Sobukwe had said, 'All we are required to do is to show the light and the masses will find the way', but this was never going to be enough to gather enough people to make an impact. On the day, the protests were disappointing.

Sobukwe and his supporters, in Orlando, protested against carrying passes and demanded that the police arrest them; the authorities agreed because there so few of them, so it was manageable. Elsewhere, most Africans went to work as normal with their passes in their pockets or they simply did not want to get involved. The often dire consequences of participating in any protest should not be forgotten. Only in Sharpeville was there a sizeable demonstration.

What triggered the massacre at Sharpeville?

The Sharpeville massacre 1960

Sharpeville was a township in Vereeniging, an industrial centre in the Transvaal, home of 37,000 Africans. Over 40 per cent were under the age of eighteen. It had first been built in 1943 to replace the township of Topville, which suffered great overcrowding, and where diseases such as pneumonia were widespread. Many people were glad to leave Topville to move to better homes, some of which had electricity and running water. The removals were halted when the local authority feared the new township was growing too close to white suburbs, but began again in 1958, when increases in land values meant the remains of Topville could be sold at a huge profit. This meant that 10,000 Africans were forcibly and rapidly moved into unfinished accommodation in the Vuka district of Sharpeville. Officially, Sharpeville was a model township with modern facilities including a library. In reality, life there was difficult.

Life in Sharpeville

Sharpeville suffered the usual problems of high unemployment and crime. Youth problems were particularly great, especially in Vuka. The schools could not cope with the influx of children and teenagers. There was mass youth unemployment, and employment opportunities were limited, with heavy manual work in factories the only real option. Local firms preferred to employ migrant workers from the British colony of Basutoland, who could be kept in hostels and paid less. Consequently, large numbers of rootless young people often drifted into gangs, antisocial behaviour and crime.

In 1959, Sharpeville received a new police station and police were energetic in checking passes, deporting illegal residents and conducting raids against illegal shebeens. It was therefore a place where resentment seethed, and its people were prime for **radicalization**. The local ANC leadership was eminently respectable and moderate in its goals. Many young people found it irrelevant to their concerns. The PAC, however, was active, particularly through the influence of the charismatic Tsolo brothers, Nyakane and Job; the former already had experience of illegal union activities. They worked tirelessly to increase its local membership, often by focusing on issues associated with women. They were also prepared to manipulate youth gangs to add muscle to persuade residents to cooperate in their activities. Although the PAC membership may have been as little as 100 at the time of the pass protest, its leaders felt confident that they could galvanize the local community into participating.

KEY TERM

Radicalization Process by which people come to adopt extreme political or religious ideas, often through undue influence from particular groups, in this case the PAC.

PAC tactics

Many residents spoke of coercion and intimidation in preparation for the anti-pass protests of 21 March. The PAC had set up a 'Task Force' of supporters to ensure maximum compliance. One tactic was to forcibly prevent bus drivers, and therefore commuters, from going to work.

SOURCE D

Excerpt from the testimony to the Wessels Commission of Inquiry of Joseph Motha, a bus driver, approached by men wearing PAC badges on Sunday 20 March 1960, quoted in *Sharpeville: An Apartheid Massacre and its Consequences* by Tom Lodge, published by Oxford University Press, Oxford, UK, 2011, p. 93.

We beg you, our people, tomorrow we must be as one. We are not going to fight the Europeans. We just want them to alter this pass law because it is hard on us. If you run away you might get hurt. We will lay our hands on the one that does not want to join us.

How persuasive might the bus driver have found the argument in Source D?

The events of Sharpeville

On Monday 21 March 1960, a crowd estimated at between 5000 and 20,000 gathered outside the police station at Sharpeville. They were peacefully protesting about having to carry passes, and demanding to be arrested for not carrying them. The police refused to arrest so many because it was impractical to do so – which was, of course, the point the protesters were making. The standoff continued all morning. Senior officers arrived to try to take control of the situation. There were 400 police, 200 white, armed with .303 rifles, and 200 African officers carrying clubs (called knobkerries).

Some accounts suggest that the 'trigger' for the massacre occurred when a drunken demonstrator, Geelbooi Mofokeng, fired his pistol in the air at the same time as one of the senior officers, Colonel 'Att' Spengler, accidentally stumbled, leading his colleagues to think he had been shot. The policemen began to fire into the crowd; they fired two volleys, one directly into the centre, killing the demonstrators at the head of the crowd, including most of the organizers, and a second higher to hit those who were fleeing. As the dust settled, it was found that 69 demonstrators had been killed and almost 200 injured; many of these would later die of their wounds. It was subsequently discovered that 70 per cent of those killed had been shot in the back.

Who was to blame for the Sharpeville massacre?

Many people have argued that the Sharpeville massacre was a premeditated attack on peaceful protesters, while others support the security forces, saying they were only trying to maintain order and protect themselves in the face of excessive provocation. The truth lies somewhere along this continuum of premeditated murder and self-defence.

More than 50 native South Africans lie dead after police opened fire on a demonstration in Sharpeville in 1960. The people were protesting against the rule that forced Africans, Indians and coloured people to carry passes.

How useful is Source E to a historian investigating the Sharpeville massacre?

Several factors contributed to the tragic events on that particular day in Sharpeville:

- The police were on edge. There had been disturbances at Sharpeville over the weekend, and nine of their colleagues had recently been killed in riots in Cato Manor (see page 181).
- The senior police officers appeared indecisive, not giving firm instructions or leadership.
- It was a hot day and the standoff had been taking place for upwards of five hours. People were getting impatient and tense.
- While the police were reluctant to make arrests, they had in fact arrested the PAC leader Nyakane Tsolo just before the shooting began. Tsolo was charismatic and had, it seemed, been able to control the crowd. It was the struggle to arrest other leaders which had prompted Spengler's stumble, which led to the first shots being fired.
- The police had earlier requested the demonstrators to adjourn to the nearby football field. They may have suggested this simply to manage the crowd more efficiently and safely – the press of thousands in a relatively confined space was dangerous in itself, particularly for the children present – but many of the demonstrators feared the police were attempting to marshal them into a killing field.

SOURCE F

Excerpt from the press statement by Dr Albertus Van Thijn, the South African High Commissioner in London, quoted in *Sharpeville: An Apartheid Massacre and its Consequences* by Tom Lodge, published by Oxford University Press, Oxford, UK, 2011, p. 326.

According to factual information now available, the disturbances at Sharpeville on Monday resulted from a planned demonstration by 20000 Natives in which the demonstrators attacked the police with weapons including firearms. The demonstrators shot first and the Police were forced to fire in self-defence and avoid more tragic results.

Compare and contrast what Sources F and G say about the events at Sharpeville.

SOURCE G

Excerpt from evidence given by David Ramohoase, one of the demonstrators, to the Truth and Reconciliation Committee, 5 August 1996, quoted in *Sharpeville: An Apartheid Massacre and its Consequences* by Tom Lodge, published by Oxford University Press, Oxford, UK, 2011, p. 6.

Many young people were gathering holding their umbrellas in their hands, they were singing Nkosi Silileli [God Bless Africa] and the other one that I can't remember … Not even one person was armed. I saw men and women and young men just holding their umbrellas because it was a hot day. Those who had guns might have had them hidden somewhere but I didn't see anyone carrying a weapon, not even a stick or knobkerrie, not even a knobkerrie. I only saw umbrellas … They were not going there to fight. They were peaceful. They didn't have anything in their hands.

The aftermath and responses to Sharpeville

Within South Africa

The lack of trust between the police and the people was exacerbated even further in the aftermath of the shootings. Police rampaged through Sharpeville: seeking out leaders, arresting the wounded in hospital, aggressively policing pass laws and arresting anyone breaking a curfew that was imposed after the massacre. Those leaders arrested were savagely beaten up in detention cells. Police officers were accused of putting rocks and weapons in the hands of the dead. They built two mounds of rocks, stones and weapons for the benefit of press photographers; these, they asserted, were carried by the demonstrators.

In the two-month period following the Sharpeville massacre, a state of emergency was declared on 30 March which saw the arrest of over 10,000 people; 2000 within the first few days. This number included Mandela and others who were still enmeshed in the Treason Trial. On 8 April, the PAC and ANC were declared illegal under the Unlawful Organisations Act. This was undoubtedly a blow for the ANC, which had not been involved in the PAC campaign. In the short term after Sharpeville there were indications of

What happened after Sharpeville?

? How useful is Source H to a historian studying the effects of the pass laws?

SOURCE H

Black South Africans line up at a counter in a government office to get their new passbooks in Johannesburg, South Africa, 7 April 1960. Hundreds of blacks, who had publicly burned their passes during recent campaign of defiance against the apartheid government, picked up new passes required by all black South Africans to return to work.

uncertainty among the white community, which the government needed to address:

- There was an increasing demand for firearms from the white population.
- On 9 April, Verwoerd was subject to an assassination attempt (see below). While he was recuperating, on 21 May the acting prime minister, Paul Sauer, asserted that change was necessary: 'The old book of South African history was closed a month ago and, for the immediate future, South Africa will reconsider in earnest and honesty her whole approach to the native question.' This was not the message most whites wanted to hear. (Sauer was not close to Verwoerd and his inner circle. When Verwoerd returned to duty on 29 May, his words were forgotten.)
- The military wings of the ANC, PAC and the African Resistance Movement comprised mainly radical, young blacks embarking on campaigns of bombing and violence, which clearly worried law-abiding citizens (see pages 225–7).
- In the years between 1960 and 1963 emigration figures exceeded those of immigration. The numbers leaving for Britain, for example, stood at 2000 in 1959 and rose to 5000 by 1962. Emigrants, moreover, tended to be members of the professional classes whose skills would be missed.
- There were economic upsets with falling share prices, and a net outflow of currency: 194 million **rand** in 1960. The amount of foreign reserves fell from R312 million to R153 million between June 1960 and May 1961.

 **KEY TERM**

Rand (currency) In 1960, South Africa decimalized its currency, moving from British sterling (pounds, shillings and pence) to rand (R) and cents.

The attempted assassination of Verwoerd

Prime Minister Verwoerd gave a speech at the Rand Easter Show on 9 April 1960, in which he asserted that the government would hold its line on apartheid. David Platt, a local farmer, fired two bullets at Verwoerd from close range. Amazingly, Verwoerd survived. Platt was subsequently diagnosed as mentally ill, although he seemed quite logical in his opposition to apartheid. He claimed to have been motivated by the sight of police manhandling pass offenders. Verwoerd's supporters meanwhile increasingly saw God's hand in his survival and recovery. It seemed to be a sign that he was chosen for God's work; ironically, Pratt also asserted that God has chosen him to carry out the assassination. Overall, Verwoerd's survival reinforced the government's commitment to apartheid and its belief that it was acting on a divine mission.

As well as this immediate aftermath, Sharpeville provoked a fierce response from the authorities, who passed measures of repression that were far more extensive than any which had gone before.

The Wessels Commission of Inquiry

The government appointed the Wessels Commission of Inquiry to investigate Sharpeville. Inevitably, it was accused of a **whitewash**. It said Africans were either too intimidated to testify, or were told what to say by the PAC. The Commission appeared reluctant to interview Africans and ignored any suggestions that the police had tampered with evidence. The Commission was, to a certain extent, critical of the police leadership (which it thought was indecisive) but did suggest that the police felt intimidated and in danger. In the overall conclusion therefore, the police were exonerated from blame. According to the Commission, they had acted in self-defence against a hostile crowd.

 **KEY TERM**

Whitewash Where a report exonerates someone without having examined all the evidence.

Sobukwe's fate

At his trial, Sobukwe refused to acknowledge the authority of the court, although he did defend himself and the PAC. He was sentenced to three years' imprisonment for inciting Africans to demand the repeal of the pass laws. This seemed extreme; clearly he was being made an example of. Worse, when the time came for his release in 1963, the government had passed the General Laws Amendment Act (see page 218), which allowed imprisonment without trial for a period of up to 90 days; by the so-called Sobukwe Clause (he was the first victim of it), it could be extended indefinitely.

Sobukwe was finally released from prison in May 1969 but sentenced to house arrest in Kimberley. It could be argued that the authorities continued to penalize him unfairly. Although he was offered a position at the University of Wisconsin in 1970 and the US government promised him a visa, he was not allowed to leave. When he developed lung cancer, from which he would die in February 1978, the authorities made continual difficulties over his going to different hospitals for treatment, or allowing him visiting rights.

The international response to Sharpeville

The government had always argued that South Africa was unique: an African country run not by European colonists but by white Africans, and that it was wealthy and efficient *because* it was run by this group. The white government, they asserted, operated for the benefit of all. They gave evidence not only of the numbers of migrant workers from other African countries, but also of the fact that the Africans in South Africa had more access to education and a higher standard of living than elsewhere on the continent. While this may be true, critics replied that it still was not anywhere near high enough, that the wealth should be shared out more fairly, and political and civic rights extended to all.

Macmillan's 'Wind of Change' speech 1960

In February 1960, a month before Sharpeville, British Prime Minister Harold Macmillan was touring southern Africa and had been invited to address the South African parliament in Cape Town. As his audience looked on, stony-faced, Macmillan made his famous 'Wind of Change' speech.

SOURCE I

Excerpt from the 'Wind of Change' speech by British Prime Minister Harold Macmillan to the South African parliament, 3 February 1960.

… the most striking of all the impressions I have formed since I left London a month ago is of the strength of this African national consciousness. In different places it takes different forms, but it is happening everywhere.

The wind of change is blowing through this continent, and whether we like it or not, this growth of national consciousness is a political fact. We must all accept it as a fact, and our national policies must take account of it.

Well you understand this better than anyone, you are sprung from Europe, the home of nationalism, here in Africa you have yourselves created a free nation. A new nation. Indeed in the history of our times yours will be recorded as the first of the African nationalists. This tide of national consciousness which is now rising in Africa, is a fact, for which both you and we, and the other nations of the western world are ultimately responsible.

As I have said, the growth of national consciousness in Africa is a political fact, and we must accept it as such. That means, I would judge, that we've got to come to terms with it. I sincerely believe that if we cannot do so we may imperil the precarious balance between the East and West on which the peace of the world depends … .

As I see it the great issue in this second half of the twentieth century is whether the uncommitted peoples of Asia and Africa will swing to the East or to the West. Will they be drawn into the Communist camp? Or will the great experiments in self-government that are now being made in Asia and Africa, especially within the Commonwealth, prove so successful, and by their example so compelling, that the balance will come down in favour of freedom and order and justice? The struggle is joined, and it is a struggle for the minds of men. What is now on *trial is much more than our military strength or our diplomatic and administrative skill. It is our way of life. The uncommitted nations want to see before they choose.*

Premier Verwoerd responded immediately.

SOURCE J

Premier Verwoerd's response to Macmillan's speech, 3 February 1960, located at: http://africanhistory.about.com/od/eraindependence/p/wind_of_change3.htm

The tendency in Africa for nations to become independent, and at the same time to do justice to all, does not only mean being just to the black man of Africa, but also to be just to the white man of Africa.

We call ourselves European, but actually we represent the white men of Africa. They are the people not only in the Union but through major portions of Africa who brought civilisation here, who made the present developments of black nationalists possible. By bringing them education, by showing them this way of life, by bringing in industrial development, by bringing in the ideals which western civilisation has developed itself.

And the white man came to Africa, perhaps to trade, in some cases, perhaps to bring the gospel; has remained to stay. And particularly we in this southernmost portion of Africa, have such a stake here that this is our only motherland, we have nowhere else to go. We set up a country bare, and the Bantu came in this country and settled certain portions for themselves, and it is in line with the thinking of Africa, to grant those fullest rights which we also with you admit all people should have and believe providing those rights for those people in the fullest degree in that part of southern Africa which their forefathers found for themselves and settled in. But similarly, we believe in balance, we believe in allowing exactly those same full opportunities to remain within the grasp of the white man who has made all this possible.

Compare and contrast the points being made in Sources I and J.

Members of the South African government may have been disturbed by Macmillan's speech and the **decolonization** going on throughout the continent. However, these developments would not deflect them from their purpose, and, indeed, disastrous events – such those taking place in the former Belgian Congo where a bloodbath and civil war were raging – only served to confirm them in their path.

The international repercussions of Sharpeville

After Sharpeville, much of the world was shocked. The United Nations had passed resolutions condemning apartheid every year since 1952, but **Security Council Resolution 134** was particularly damning, blaming the shootings on the system of apartheid and asserting that violence would continue until apartheid was ended. Despite the economic turbulence, countries which did business with South Africa were reluctant to antagonize it. For example, Britain, along with France, abstained from the United Nations Resolution.

 **KEY TERM**

Decolonization Colonies winning their independence.

Security Council Resolution 134 A United Nations resolution condemning the South African government for the Sharpeville massacre.

Commonwealth
Association of members and former members of the British Empire.

Commonwealth Conference An annual meeting of members of the Commonwealth or former British Empire.

Maoris Indigenous peoples of New Zealand.

In October 1960, white South Africans went to the polls to decide whether they wanted to sever political ties with Britain and form a republic. With a 90 per cent turnout, it was a close call, with 52 per cent opting for republic status. It was perhaps inevitable that South Africa would leave the **Commonwealth**. In June 1961, Verwoerd attended his final **Commonwealth Conference**. He withdrew South African membership in the face of criticism over apartheid; one of the main stumbling blocks to continued membership was Verwoerd's refusal to accept diplomats from newly independent African countries; it would, he said, lead to Pretoria being overcrowded with embassies. Privately, he acknowledged that African diplomats in an apartheid state could cause problems.

South Africa's withdrawal from the Commonwealth did nothing to diminish its economic or cultural ties with Britain. Indeed, of the white dominions, it was New Zealand which presented the most diplomatic problems, as South Africa refused to allow **Maoris** to be included in the visiting All Blacks rugby teams. The acquiescence in excluding the Maori players led to the biggest demonstrations in New Zealand's history. South Africa, however, did not care much, particularly if it meant its side had a greater chance of winning.

Nor were they concerned over much when the president of the ANC, Chief Albert Luthuli, won the Nobel Peace Prize in December 1961. The authorities protested that it was a bizarre choice but allowed the veteran anti-apartheid protester to attend the ceremony in Oslo.

Luthuli's Nobel Peace Prize 1961

Luthuli joined colleagues in the dock during the Treason Trial (see page 192). He was given ten days' grace in December 1961 from his banning orders to travel to Oslo to collect his Nobel Peace Prize. As the 1960s progressed, he was increasingly marginalized and ill, meeting his end in July 1967 after being run over by a freight train.

SOURCE K

? Explain the message Chief Luthuli is sending in Source K.

Excerpt from Chief Luthuli's Nobel Peace Prize acceptance speech, 10 December 1961, located at: www.anc.org.za/show.php?id=4732

I recognise, however, that in my country, South Africa, the spirit of peace is subject to some of the severest tensions known to man. For that reason South Africa has been and continues to be in the focus of world attention. I therefore regard this award as a recognition of the sacrifices by my people of all races, particularly the African people, who have endured and suffered so much for so long. It can only be on behalf of the people of South Africa, especially the freedom-loving people, that I accept this award. I accept it also as an honour, not only to South Africa, but to the whole continent of Africa, to all its people, whatever their race, colour or creed. It is an honour to the peace-loving people of the entire world, and an encouragement to us all to redouble our efforts in the struggle for peace and friendship.

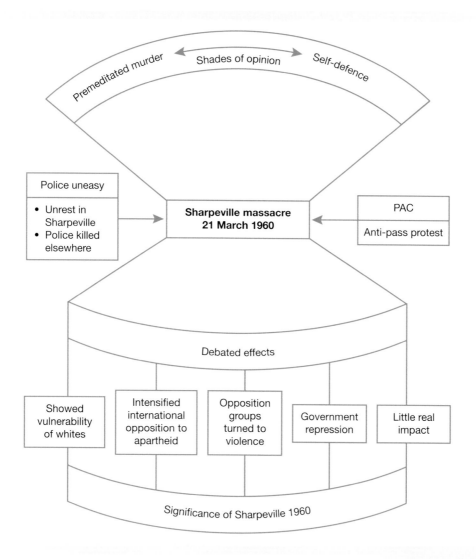

SUMMARY DIAGRAM

The significance of the Sharpeville massacre

② Key debate

▶ *Key question: How has the Sharpeville massacre been interpreted?*

Sharpeville was not the only time white police had fired into an African crowd; this had happened before (see page 145) and since. On the very same day as the events at Sharpeville, as they received news of it, thousands of Africans demonstrated at Langa Flats bus station in Cape Town. The police charged with tear gas, batons and guns; three demonstrators were killed and 27 injured. It was also not the scale of deaths at the hands of armed police;

Enoch Mgijilma In May 1921, 1000 supporters of Mgijilma, a religious prophet, settled in an area of the Eastern Cape. Their aim was to form their own community – unfortunately on land to which they had no claim. Law enforcement officers arrived to evict them. When they refused to leave, the officers opened fire.

Black Consciousness Movement based on Black Power in the USA in which African people increasingly took pride in their culture and identity. This was particularly associated in South Africa with the influence of Steve Biko and the South African Student Association (SASA).

in 1921, five detachments of troops and police had killed 189 supporters of **Enoch Mgijilma**. Regardless, Sharpeville was a hugely significant event in that it showed the world how far removed South Africa was from the rest of the world. Although the Civil Rights Movement in the USA, in particular, had seen, and would see, its own share of violence during the 1960s, at least the US presidents during that period had somewhat listened and legislated in support of the protesters. In South Africa, this was not an option. The government saw decolonization elsewhere but would not be moved from its position of apartheid, which would not end until 1994.

There is little doubt that Sharpeville was significant, but some doubt as to in what way. Veteran South African Communist Joe Slovo asserted in 1975 that it was a turning point. PAC activist David Sibeko felt it showed the vulnerability of whites, and fellow activist Nyakane Tsolo argued that Sharpeville led Africans to lose their fear of the whites. Others are more dubious; the historian Tom Lodge acknowledges that the massacres shocked the world but reminds us that accelerated action against the regime did not begin until ten years later with the **Black Consciousness** protests and extensive labour unrest in 1973. However much Sharpeville alerted the world to the evils of apartheid, there was no real change. Writing in 1969, historian G.H.L. Lemay said, 'In the event Sharpeville was merely an incident, a turning point at which no-one turned.'

Sharpeville after the massacre

In 1998, Joyce Mokhesi wrote movingly about the impact of growing up there after the 1960 massacre. Two hundred and sixteen families and 500 children were directly affected by the events of 21 March. Parents, however, did not discuss it with their children, in part to protect them from politicization and militancy. As late as 1976, some children did not know how or when their parents had died. The residents sought to forget. One priest, Father Rudolph O'Flynn, did hold memorial services until he was deported in 1963 but his successors discontinued the practice. Not until the growth of the Black Consciousness movement in the 1970s was the massacre formally remembered.

SOURCE L

Excerpt from *In the Shadow of Sharpeville: Apartheid and Criminal Justice* by Peter Parker and Joyce Mokhesi Parker, published by New York University Press, New York, USA, 1998, p. 24. Mokhesi grew up in Sharpeville and is writing of her parents' generation in the 1960s.

Their silent grief smothered our knowledge. They tried to protect us from our heritage. They wished to free us of the anger they would not feel. They were the last generation of Azania [African name for South Africa] to live expecting peace. They hoped the path of forgetting would give us, their children, a peace they could not feel.

? Explain the point Mokhesi is making in Source L.

Lodge has also written of the legacy within Sharpeville to argue that the silence and lack of political guidance of the parents in the 1960s helped to frame the militancy of the youth of the ensuing decades.

The culpability of the police

For the authorities, Sharpeville was an example of the propensity of Africans for violence and the need to keep them in check. This view was reflected in the Wessels Commission report (see page 211) and was perpetuated by right-wing groups thereafter. A 1988 *A History of Communism in South Africa*, for example, has large mobs of armed blacks panicking the handful of officers into opening fire. This view was largely discredited by the first account of the Sharpeville massacre written by Bishop Ambrose Reeves and featuring photographs by Ian Reed. The latter appear to show a largely good-humoured crowd and later a mass of bodies shot in the back; the former refutes allegations about the hostility of the crowd and argues that the racist reflexes of the white police were responsible for their opening fire. Writing in 2001, Philip Frankel interviewed many surviving perpetrators and demonstrators to arrive at a slightly different conclusion: the massacre was not premeditated but was a consequence of 'terror and error' – poor leadership from both sides but with a well-armed security force prepared to use their weapons.

Government responses

Frankel goes on to examine the government responses and argues that after Sharpeville the state could neither any longer justify apartheid as any kind of benign system, nor tolerate anything but the most timid resistance – hence the future oppressive measures. In 2007, historian Brian Martin considered Sharpeville in the context in which governments try to cover up mistakes and how, when they fail, they come back to haunt them. He argues that while most Africans saw the authorities simply acting in the brutal way they had come to expect, the international community was shocked, particularly by Reed's images. Because many whites were so racist and denigrated the lives of Africans, they were shocked in turn by the world's response. While the robust response of the authorities discouraged African resistance, it galvanized criticism elsewhere – particularly when overt racism was diminishing in other countries and former colonies were gaining their independence.

The wider picture

In 2011, writing over space and time, Lodge attempted to place Sharpeville in a wider context, examining its place in the lexicon of apartheid. In this context, Lodge discusses the position of Africanism in the African resistance movement, showing that the PAC, newly formed, needed to assert itself, as exemplified by the arm twisting to make people comply on 21 March 1960. He showed Sharpeville within its historical context to examine its impact on future developments, notably the anti-apartheid movement abroad. There is little debate that Sharpeville did shock international opinion, although how

Given the language used by white South Africans to defend apartheid, how do you imagine they might have justified the actions of the police at Sharpeville? (Language, Emotion, Perception, Logic, Ethics)

far this translated into action is open to question. Historian Christopher Saunders has an interesting take on its impact on a generation of South African historians who moved to university positions abroad and collectively wrote more critical versions of South African history.

Government policies 1958–64

> ▶ **Key question:** *What was the impact of the main government policies against opposition groups?*

As apartheid continued to be implemented, protest groups felt the injustice more keenly.

How did the government continue apartheid?

The main government policies

Government policy towards the continuation and development of apartheid took two forms:

- repression
- the development of separate territories through the creation of Bantustans.

Repression

The new minister of justice, John Vorster, appointed in July 1961, instituted a new part-time Police Reserve Unit. This was to morph into the feared Security Police. He also set up secret, quasi-legal bodies to co-ordinate security matters and undertake 'dirty tricks' such as assassinations of opposition figures. These were to formally integrate in 1969 into the Bureau for State Security (BOSS), although their activities remained state secrets.

Other measures followed:

- The Sabotage Act 1962 not only carried the death penalty for acts of sabotage but also placed the onus on the accused to prove themselves innocent; guilt was implied.
- In 1963, the government passed the General Laws Amendment Act. This allowed the authorities to arrest anyone for 90 days without having to bring charges against them or even giving them access to a lawyer. Once the initial 90-day period was up it could be extended for a further 90 days *ad infinitum*.
- The so-called Sobukwe clause (see page 211) allowed the security forces to keep people in prison beyond the end of their sentence.
- Now that there was no effective check on their activities, the security forces increasingly resorted to torture to extract confessions, particularly through the use of electric shocks. This was allowed under the 1962 Sabotage Act.

- The authorities set up a network of spies and informers to infiltrate opposition groups and if necessary to act as *agents provocateurs*. These people were sometimes motivated by money, but also because they feared that resistance to apartheid was useless and all Africans suffered for the actions of a few.
- In 1963, a new radio network was set up offering direct communication between more than 1000 police stations and police headquarters in Pretoria to facilitate rapid response to incidents.
- Finally, the Bantu Laws Amendment Act 1964 empowered the authorities to deport any African from any urban area or white farming area for any reason whatsoever. It also allowed the minister for Bantu affairs to establish quotas in particular areas or industries, and deport unemployed Africans back to their homelands. This was a draconian measure which gave the authorities complete power over Africans in 'white' South Africa. Anyone who caused problems or it was felt had the potential to do so could be removed.

SOURCE M

Excerpt from *117 Days* by Ruth First, published by Penguin Classics, London, UK, 2009. First was an anti-apartheid activist married to Communist leader Joe Slovo. She was arrested and rearrested under the 90-day law before escaping to Britain. She was assassinated, probably by the South African security forces, in 1982. Here First discusses her interrogators.

Swanepoel was squat, bullfrog like. His face glowed a fiery red that seems to point to the bottle, but he swore he has never drunk so it must be his temper burning through for Swanepoel's stock in trade was bullying. Higher in rank yet deferring to Swanepoel's belligerence was Van Zyl, a lumbering large man who tried persuasion in a sing song voice … On Sundays he was lay preacher, on weekdays he was Swanepoel's interrogation partner. The two of them peddled a mixture of noisy vulgar abuse and suspect avuncular wheedling …

Swanepoel's stock in trade was to bully and taunt …

'You're an obstinate women Mrs Slovo. But remember this. Everyone cracks sooner or later. It's our job to find the cracking point. We'll find yours too.'

Is Source M useful to a historian investigating interrogations against anti-apartheid activists? **?**

The impact of government repression

These powers together effectively allowed the security forces to do whatever they wanted, to whomever they wanted to do it, for as long as they wanted to do it, with no fear of redress. They could also ban people from public meetings, or from publishing anything they deemed inflammatory. The South African government essentially placed itself on a war footing. The Defence Budget rose from R44 million to R255 million between 1961 and 1966. An Armaments Production Board was set up in 1964 to co-ordinate arms production; R33 million was invested in domestic arms manufacture and firms began to produce foreign-designed weapons, and later on to develop their own. In 1960, **conscription** was introduced for whites.

 **KEY TERM**

Conscription Compulsory membership of the armed forces for certain periods of time.

In theory, all the white population would know how to defend themselves in the event of insurgency. South Africa became something of an armed camp.

Bantustans

Verwoerd's government had plans to solve the racial problems beyond mere repression. The idea was to develop the policy that Africans should live on tribal reserves and only enter 'white South Africa' as migrant workers, so that the Africans' tribal homelands became Bantustans (see below).

The National Government under Verwoerd had three fundamental beliefs:

● That it was fulfilling God's divine purpose – confirmed, of course, by the prime minister's recovery after the abortive assassination attempt (see page 210).
● That every people had a right to existence.
● That national aspirations should be fulfilled within one's own country.

The last belief meant that people could not aspire to belong to a country of which they were not citizens, and whose values and customs were alien to them. The idea was based on the notion not only that whites and Africans were different, but also that people of different ethnic origins were different, as indeed were Africans of different tribal origins. All then should have their own Bantustans in which they could achieve their own national identities, by adopting a society and culture which suited their own traditions.

What can you infer from Source N about the creation of Bantustans?

SOURCE N

Excerpt from 'Speeding Bantustan Development – From Our Own Correspondent', *The Times*, 15 April 1961. *The Times* is a British newspaper.

Die Landstem, *the independent newspaper, said that it had information that Dr Verwoerd planned to divide South Africa into separate states and give seven Bantu states political freedom within their own parliaments and constitutions. The South African republic would then propose a 25 year treaty of friendship and cooperation in external relations.* Die Landstem *said that Dr Verwoerd had told the newspapers he controlled* Die Transvaler *and* Dagbreek *to prepare nationalists [supporters of the national party] for this.*

The creation of Bantustans

The 1958 Bantu Self-Government Act laid the basis for the creation of eight Bantustans. This was not a new idea (see page 125). Afrikaners of extremist views had long suggested total separation of the different races, with Afrikaners themselves doing the unskilled work previously reserved for Africans. Malan had argued this was impractical; Verwoerd had been one of its proponents and indeed had once said South Africa should choose 'to be poor and white rather than rich and multi-racial'. He may have tempered his views, as South Africa did eventually become wealthy for its white inhabitants (see page 235). He accepted the continuing need for cheap African labour, but he was adamant there was no place for Africans in white society.

Verwoerd may also have been influenced by the decolonization which was happening in Africa; Ghana had become independent from Britain in March 1957, Guinea from France in October 1958, and it was clear that other countries would shortly follow. The idea of Bantustans was a South African take on decolonization. The African homelands, currently governed as types of colonies with tribal chieftains assisted by white officials, would henceforth through the Promotion of the Self-Government Act 1958 be prepared for full independence, to become fully self-governing and self-financing. Apartheid supporters could not understand how South Africa could possibly be accused of racism under this policy.

Transkei: an independent Bantustan?

The creation of Bantustans and how they fared lie mainly outside the timespan of this book. However, Transkei, the first Bantustan to be created in May 1963 as a self-governing state (it received full 'independence' in 1976), is a suitable case to investigate how effectively this policy worked.

Transkei already had a quasi-parliament, the Territorial Assembly, which was a legislature of 110 members, 65 of whom were appointed chieftains and 45 elected through a democratic franchise. The chiefs were already in the majority but they also controlled the management of elections to ensure, in theory, that compliant delegates were returned to parliament. However, in 1963, the three main chieftains were in disagreement. The Democratic Party, which demanded South African citizenship and an end to apartheid, won 38 out of the 45 elected seats in Transkei. Nevertheless, the powerful Kaiser Matanzima could still control parliament through his control of sufficient numbers of chieftains. He relied on coercion and declared a state of emergency which continued for much of the lifespan of Transkei. He attempted to prevent unrest and banned opposition groups through Proclamation R400, which allowed unlimited detention.

No other government recognized Transkei: it was condemned by the United Nations and faced considerable unrest from the activities of Poqo, the military wing of the PAC (see page 227), for example the assassination of Matanzima's supporters. Matanzima himself survived multiple assassination attempts. Transkei never achieved anything like economic independence from South Africa and it continued much as before, as a reservoir for cheap labour. As an independent state, Transkei remained a sham.

However well-intentioned Verwoerd was with the Bantustans policy, it clearly did not achieve its objectives and never won acceptance either outside South Africa or from opponents of apartheid within. With the rise in the government's determination to separate black Africans from white, opposition groups became more militant, with the beginnings of violent protest and armed struggle.

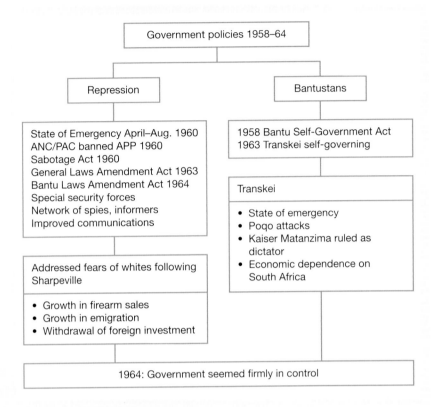

```
                    ┌─────────────────────────────────┐
                    │  Government policies 1958–64     │
                    └─────────────────────────────────┘
           ┌──────────────────┴──────────────────────┐
  ┌─────────────────┐                      ┌─────────────────┐
  │   Repression    │                      │   Bantustans    │
  └─────────────────┘                      └─────────────────┘
```

State of Emergency April–Aug. 1960
ANC/PAC banned APP 1960
Sabotage Act 1960
General Laws Amendment Act 1963
Bantu Laws Amendment Act 1964
Special security forces
Network of spies, informers
Improved communications

1958 Bantu Self-Government Act
1963 Transkei self-governing

Transkei

• State of emergency
• Poqo attacks
• Kaiser Matanzima ruled as dictator
• Economic dependence on South Africa

Addressed fears of whites following Sharpeville

• Growth in firearm sales
• Growth in emigration
• Withdrawal of foreign investment

1964: Government seemed firmly in control

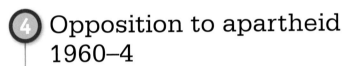

④ Opposition to apartheid 1960–4

▶ *Key question: Why did opposition groups engage in an armed struggle?*

Umkhonto we Sizwe or Spear of the Nation (MK) The armed wing of the ANC.

> **What factors were behind the decision to begin the armed struggle?**

The two biggest developments among opposition groups during the period 1960–4 were the decision to adopt an armed struggle against apartheid and the Rivonia Trial. Although Mandela had been contemplating a militant strategy since the early 1950s, as late as 3 August 1960, in his testimony at the Treason Trial, he reaffirmed the ANC commitment to non-violence. The movement's decision to use violence was not taken lightly.

The move from non-violent protest to violent protest

While the Sharpeville massacre undoubtedly had some influence on the ultimate decision, it was simply one of a number of fast-moving factors and final realizations that led to the creation of **Umkhonto we Sizwe or Spear of the Nation (MK)** in June 1961. The PAC had already created Poqo, whose activities were more militant still.

Government deceit

The government was increasingly devious. One such example is the events on 30 March 1960, when PAC activist Philip Kgosona organized a peaceful protest of 30,000 marching on the parliament building at Cape Town. The legislature was in session, ironically debating the state of emergency (see page 209). Police persuaded Kgosona to ask the demonstrators to disperse. They promised to organize a meeting between him and the minister of justice that evening. Kgosona complied, but when he turned up for the meeting he was arrested.

Ineffectiveness of non-violent mass demonstrations

Opposition leaders finally realized that peaceful protest had never worked and was never going to work. The ANC, in response to the Sharpeville massacre, decided that its leaders should publicly burn their pass books and invite arrest. The president, Chief Luthuli (see page 187), did so, as did Mandela and others. When pass burning became more widespread, the police commissioner ordered the suspension of arrests for not carrying passes. Some felt that the government was on the defensive and that the apartheid system was faltering. It was, however, no victory. Soon the system was even more vigorously enforced, with Africans being told they could no longer draw pensions without their pass. Many were forced to queue to reapply for passes while their benefits were suspended.

What is the message of Source O?

SOURCE O

A cartoon by Pat Oliphant commenting on arrests for breaching the pass laws, 1962. Oliphant is a celebrated Australian cartoonist.

The final peaceful protest

There had been an All-in-Africa conference held at Pietermaritzburg on 25–26 March 1961, attended by 1400 delegates representing 145 religious, cultural and political groups. They called for a convention to discuss an end to apartheid, and threatened the government with mass action in the form of 'stayaways' and demonstrations at the end of May 1961 if this was not granted. The government ignored the demand.

The ANC's direct action planned for 29–31 May failed. The timing was chosen to coincide with the celebrations to commemorate South Africa finally becoming a republic (see page 214). Although the government had banned meetings and harassed those suspected of organizing the action, and the ANC had been illegal since 8 April 1960 (see page 209), it mobilized the army and police, ready for insurrection. The PAC meanwhile refused to participate because it was a multiracial activity; it told its supporters to go to work as normal.

There was a poor response to the demonstration. This failure helped to convince leaders that peaceful demonstration had finally had its day.

Increasing government violence

The security forces had always been prepared to use violence. Indeed, violence was widespread in many rural areas, for example, in East Pondoland, where the rebellion led by the **Intaba** movement had been defeated by superior government forces and military hardware. The decision to begin an armed struggle was to some degree a case of leaders catching up with the demands of their supporters. The ANC remained conscious that it had not been effective in rural areas and had not given any military support to Intaba; the formation of an armed wing could eventually provide this sort of assistance in future conflicts.

Mandela and Communism

During the 1960 state of emergency, defendants in the Treason Trial were incarcerated when not in court and found it difficult to access their lawyers, particularly if they were of a different racial group. For this reason, until the state of emergency was lifted in August 1960, they conducted their own defence. Mandela used the opportunity to expound ANC policy and spoke of its relationship with Communism:

SOURCE P

Excerpt from *Long Walk to Freedom* by Nelson Mandela, published by Abacus, London, UK, 2013, p. 297.

The state was determined to prove that I was a dangerous violence-spouting Communist. While I was not a communist or a member of the party I did not want to be seen as distancing myself from my communist allies. Although I could have been sent to jail for voicing such views, I did not hesitate to reaffirm the tremendous support the communists have given us.

KEY TERM

Intaba Resistance movement in East Pondoland; Intaba is an African word for 'mountain'.

?
Compare Source P to Source P in Chapter 4, page 146. How similar is the message offered?

Comrade Mandela?

Since his death in December 2013, Communist groups in South Africa have claimed that despite what he said to the contrary, Nelson Mandela, and indeed most of the ANC leadership, were in fact secret members of the Communist Party, but this has not so far been verified.

Violent protest 1961–4

Mandela co-founded the military branch of the ANC, Umkhonto we Sizwe (Spear of the Nation), in June 1961. Clearly, it could not wage all-out war. It was decided that initially it would commit acts of sabotage on property such as government installations; the intention was to avoid loss of life. The emphasis was war on a system, not people. However, a second phase would involve volunteers training for **guerrilla warfare**. The overall aim, according to Mandela, was to make an apartheid government impossible.

The beginning of Umkhonto we Sizwe

Much stress was laid on seeing the Spear of the Nation as independent from the ANC. The word 'independent' was emphasized throughout its manifesto. Members from the outlawed CPSA/SACP, and members of SAIC, reluctantly forgoing their commitment to non-violence, also joined. It was organized through a national high command which had overall control over strategy, training and finance, and regional commands which were to commit acts of sabotage in their local areas. Others, meanwhile, trained in guerrilla warfare.

The decision to adopt the armed struggle was ultimately taken because the leaders saw no alternative; it was seen as a response to government violence and brutality as much as the fact that the government refused to listen to peaceful demands. Mandela had written that ultimately the government set the agenda for the type of protest: if the government responds to peaceful protest with violence, passive resistance has failed.

← **How did the opposition groups use violence as protest?**

 **KEY TERM**

Guerrilla warfare Fighting using techniques such as ambush and bombings, avoiding direct large-scale conflict.

SOURCE Q

Excerpt from an interview in *The Guardian*, June 1983, where Oliver Tambo explained the decision to use violence. Tambo was an ANC leader who left South Africa in 1960 to lead its campaign from abroad. *The Guardian* is a British newspaper.

For decades we did not think violence had a role to play in the ANC struggle; not until the national party came to power in 1948 and was physically violent. The obvious thing was to respond with violence, but then we thought that perhaps that was what they wanted – that they would use our violence to rally whites around them. …

But as the years went by, violence increased. We saw more armed police – with pistols at first then Sten guns [a type of machine gun]. Then tanks came. Women's demonstrations were put down with tanks. As we approached the 1960s our people asked – where do we go from here? In 1960, when the ANC leadership were still insisting on non-violence, on discipline, that we must get the support of the white electorate – the white electorate continued to support the regime. Then we had the Sharpeville shootings (67 Blacks killed, 187 wounded). Even after that we decided to continue with non-violence.

In 1961 we called a strike to protest against the formation of a Republic in South Africa because the government had failed to respond to our call for a national convention. But the army was mobilised on a scale not seen since the Second World War – against a peaceful strike …

We decided then to embrace violence as a method of struggle.

SOURCE R

Extract from the manifesto of Umkhonto we Sizwe, published 16 December 1961, located at: www.anc.org.za/show.php?id=77.

The time comes in the life of any nation when there remain only two choices: submit or fight. That time has now come to South Africa. We shall not submit and we have no choice but to hit back by all means within our power in defence of our people, our future and our freedom. The government has interpreted the peacefulness of the movement as weakness; the people's non-violent policies have been taken as a green light for government violence. Refusal to resort to force has been interpreted by the government as an invitation to use armed force against the people without any fear of reprisals. The methods of Umkhonto we Sizwe mark a break with that past.

We are striking out along a new road for the liberation of the people of this country. The government policy of force, repression and violence will no longer be met with non-violent resistance only! The choice is not ours; it has been made by the Nationalist government which has rejected every peaceable demand by the people for rights and freedom and answered every such demand with force and yet more force! Twice in the past 18 months, virtual martial law has been imposed in order to beat down peaceful, non-violent strike action of the people in support of their rights. It is now preparing its forces – enlarging and rearming its armed forces and drawing the white civilian population into commandos and pistol clubs – for full-scale military actions against the people. The Nationalist government has chosen the course of force and massacre, now, deliberately, as it did at Sharpeville.

Umkhonto we Sizwe will be at the front line of the people's defence. It will be the fighting arm of the people against the government and its policies of race oppression. It will be the striking force of the people for liberty, for rights and for their final liberation! Let the government, its supporters who put it into power, and those whose passive toleration of reaction keeps it in power, take note of where the Nationalist government is leading the country!

How far does Source Q support the arguments in Source R over the movement to armed opposition?

Umkhonto we Sizwe began its campaign on 16 December 1961, to coincide with Covenant Day. Africans called this Digane Day, after a famous Zulu king (see page 125). Bombings took place in government buildings in Durban and Port Elizabeth, including an electricity substation. In the next eighteen months, 200 attacks took place.

Which opposition groups participated in the armed struggle?

Alongside Umkhonto we Sizwe, other opposition groups fought in the armed struggle against apartheid.

African Resistance Movement

The African Resistance Movement, a group comprised mainly of radical whites, meanwhile committed similar bombing attacks which saw most of their members arrested for sabotage in July 1964. Possibly because they were white or coloured, their sentences ranged from just seven to fifteen years, apart from John Harris, who had bombed Johannesburg railway station, causing loss of life. He was executed in April 1965.

Poqo

Poqo, the military wing of the PAC, was the most violent of the armed movements and perhaps the nearest to a terror organization. Particularly strong in the townships of Mbekweni near Paarl, and Langa by Cape Town, it was organized into secret cells, with members unaware of others outside their own groups. It was far more prepared to operate using methods of terror and intimidation than the other groups (see page 224), and also targeted whites whom it saw as an enemy. This, of course, made it particularly dangerous and worrying for the security forces who, because of its secrecy, found it difficult to penetrate.

In keeping with PAC philosophy, membership of Poqo, an African word meaning 'pure', was limited to Africans. They targeted African policemen, local chiefs whom they saw as collaborators, and any suspected of being informers. They were also happy to kill any whites who came their way, for example, a family with two teenage daughters who were camping in the Transkei in February 1963. The Transkei indeed was a particular centre for their activities; they were responsible for most of the assassinations referred to on page 221. Their most ambitious venture perhaps was the concerted assault on the town of Paarl on 22 November 1962, when a mob of 250 supporters, armed with axes and homemade weapons, attacked the police station and brutally hacked two young white people to death.

By 1964, Poqo members were arguing among themselves, and effective police work and harsh penalties including executions for any captured ended their prominence. It remained dormant and re-emerged as the Azanian People's Liberation Army (APLA) in 1968.

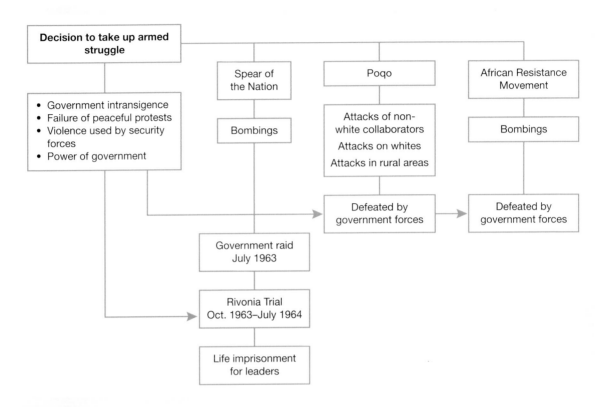

Opposition to apartheid
1960–4

Black Pimpernel Referring
to the Scarlet Pimpernel, the
elusive hero of Baroness
Orczy's novels set in the
French Revolution.

How significant was
the Rivonia Trial?

⑤ Official responses to violent protest

▶ *Key question: How effectively did the authorities react to violent protest?*

The authorities reacted resolutely to violent protest by the expansion of the security forces (see page 218) and the Rivonia Trial, at which most ANC leaders were accused of treason and threatened with capital punishment.

The Rivonia Trial

After Nelson Mandela was acquitted after the Treason Trial, he went underground, working secretly, popping up at meetings and being known as the '**Black Pimpernel**' because the authorities could not trace him. Often he was disguised as a chauffeur because this allowed him to drive unchallenged and on accasion he was accompanied by white sympathizers, usually members of the outlawed Communist Party, who could act as his employers.

He spent a great deal of time hiding at a farm called Liliesleaf in the Johannesburg district of Rivonia, where he acted as a handyman; the farm was secretly owned by the Communist Party. It was here, for example, that he helped to plan the formation and activities of Spear of the Nation.

Mandela's capture

Early in 1962, Mandela set out for Africa and London seeking support and funds. It was the first time he had been abroad, and he mentioned how surprised he was to see white and black people mixing together in apparent harmony in Tanzania. Mandela was lionized on his journey; he met political leaders in London, spoke at international conferences. In Addis Ababa, Ethiopia, he explained why the armed struggle was necessary and how he feared South Africa was on the brink of civil war. It was here that he received military training himself. On his return to South Africa, while travelling around to post-tour briefing meetings, he was finally arrested in August 1962.

Mandela was accused of incitement to strike and travelling abroad without a passport. Grateful that he was not yet associated with the Spear of the Nation, he realized defence was fruitless as the prosecution brought witnesses who could verify all the accusations. Therefore, he turned his defence instead into a further justification of the struggle. He was sentenced to five years in prison without parole.

The Rivonia Trial

While Mandela was in prison at Robben Island, the security forces on 11 July 1963 raided Liliesleaf Farm. Here they found not only Spear of the Nation operatives and caches of weapons but over 250 incriminating documents. Some of these appertained to Mandela's role; he had asked for them to be destroyed but they had been kept as valuable historical documents. Mandela therefore became the prime defendant in the Rivonia Trial which began in October 1963. The trial attracted great publicity, was reported in many countries, and attracted large crowds each day, mainly in support of the defendants.

At first it seemed the elements of farce from the Treason Trial might reappear. The prosecutor, Percy Yutar, alleged Mandela had committed acts of sabotage while he was in fact locked away on Robben Island. However, dangerous state witnesses appeared, including Bruno Mtolo, a former Spear of the Nation activist. He recorded with credibility how he had conducted acts of sabotage, although he did go on to make accusations he could not substantiate, such as the ANC and Spear of the Nation both being fronts for the Communist Party. However, the state had enough evidence to be sure of its case, for example papers relating to Operation Mayibuye, a plan for the commencement of guerrilla warfare. It did no good to suggest that the plan had not yet been adopted; the fact that it existed was enough. Denis Goldberg, a white member of the Spear of the Nation, moreover, was shown

A crowd outside the Palace of Justice in Pretoria gives the thumbs up to a prison van carrying defendants as the Rivonia Trial opens in 1963.

What impression does Source S give of the significance of the Rivonia Trial?

to have been negotiating for enough high explosives and parts to manufacture 20,000 hand grenades. While the defendants and their lawyers may have been able to outwit the prosecution in wordplay in the witness box, the evidence was overwhelming. It was inevitable that Mandela would be found guilty and the penalty for sabotage could be death.

The highlight of the trial was undoubtedly the four-hour speech by Mandela in which he admitted the charges that he belonged to the ANC and Spear of the Nation, and again justified the ANC struggle against apartheid.

SOURCE T

Excerpt from Nelson Mandela's opening speech at the Rivonia Trial, located at: www.anc.org.za/show.php?id=3430.

How useful is Source T to a historian studying the reasons for the struggle against apartheid?

The lack of human dignity experienced by Africans is the direct result of the policy of white supremacy. White supremacy implies black inferiority. Legislation designed to preserve white supremacy entrenches this notion. Menial tasks in South Africa are invariably performed by Africans. When anything has to be carried or cleaned the white man will look around for an African to do it for him, whether the African is employed by him or not. Because of this sort of attitude, whites tend to regard Africans as a separate breed. They do not look upon them as people with families of their own; they do not realize that they have emotions – that they fall in love like white people do; that they want to be with their wives and children like white people want to be with theirs; that they want to earn enough money to support their families properly, to feed and clothe them and send them to school. And what 'house-boy' or 'garden-boy' or labourer can ever hope to do this? …

Above all, we want equal political rights, because without them our disabilities will be permanent. I know this sounds revolutionary to the whites in this country, because the majority of voters will be Africans. This makes the white man fear democracy.

But this fear cannot be allowed to stand in the way of the only solution which will guarantee racial harmony and freedom for all. It is not true that the enfranchisement of all will result in racial domination. Political division, based on colour, is entirely artificial and, when it disappears, so will the domination of one colour group by another. The ANC has spent half a century fighting against racialism. When it triumphs it will not change that policy.

This then is what the ANC is fighting. Their struggle is a truly national one. It is a struggle of the African people, inspired by their own suffering and their own experience. It is a struggle for the right to live.

All the defendants conducted themselves effectively during the trial, and the judge took three weeks to reach a verdict, that of life imprisonment. Most of the leadership of the ANC and Spear of the Nation had been caught up in the Rivonia Trial. As the defendants departed for prison on Robben Island, the government may have been convinced that it had defeated the most significant challenge to its regime. The judge, however, may have been influenced in part by the international response, which was overwhelmingly for the release of the defendants and the end to apartheid.

International response to the Rivonia Trial

The Rivonia Trial attracted worldwide attention. The United Nations called for the defendants to be released, while dockworkers in several countries threatened to refuse to handle South African goods in the ports. The leader of the Soviet Union, Leonid Brezhnev, joined US Congressmen and British

MPs in calling for clemency while 50 of the latter led a protest march in London. Verwoerd claimed to have been unmoved by international protest and even said he had thrown appeals from foreign leaders into the bin. However, as anti-apartheid activist Peter Hain has argued, this formed the context in which Judge Quartus de Wet had to deliver his verdict – and indeed the international concerns about the Rivonia Trial led to widespread protests against apartheid, and sanctions against South Africa, in the years to come.

? Explain the meaning of Source U.

SOURCE U

A cartoon from *Nelson Mandela: A Life in Cartoons* edited by **Harry Dugmore, Stephen Francis** and **Rico Schacherl**, published by **David Philip Publishers, Claremont, South Africa, 1999. Francis and Schacherl produce the daily South African comic strip 'Madam & Eve', which Dugmore founded. The artist, J.H. Jackson, was a well-known South African cartoonist. This cartoon dates from 1959.**

South Africa in 1964

▶ *Key question: How effectively was apartheid entrenched by 1964?*

By 1964, leaders of the opposition groups were either exiled or in prison. The government remained firmly in control via a raft of repressive legislation, as summarized in Table 6.1.

Table 6.1 Summary of apartheid legislation 1948–64

Legislation	Summary
Prohibition of Mixed Marriages 1949 and Immorality Act 1950	• Mixed marriages and sexual relations between members of different racial groups were made illegal. • Whites could be imprisoned for disobeying the latter, although their punishment was not usually as severe as for members of other groups, including their sexual partners.
Group Areas Act 1950	• Required registration of all land ownership, and gave the government the authority to designate particular areas for racial groups, and to remove other groups by force. • Responsible for the forced removal of as many as 3.5 million Africans between 1960 and 1983, with over 1 million of these being moved from urban areas back to the homelands.
Suppression of Communism Act 1950	• Defined Communism as any scheme aimed 'at bringing about any political and social and economic change within the Union by the promotion of disturbance and disorder'. • This Act could be used for imprison anyone for more or less anything the authorities deemed subversive. • It could also ban organizations and indeed individuals from contacting others for periods of up to five years, by the use of banning orders. For many, this meant house arrest. • The CPSA dissolved itself (see page 184) and became an illegal organization, the South African Communist Party (SACP). Some white members also formed the Congress of Democrats (see page 185).
Natives Resettlement Act 1951	• Enabled the government to specifically move Africans from anywhere in and next to Johannesburg to any other area.
1951 Bantu Authorities Act	• Reinforced that home areas for Africans and the only places they were entitled to live were their 'tribal reserves' set out in the 1911 and 1936 legislation (see page 165). • Led to the abolition of the Native Representative Council (see page 126). • The tribal reserves were to be governed by tribal leaders designated by the government.
Separate Representation of Voters Act 1951	• Malan's government decided to remove the vote from coloured people because it believed only whites should be allowed to participate in elections. The problem was that their right to vote was protected by the 1910 Constitution. This led to a constitutional crisis.
Native Laws Amendment Act 1952, also known as the Abolition of Passes and Co-ordination of Documents Act	• Regulated the use of passes by Africans throughout South Africa, by officially abolishing existing passes and replacing them with standardized reference books. • All Africans had to carry reference books at all times. • Neither African men nor women could remain in urban areas for 70 hours after their permits had expired. • No African could live permanently in an urban area unless he had been born there, or lived there for over fifteen years or been with the same employer for over ten years. • National reference books were issued, replacing the regional ones. It was a criminal offence not to carry them.

Legislation	Summary
Bantu Education Act 1953	• Moved control of African education from the Ministry of Education to the Ministry for Native Affairs. • Removed state subsidies from mission schools, so most were forced to close. • Expanded the government-run system and set a limited vocational-based curriculum.
Public Safety Act 1953	• Allowed the government to call a state of emergency for up to twelve months in the first instance, with the power to renew it indefinitely.
Criminal Law Amendment Act 1953	• Anyone accompanying a person found guilty of a crime would automatically be presumed guilty also and have to prove their innocence.
Native Labour Act 1953	• Africans were not allowed to join trade unions or take part in strikes. This Act led to 'stayaway' protests to circumvent the ban on strikes (see page 184).
Riotous Assemblies Act 1956	• Passed as a response to the mass meeting at Kliptown (see page 190). Any open-air meetings could be banned if the minister of justice felt they endangered peace or fomented hostility between white and other groups.
Bantu Self-Government Act 1958	• Laid the basis for the creation of eight Bantustans.
Extension of Universities Act 1959	• Banned the English-language universities from accepting African students. By way of recompense, three new strictly segregated colleges were opened for coloured, Indian and Zulu students, and another for Africans in the Transvaal. Fort Hare remained under a new and more conciliatory principal for Xhosa-speaking students only.
Promotion of Self-Government Act 1959	• Turned local chieftains into government agents rather than representatives of the people. Government officials gained the right to attend all meetings and, if necessary, to dismiss the African officials. • The policy was developing into the idea of grand apartheid in which these tribal areas would become Bantustans, ostensibly independent but under close supervision from Pretoria.
State of Emergency 1960	• Over 10,000 people were arrested, 2000 within the first few days, in the aftermath of Sharpeville.
Unlawful Organisations Act 1960	• PAC and ANC were declared illegal.
Sabotage Act 1962	• Carried the death penalty for acts of sabotage; offenders presumed guilty until found innocent. • Now that there was no effective check on their activities, the security forces increasingly resorted to torture to extract confessions, particularly through the use of electric shocks.
General Laws Amendment Act 1963	• Allowed the authorities to arrest anyone for 90 days without having to bring charges against them or even giving them access to a lawyer. Once the initial 90-day period was up it could be extended for a further 90 days *ad infinitum*.
Bantu Laws Amendment Act 1964	• Empowered the authorities to deport any African from any urban area or white farming area for any reason whatsoever. • Also allowed the minister for Bantu affairs to establish quotas in particular areas or industries and deport unemployed Africans back to their homelands.

South Africa grew eminently confident in the 1960s:

- Investment returned and so did the white immigrants.
- Foreign investors could get 15–20 per cent return on their outlays.
- Average economic growth was six per cent a year.
- The number of white people employed in manufacturing increased from 957,000 to 1,181,000 between 1960 and 1966.
- The white population rose from 3.09 million to 3.77 million over the course of the decade, largely as a result of immigration.
- Per capita income among whites rose by almost 50 per cent during the 1960s, from R22,389 to R32,779.

Life was good for most whites; a pleasant climate all year round, wonderful scenery and beaches, barbecues and sport, full employment. As a group, white Africans were to rival white Californians as the most wealthy people on the planet.

When Verwoerd was eventually assassinated in 1966, the even more hardline John Vorster took his place and South Africa was a fearful and repressive police state for many people.

Postscript: the end of apartheid

Of course, this state of affairs could not last. South Africa had been protected by a barrier of friendly colonial powers; when countries such as Angola, Mozambique and Zimbabwe won their independence over the course of the 1970s this changed to a frontier of hostile enemies from where opponents could easily infiltrate into South Africa and fight an increasingly successful guerrilla war. From the 1970s, sanctions were imposed, the Black Consciousness movement effected internal rebellion and the days of apartheid were numbered.

In 1976, protests concerning government efforts to introduce teaching through the medium of Afrikaans in African schools escalated into a massive insurrection, with young people particularly involved. During the 1980s, Prime Minister P.K. Botha introduced limited reforms such as legalizing African trade unions and reducing petty apartheid, but this was too little, too late. Even though the pass laws were abolished in 1986, Africans still earned far less than whites and lacked political representation. Botha's attempts to divide coloureds and Indians from Africans by allowing them some political rights were largely dismissed as a cynical ploy.

By the late 1980s, South Africa was becoming ungovernable, with African groups such as the Zulu group Inkatha and militants within the ANC fighting each other, and far-right groups such as the Afrikaner Weerstandbeweging (AWB) threatening an armed struggle to maintain apartheid. Many were advocating Nelson Mandela and his colleagues be released from prison, although there were doubts over whether they would be able to control the new generation of anti-apartheid protesters.

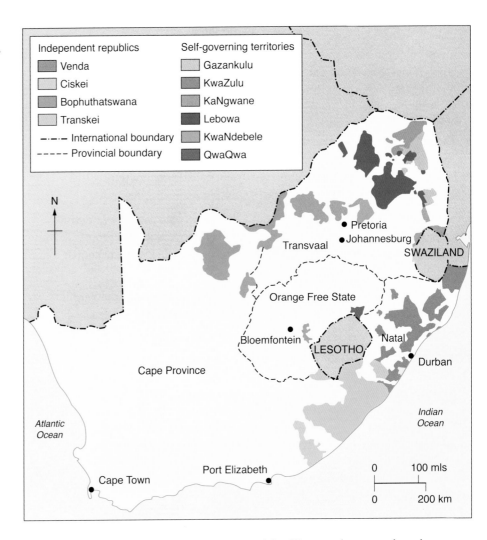

Figure 6.1 Bantustans in 1989. Just four homelands, including Transkei, had become 'independent'.

Independent republics
- Venda
- Ciskei
- Bophuthatswana
- Transkei

–·–·– International boundary
– – – – Provincial boundary

Self-governing territories
- Gazankulu
- KwaZulu
- KaNgwane
- Lebowa
- KwaNdebele
- QwaQwa

N

Pretoria
Johannesburg
Transvaal
SWAZILAND

Orange Free State

Bloemfontein
LESOTHO
Natal
Durban

Cape Province

Atlantic Ocean

Indian Ocean

Cape Town
Port Elizabeth

0   100 mls
0   200 km

It was felt that having been imprisoned for 25 years they were largely forgotten within South Africa and out of touch. This, however, was not the case.

Nelson Mandela

The ANC leaders were released in 1990, with Nelson Mandela, in particular, enjoying the charisma that enabled him to have the authority to at least partially stifle the violence and negotiate with the leaders of the National Party to secure a peaceful transition to democratic rule. While this process was not easy – members of the Zulu Inkatha group regularly attacked ANC supporters, and the ruler of the Bantustan of Ciskei ordered his troops to fire on peaceful protesters in September 1992 – free elections finally took place in April 1994, with the ANC winning 62.5 per cent of the seats and Mandela becoming president of a multiracial democratic South Africa. He remained president until his retirement in 1999. In 2013, when he was 95 years old, he died of a respiratory infection. His death was mourned around the world.

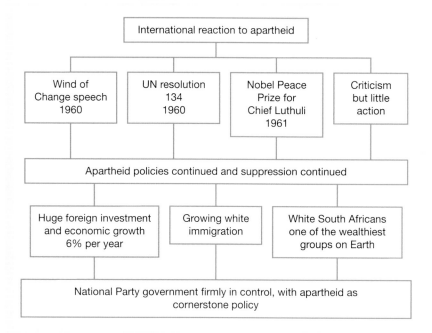

```
                    ┌─────────────────────────────────────────┐
                    │   International reaction to apartheid      │
                    └─────────────────────────────────────────┘
```

| Wind of Change speech 1960 | UN resolution 134 1960 | Nobel Peace Prize for Chief Luthuli 1961 | Criticism but little action |

```
        ┌─────────────────────────────────────────────────────────┐
        │  Apartheid policies continued and suppression continued    │
        └─────────────────────────────────────────────────────────┘
```

| Huge foreign investment and economic growth 6% per year | Growing white immigration | White South Africans one of the wealthiest groups on Earth |

```
        ┌─────────────────────────────────────────────────────────┐
        │ National Party government firmly in control, with apartheid as │
        │                   cornerstone policy                        │
        └─────────────────────────────────────────────────────────┘
```

SUMMARY DIAGRAM

Official responses to violent protest

Chapter summary

Protests and action up to 1964

The massacre at Sharpeville acted in many ways as a catalyst in the decision to begin an armed struggle. It was born out of a split in opposition groups, with the more Africanist PAC breaking away from the ANC and calling for anti-pass protests in March 1960. Police opened fire at Sharpeville, although there is much debate about whether this was premeditated or an act of panic in the face of a huge and hostile crowd. The government responded with repressive legislation including the right to hold suspects for 90 days and more without change. It also went ahead with the Bantustan programme of setting up independent homelands for Africans. Opposition groups meanwhile turned to an armed struggle. The ANC set up the Spear of the Nation, which initially committed acts of sabotage and tried to avoid loss of life, while Poqo was more extreme and actually targeted whites. Much of the ANC leadership was tried at Rivonia and with mass arrests, and an effective campaign against Poqo, the government seemed to have defeated the opposition by 1964. While international opinion was hostile, particularly after the Sharpeville shootings, investment in South Africa and white immigration returned and apartheid remained firmly entrenched.

Examination practice

The following are exam-style questions for you to practise, using sources from Chapters 5 and 6. Sources can be found on the page references given.

The questions also reflect the numbering style of the exam (there are no questions 1–12; questions for Rights and protest begin at Question 13).

PAPER 1 PRACTICE QUESTIONS FOR CASE STUDY 2 (USING SOURCES FROM CHAPTER 5)

See Chapters 1 and 2 for advice on answering Questions 13 and 14.

The sources and questions relate to the creation of townships and forced removals.

Source E: page 129

Source I: page 135

Source G: page 133

Source L: page 139

13 a) Why, according to Source L, have the Bantus (black South Africans) failed to prosper? [3 marks]

13 b) What message is conveyed by Source G? [2 marks]

14 With reference to its origin, purpose and content, analyse the value and limitations of Source E for historians studying townships and forced removals. [4 marks]

15 Compare and contrast what Sources E and I indicate about the conditions in black African communities. [6 marks]

16 Using the sources, and your own knowledge, explain why the South African government wanted to remove hundreds of thousands of South Africans from where they lived. [9 marks]

PAPER 1 PRACTICE QUESTIONS FOR CASE STUDY 2 (USING SOURCES FROM CHAPTER 6)

See Chapters 1 and 2 for advice on answering Questions 13 and 14.

The sources and questions relate to increasing violence against protesters.

Source E: page 208

Source Q: page 225

Source G: page 209

Source R: page 226

13 a) What, according to Source G, suggests that the demonstrators were peaceful? [3 marks]

13 b) What message is conveyed by Source E? [2 marks]

14 With reference to its origin, purpose and content, analyse the value and limitations of Source R for historians studying the decision to take up arms against the South African government. [4 marks]

15 Compare and contrast how Sources Q and R describe the actions of the South African government. [6 marks]

16 Using the sources and your own knowledge, analyse the ways in which South African blacks fought against the government from 1948 to 1964. [9 marks]

Case Study 2: Timeline

1910	**May:** Creation of the Union of South Africa
1912	**Jan:** Formation of the South African Native National Congress (SANNC), renamed the African National Congress (ANC) in 1923
1913	**June:** Natives Land Act
1919	Industrial and Commercial Union (ICU) formed
1921	South African Indian Congress (SAIC) formed
1923	**June:** Urban Areas Act
1927	**Sept:** Native Administration Act
1935	**March:** All-African Convention formed
1936	**Aug:** Native Trust and Land Act
1938	**Dec:** Celebration of centenary of the Great Trek
1944	**April:** Youth League of the ANC formed
1947	**March:** 'Three Doctors' Pact' between ANC and SAIC
1948	**May:** National Party electoral victory
1950	**July:** Population Registration Act **July:** Group Areas Act
1951	**July:** Bantu Authorities Act
1952	Native Laws Amendment Act **April–Dec:** Defiance Campaign
1953	Reservation of Separate Amenities Act
1954	**Jan:** Bantu Education Act **April:** Federation of African Women formed
1955	**Feb:** Destruction of Sophiatown **June:** Freedom Charter adopted
1956	**March:** Separate Representation of Voters Act passed **April:** Tomlinson Committee reported **Dec:** Mass arrests in preparation for the Treason Trial
1957	**Jan–June:** Alexandra bus boycott **April:** Zeerust protests began

1959	**April:** Pan African Congress (PAC) formed **Aug:** Treason Trial finally began Extension of Universities Act Promotion of Self-Government Act **Feb:** 'Wind of Change' speech
1960	**March:** Sharpeville massacre **April–Aug:** State of emergency declared **April:** ANC and PAC made illegal **April:** Assassination attempt on Prime Minister Hendrik Verwoerd
1961	**Jan:** East Pondoland rebellion suppressed **March:** Treason Trial ended **March:** South Africa became a republic **June:** Spear of the Nation (MK) formed **June:** South Africa left the Commonwealth **July:** John Vorster appointed minister of justice **Dec:** Chief Luthuli, president of the ANC, won the Nobel Peace Prize
1962	**Aug:** Nelson Mandela arrested **Dec:** First ANC bombings on government buildings **June:** Sabotage Act **Nov:** Poqo attack on town of Paarl
1963	**May:** General Laws Amendment Act – 90-day rule **May:** Transkei became the first self-governing Bantustan **July:** Government raid on Liliesleaf Farm **Oct:** Rivonia Trial began
1964	Bantu Laws Amendment Act **June:** Rivonia Trial ended – defendants found guilty and sentenced to life imprisonment

Glossary

13th Amendment   This Amendment to the Constitution abolished slavery.

14th Amendment   This guaranteed 'equal protection of the law' to all citizens.

15th Amendment   This granted the suffrage to black men. (Women, black and white, were granted the right to vote in 1920.)

1910 Constitution   The key document which set out how South Africa was to be governed and what powers it possessed as a dominion within the British Empire.

Accoutrements   Facilities.

African Nationalism   The movement within Africa for independence from colonial powers such as Britain and for civil and political rights in South Africa.

African People's Organisation (APO)
An organization for coloured South Africans opposing apartheid.

Africanism   The policy of black Africans fighting for civil and political rights without help from whites or other racial groups.

Africans   The original black population of Africa.

Afrikaners   Descendants of immigrants to South Africa mainly from the Netherlands and Germany.

Allies   The USA, the UK, France, the USSR and other countries who supported them during the Second World War.

Amendments   Under the Constitution, Congress could make changes, in the form of new clauses, to the Constitution. Each Amendment required a two-thirds majority in Congress and approval by 75 per cent of the states.

Anathema   Complete hostility to something.

Anti-pass protests   Protests against the requirement to carry passes which proliferated during the 1950s, especially when the government tried to force African women to carry them.

Apartheid   Strict separation of different racial groups. It is an Afrikaans word, meaning 'separate' or 'apartness'.

Attorney general   Head of the Justice Department in the federal government.

Baaskap   Afrikaner term used to describe their power over so-called 'inferior' races loosely meaning: 'do as I say because I'm the boss'.

Bail   A payment demanded by a court of law in order to release a person awaiting trial. If not paid, the person must stay in custody.

Banning orders   Orders by which individuals or groups were banned from certain areas or from contacting others, or forced to live in specific areas.

Bantu   An African people who speak a common group of languages. In the apartheid era, the white minority used 'Bantu' or 'native' to refer to Africans in South Africa, often in a derogatory way.

Betterment   First used in the Betterment Proclamation of 1939 to describe government-driven improvements in agriculture and living conditions in the homelands.

Black Consciousness   Movement based on Black Power in the USA in which African people increasingly took pride in their culture and identity. This was particularly associated in South Africa with the influence of Steve Biko and the South African Student Association (SASA).

Black nationalists   Those who believed that black people should seek separation from, not integration with, whites. Many of them criticized the policy of non-violence.

Black Pimpernel   Referring to the Scarlet Pimpernel, the elusive hero of Baroness Orczy's novels set during the French Revolution.

Black Power   A movement that emphasized black racial pride and the importance of blacks creating their own political and cultural institutions.

'Black spots'   Areas outside the land officially designated for settlement by black Africans where they nevertheless managed to acquire land.

Boycott   A refusal to have anything to do with a person or an organization, in this case the Montgomery bus company.

Broerderbund   An influential Afrikaner organization promoting apartheid. Most key Afrikaner figures in politics, industry and civic life belonged to it.

Bureaucracy   Members of the administration which implemented government policies.

Cape The southernmost province of South Africa, originally Cape Colony, part of the British Empire.

Charter of the United Nations Document outlining the aims and organization of the United Nations, including racial equality and social and economic justice for all. The United Nations was formed in 1945 to promote cooperation among nations worldwide.

Civil Rights Movement A range of social and political movements in the USA whose goal was to end racial segregation and discrimination against black Americans and ensure legal, social and political equality for them.

Coalition A partnership between different political parties to try to win elections together.

Cold War The state of tension, primarily between the USA and the Soviet Union, that existed from the late 1940s to the late 1980s.

Commonwealth Association of members and former members of the British Empire.

Commonwealth Conference An annual meeting of members of the Commonwealth or former British Empire.

Communist A person who believes that the planning and control of the economy should be by the state and people should be rewarded according to the value of their contribution.

Communist Party of South Africa (CPSA) Communist Party believing in ideas such as state ownership of industry and equality for everyone.

Confederacy A loose alliance of states that resented what they saw as increasing domination by the federal government and sought more autonomy. Their supporters were known as the Confederates.

Congress The national, or federal, law-making body.

Congress of Racial Equality (CORE) An interracial civil rights group founded by James Farmer and other students in Chicago in 1942.

Conscription Compulsory membership of the armed forces for certain periods of time.

Constitution The rules and regulations by which a country's government works.

Council of Non-European Trade Unions (CNETU) African trade union formed in 1941.

Covenant Solemn oath, in this sense the agreement apparently made between God and the Boers in 1838.

Decolonization Colonies winning their independence.

Deep South Used to denote the states which had been most dependent on plantation agriculture, sometimes referred to as the Cotton Belt, and which had formed the core of the Confederacy. It is usually thought to include states such as Alabama, Louisiana, Mississippi and South Carolina.

Delegations Groups meeting those in authority to make specific requests.

Department of Native Affairs The government department that regulated the lives of black citizens.

Desegregation The (process of) ending of segregation or the implementation of integration.

Direct action Action to protest something, for example a march or demonstration.

Disenfranchised Deprived of the right to vote.

Dominion Largely self-governing country within the British Empire, recognizing the monarch as head of state.

Dutch East India Trading Company Company established in 1602 to conduct trade with Asia. It used the Cape as a supply post for vessels *en route* to and from Asia.

Dutch Reformed Church Afrikaner Church which supported apartheid.

Electoral register Before people were allowed to vote, they had to apply to be put on the electoral register (a list of names and addresses).

Enoch Mgijilma In May 1921, 1000 supporters of Mgijilma, a religious prophet, settled in an area of the Eastern Cape. Their aim was to form their own community – unfortunately on land to which they had no claim. Law enforcement officers arrived to evict them. When they refused to leave, the officers opened fire.

Fascist dictatorships Racist and nationalist regimes, in this case Hitler's Nazi Germany and Benito Mussolini's Fascist Italy.

Federal Bureau of Investigation (FBI) The main investigative branch of the federal Department of Justice.

Federal system of government A system in which power is shared between central and state governments.

First World War   The 1914–18 war fought between the Allied Powers, notably Britain, France, Russia and from 1917, the USA, and the Central Powers dominated by Germany.

Forced removals   Where black, coloured or Indian people were removed from areas designated 'whites only' and forced to live in locations or townships, usually on the edge of urban areas.

French Revolutionary and Napoleonic Wars
A series of wars fought between France and Britain and their respective allies between 1792 and 1815.

Ghetto   An area inhabited overwhelmingly by (usually poor) members of one race or ethnic group.

Gold rush   Migration of people to an area to find gold and become rich.

Grassroots   An activity or a movement rooted in local, community politics.

Great Society   Johnson's plan to decrease poverty and inequality in the USA.

Great Trek   The movement of Boer farmers into the vast South African interior, away from British rule, which began in 1834.

Guerrilla warfare   Fighting using techniques such as ambush and bombings, avoiding direct large-scale conflict.

Hinterland   A remote area of a country, generally away from coastal regions.

Homelands   Areas laid aside for Africans to live in according to their tribal groups.

Ideologue   Someone completely committed to a certain belief, in this case, apartheid.

Indigenous   Native to an area.

Influx control   Methods used to control African migration into urban areas, such as the pass laws.

Intaba   Resistance movement in East Pondoland; Intaba is an African word for 'mountain'.

Integrationalist   Made up of different groups, in this case of all races in South Africa.

Interstate transport   Transport which crossed state boundaries and was therefore the responsibility of the federal government, specifically the Interstate Commerce Commission.

Interwar years   The years between the First (1914–18) and the Second World Wars (1939–45).

'Jim Crow' laws   Named after a comic, stereotypical character, these laws were passed by southern states in order to 'legalize' segregation.

Kaffir   Derogatory name given to black Africans.

Kraals   Name given to African collections of farms where families or close members of tribal groups may live together.

Ku Klux Klan (KKK)   A secret terrorist society formed by ex-Confederate soldiers in 1865 in order to maintain white supremacy.

Legislature   The elected, law-making body in each state (the state equivalent of Congress).

Litigation   Taking a case to a court of law.

Locations   Townships reserved for Africans on the edge of urban centres.

Lynching   Unlawful killing, mostly by hanging, usually of black people.

Maoris   Indigenous peoples of New Zealand.

Mbaqanga music   Throbbing African jazz-type music with Zulu roots.

Minstrel   A member of a band of entertainers with blackened faces who performed songs and music ostensibly of black American origin.

Mission schools   Schools run by various Churches to educate African children.

Montgomery Improvement Association (MIA)
The organization that co-ordinated the Montgomery Bus Boycott.

Nation of Islam (NOI)   A religious movement founded in 1930. Its leader was Elijah Muhammad and its main stated goal was to improve the lives of African-Americans in the USA.

National Association for the Advancement of Colored People (NAACP)   The oldest and largest civil rights organization. It is still active today.

Nazi Germany   The German regime under Adolf Hitler.

Pan Africanist Congress (PAC)   Black African organization that set up an Africanist agenda, in which the government of South Africa should comprise only black Africans.

Pass books   Internal passports to restrict the movement of people.

Passive resistance   Non-violent opposition.

Pastoral environment   Rural life based on small-scale agriculture or animal husbandry.

Petitioned   Presented an appeal bearing the signatures of as many supporters as possible.

Pickets   A method of protest whereby groups of people gather to stop people from going into an institution or a location.

Policy of non-cooperation   Civil disobedience, for example leaving pass books at home or entering white-only facilities.

Poll tax   A tax levied on would-be voters, which made it harder for blacks (who were usually poorer) to vote.

Polyglot   Someone fluent in different languages.

Pre-fab construction   Houses made from prefabricated parts.

Proportional representation   The concept that the government of a country must be proportionally represented. In this sense Sobukwe meant that Africans, as the overwhelming racial majority, should govern South Africa.

Race Classification Board   Board charged with deciding which race a person belonged to.

Radicalization   Process by which people come to adopt extreme political or religious ideas, often through undue influence from particular groups, in this case the PAC.

Rand   The goldmining areas in the Transvaal, known more correctly as Witwatersrand.

Rand (currency)   In 1960, South Africa decimalized its currency, moving from British sterling (pounds, shillings and pence) to rand (R) and cents.

Reconstruction   The process of rebuilding and reforming the Confederate states and restoring them to the Union.

Regional Service Councils   Groups of local councils which shared certain functions.

Republic   Country without a monarch at its head, usually led by a president.

Second Boer War   (South African War) between Britain and the Boers between 1899 and 1902. The Boers wanted complete independence from Britain, who wanted to expand to control the gold and diamond industries in the Transvaal.

Second World War   Fought from 1939 and 1945 between the Allies, primarily the USA, the UK, France and the USSR (Union of Soviet Socialist Republics, or the Soviet Union), and Nazi Germany, Japan and their allies.

Security Council Resolution 134   A United Nations resolution condemning the South African government for the Sharpeville massacre.

Segregation   The separation of people by race in schools, public spaces and transport.

Seventh Day Adventists   Religious group who see Saturday as the Sabbath.

Shanty towns   Areas made up of temporary, often inadequate accommodation and lacking proper facilities such as sanitation or supplies of fresh water.

Sharecroppers   Ex-slaves (freedmen) who rented land and, in return, shared their crop with the landowner.

Shebeens   Often African women earned an income by brewing and selling beer in these illegal drinking dens. The government deemed them illegal because they ran and profited from official beer halls (where only weak beer with an alcoholic content of two per cent was sold), and because they feared that drunken Africans might rampage.

Southern Christian Leadership Conference (SCLC)   A non-violent civil rights organization founded by Martin Luther King Jr.

Southern Manifesto   A statement of defiance against the 1954 *Brown* ruling which was signed by most southerners in Congress.

Soviet Union   The leading Communist country from 1922 to 1991.

Soweto   Acronym for South Western Townships, the African townships on the edge of Johannesburg.

States' rights   The rights which the Constitution reserves for the states as opposed to the federal government.

Stayaway   Where workers protested by staying at home rather than actually going on strike.

Student Nonviolent Coordinating Committee (SNCC)   The student-run organization formed after the 1960 sit-ins.

Suffrage   The right to vote.

Supreme Court   The highest court in the USA. Its primary role was to interpret the Constitution.

Taboo   Something which custom or convention prohibits.

Think tanks Groups of experts formed to give advice on issues.

Townships Areas where black people lived separately from other races.

Transient migration Temporary resettlement or movement, for example as guest workers. The government also called migrants temporary sojourners.

Transvaal Indian Congress Branch of the South African Indian Congress (SAIC) based in Transvaal.

Umkhonto we Sizwe or Spear of the Nation (MK) The armed wing of the ANC.

United Nations (UN) An organization formed in 1945, the main aim of which was to solve international disputes.

White Citizens' Councils Organizations set up to maintain segregation. The first one was in Mississippi but they soon spread across the Deep South.

White-collar Professional jobs such as administrators.

White supremacy The belief that whites are superior to other races.

Whitewash Where a report exonerates someone without having examined all the evidence.

Further reading

Works that are useful for the whole of Case Study I

Carson, C. and others, editors, *The Eyes on the Prize Civil Rights Reader*, Penguin, 1991.
A highly recommended book containing hundreds of primary sources as well as useful commentaries by different historians.

Carson, C., *In Struggle: SNCC and the Black Awakening of the 1960s*, Harvard University Press, 1981.
A history of the SNCC and its impact which views the organization as the cutting edge of the Civil Rights Movement.

Cook, R., *Sweet Land of Liberty? – The African-American Struggle for Civil Rights in the Twentieth Century*, Pearson, 1998.
An incisive and critical evaluation of many aspects of the struggle for civil rights. Particularly useful in its analysis of the importance of African-American leadership and of grassroots campaigning.

Dierenfield, B., *The Civil Rights Movement*, Pearson, 2008.
One of the Seminar Series, this is a clear, chronologically organized account, just one step up from an IB level textbook. It has brief pen portraits of key players in the movement in the margins and a very thorough glossary.

Dudziak, M., *Cold War Civil Rights*, Princeton University Press, 2000.
This book examines the impact of international relations, particularly the Cold War, on civil rights in the USA.

Fairclough, A., *Better Day Coming: Blacks and Equality, 1890–2000*, Penguin, 2002.
An account of the Civil Rights Movement from its earliest days, with very good chapters on the 1950s and 1960s.

Lawson, S. and Payne, C., *Debating the Civil Rights Movement, 1945–1968*, Rowan & Littlefield, 1998.
This book contains two long, interpretative essays (40 pages each) on the Civil Rights Movement, one looking at it from above, from a national perspective, and the other from below, 'from the trenches'. It also contains some key documents. Highly recommended.

Marable, M., *Race, Reform and Rebellion, The Second Reconstruction in Black America, 1945–1990*, University Press of Mississippi, 1991.
A critically vigorous account of the struggle for civil rights, by a highly respected African-American historian.

Sitkoff, H., *The Struggle for Black Equality, 1954–1992*, Hill & Wang, 1993.
A lively narrative by an acknowledged expert in African-American history.

Racism and white supremacy

Franklin, J.H. and Moss, A., *From Slavery to Freedom – A History of African-Americans*, McGraw-Hill, 1994.
A huge, wide-ranging and authoritative account first published in 1947, this edition goes up to the early 1990s.

Trotter, J.W., *The African-American Experience, Volume 1 – Through Reconstruction*, Houghton Mifflin, 2001.
An account of the African-American experience from the days of slavery to the early twentieth century.

Williams, J., *Eyes on the Prize, America's Civil Rights Years, 1954–1965*, Penguin, 1987.
A very readable, richly-illustrated book written to accompany the television series of the same name.

Protests and action: from Montgomery to the Civil Rights Act

Branch, T., *Parting the Waters: America in the King Years, 1954–1963*. Simon & Schuster, 1989.
Acclaimed first volume in a trilogy on King. In-depth and exhaustively researched.

Branch, T., *Pillar of Fire: America in the King Years, 1963–1965*. Simon & Schuster, 1999.
Second volume in the trilogy covering the pivotal civil rights years.

Jackson, T., *Becoming King – Martin Luther King Jr. and the Making of a National Leader*, University Press of Kentucky, 2008.
A study of King's role in the Montgomery Bus Boycott and of how it changed him and shaped his development as a civil rights leader.

Norrell, R., *The House I Live In – Race in the American Century*, Oxford University Press, 2005.
A social as well as a political history, this book is particularly useful on how white supremacy was established and maintained in the face of American values of liberty and equality.

Oates, S., *Let the Trumpet Sound – A Life of Martin Luther King*, Payback Press, 1998.
This is one of several good biographies of King.

Polenberg, R., *One Nation Divisible – Class, Race and Ethnicity in the United States since 1938*, Penguin, 1980.
As the title suggests, this book shows how divisive the issue of race was in twentieth-century America.

The achievement of the Civil Rights Movement

Dallek, R., *Lyndon B. Johnson, Portrait of a President*, Penguin, 2005.
A much-praised biography by a historian who has written widely on President Johnson.

Malcolm X and Haley, A., *The Autobiography of Malcolm X*, Penguin, 1968.
This book was published shortly after the death of Malcolm X and was jointly written with Alex Haley, who later wrote a famous book, *Roots*, about a black American family's African origins.

Marable, M., *Malcolm X, A Life of Reinvention*, Allen Lane, 2011.
This is the definitive account of the life and significance of Malcolm X, by a renowned expert.

Purdum, T., *An Idea Whose Time Has Come: Two Presidents, Two Parties, and the Battle for the Civil Rights Act of 1964*, Henry Holt & Co., 2014.
Published on the fiftieth anniversary of the passing of the Civil Rights Act, this book focuses on the passage of the bill through Congress.

Works that are useful for the whole of Case Study 2

Beinart, W., *Twentieth Century South Africa*, Oxford University Press, 1994.
Readable, informative, particularly strong on social and economic aspects and what was going on in rural areas.

Clark, N.L. and Worger, W.H., *South Africa: The Rise and Fall of Apartheid*, Pearson, 2004.
Thorough account aimed at students, with a useful collection of documents.

De Villers, M., *White Tribe Dreaming*, Viking Penguin, 1988.
The history of South Africa as seen through the eyes of an Afrikaner family.

Dubow, S., *The African National Congress*, Sutton Pocket Histories, 2000.
A short but comprehensive history of the ANC.

Dubow, S., *Apartheid 1948–1994*, Oxford Histories, 2014.
Contextualizes apartheid in a global and local perspective and considers resistance within the context of governmental power.

Giliomee, H., *The Afrikaners: Biography of a People*, University of Virginia Press, 2013.
Highly praised history, particularly useful for seeing apartheid from the Afrikaner perspective.

Gunther, J., *Inside Africa*, Hamish Hamilton, 1955.
Thorough account of South Africa in the mid-1950s including interviews with most of the government and opposition leaders.

Hain, P., *Sing the Beloved Country*, Pluto Press, 1996.
Highly readable account from a former anti-apartheid activist, particularly useful for the fight against apartheid in the period covered by this book, in which his parents were involved.

Hain, P., *Mandela*, Octopus Books, 2010.
A short but complete biography of Nelson Mandela.

Joseph, H., *Side by Side*, Zed Books, 1986.
Autobiography by one of the most noted anti-apartheid activists.

Mandela, N., *Long Walk to Freedom*, Abacus, 2013.
Essential background reading, a very well-written autobiography almost impossible to put down, and exhaustive in its coverage of the fight against apartheid in the period covered by this book.

Meli, F., *A History of the ANC: South Africa Belongs to Us*, James Currey, Woodbridge, 1989.
A history of the ANC by one of its leaders in the 1980s.

Thompson, L., *A History of South Africa*, Yale University Press, 1990.
Detailed and comprehensive history.

United Nations, *The United Nations and Apartheid, 1948–1994*. United Nations Blue Book Series, 1994.
An examination of how the UN tackled apartheid. Over 200 key documents in the book.

Walsh, F., *A History of South Africa*, HarperCollins, 2000.
Thorough and authoritative, offering challenging perspectives on many aspects of South African history.

The creation of the apartheid state

Paton, A., *Cry, The Beloved Country*, Penguin, 1971.
One of the masterpieces of South African literature, originally written in 1948, this is an ostensibly simple story of a rural church minister searching for his errant son in Johannesburg but covers every aspect of apartheid and its impact. Filmed twice and turned into a musical, 'Lost in the Stars'. Essential background reading.

Sparks, A., *The Mind of South Africa: The Story of the Rise and Fall of Apartheid*, Heinemann, 1990.
Excellent account of apartheid seen in terms of the Afrikaner mindset.

The development of apartheid

Evans, I., *Bureaucracy and Race: Native Administration in South Africa*, University of California Press, 1997.
An analysis of the Department of Native Affairs showing how far apartheid needed an effective system of bureaucracy as much as repression to implement it.

Huddleston, T., *Naught for Your Comfort*, Collins, 1987
Powerful and evocative memoir from an anti-apartheid activist who served as a priest in the Sophiatown area – originally published in 1956; essential background reading.

Spink, K., *Black Sash: The Beginnings of a Bridge in South Africa*, Methuen, 1991.
An account of Black Sash, which changed from a being an organization of middle-class ladies protesting constitutional reform to one of the most noted anti-apartheid groups in South Africa.

Protest and action

First, R., *117 Days*, Penguin, 2009.
At times harrowing account by an anti-apartheid activist of being subject to the 90-day imprisonment rule in the early 1960s.

Frankel, P., *An Ordinary Atrocity: Sharpeville and its Massacre*, Yale University Press, 2001.
A reconstruction of the events at Sharpeville through interviews with both perpetrators and demonstrators.

Lodge, T., *Sharpeville: An Apartheid Massacre and its Consequences*, Oxford University Press, 2011.
The massacre seen in a wider context and therefore thorough in its coverage of many of the issues facing South Africa at the time of the massacre and in the years afterwards: essential reading

Reeves, A., *Shooting at Sharpeville: The Agony of South Africa*, Houghton Mifflin, 1961 (available at https://archive.org/details/shootingatsharpe002466mbp).
An impassioned account of the massacre, accompanied by powerful photographs.

Internet and film resources

- *A World Apart* (1988). Intensely moving film based in part on the life of Ruth First but focusing on the impact her activities had on her family.
- BBC television programmes about apartheid, for example a *Panorama* documentary from 1957: www.bbc.co.uk/archive/apartheid/
- *Cry the Beloved Country* (1952 and 1995). Both versions of this film are worth seeing.
- *Eyes on the Prize* (1987). Comprehensive and moving 14-hour PBS documentary on the Civil Rights Movement.
- *Freedom Riders* (2010). Award-winning PBS documentary on the brave efforts to break the grip of segregation in the South.
- *Goodbye Bafana* (2007). A minor masterpiece about Nelson Mandela's developing relationship based on trust with one of his prison warders. (Titled *The Color of Freedom* in the USA.)
- John F. Kennedy Presidential Library and Museum: www.jfklibrary.org/Asset-Viewer/LH8F_0Mzv0e6Ro1yEm74Ng.aspx
- *King: A Filmed Record … Montgomery to Memphis* (1970). Gripping three-hour documentary on King.
- Lyndon B. Johnson Presidential Library: www.lbjlibrary.org/
- *Mandela: Long Walk to Freedom* (2013). Big budget biopic based on Nelson Mandela's autobiography.
- *Malcolm X* (1992). Spike Lee's absorbing biopic of Malcolm X.
- Official ANC site with lots of primary material source relating to the struggle against apartheid: www.anc.org.za/

- Scholars Online, part of The Choices Program, Brown University, USA: www.choices.edu/resources/scholars_civilrights.php
- *Selma* (2014). A moving historical drama covering a critical three-month period in the Civil Rights Movement in 1965.
- Several important Malcolm X documents are at: www.hartford-hwp.com/archives/45a/index-bda.html
- South African History Online. Exhaustive educational site with documents, histories, biographies, timelines and some very useful analytical essays: www.sahistory.org.za/
- The Heart of Hope. Thorough coverage of Nelson Mandela's life in terms of documents, interviews and analysis, hosted by journalist Padraig O'Malley: www.nelsonmandela.org/omalley/index.php/site/q/03lv00000.htm
- The King Center possesses a tremendous number of digital documents on Dr King. See: www.thekingcenter.org/
- The Library of Congress has created a useful tool for teachers entitled *The Civil Rights Act of 1964: A Long Struggle for Freedom*. Free download of PDF can be located at: www.loc.gov/teachers/newsevents/idea-book/

Internal assessment

The internal assessment is a historical investigation on a historical topic. Below is a list of possible questions that could warrant further investigation. They have been organized by case study.

Case Study 1: The civil rights movement in the United States 1954–1965

1 To what extent did the Supreme Court Decision in *Sweatt* v. *Painter* (1950) influence *Brown* v. *Board of Education* (1954)?
2 To what extent were 'separate' school facilities 'equal' in Mississippi?
3 How did Virginia's Board of Education respond to the *Brown* v. *Board of Education* Supreme Court decision and with what effect?
4 How and why did Martin Luther King Jr agitate against the US war in Vietnam?
5 What impact did the Greensboro sit-in in 1960 have on segregated restaurants?
6 How was Lyndon Johnson able to steer the 1964 Civil Rights Act through Congress?
7 How and why did Malcolm X's racial views change in the 1960s?
8 To what extent were the FBI's attempts to destroy the reputation of Martin Luther King Jr successful?

Case Study 2: Apartheid South Africa 1948–1964

1 Why did the South African Indian Congress become more radical in the 1940s?
2 To what extent were the efforts of Umkhonto we Sizwe successful?
3 How did the international community react to the introduction of apartheid in South Africa?
4 What specific social and economic factors led to the declaration of the first apartheid laws in 1948?
5 What impact did the 1958 Bantu Self-Government Act have on South Africans living in townships?
6 How effective were the efforts of South African security forces in silencing critics of the white regime from 1948 to 1964?
7 To what extent did the Rivonia Trial damage the ANC?
8 To what extent was the Black Sash movement effective in combatting apartheid?

Index

Police Reserve Unit, *see* Security Police

Poll tax 20, 26, 28

Poqo 221, 227

Posters, use in exam questions 112

Potato boycott 181

Project Confrontation 61

Promotion of Self-Government Act 195, 221

Purified National Party 131, 132, *see also* Malan, Daniel François

R

Racial terminology 12, 13, 123

Randolph, A. Philip 26, 43, 66–7, 68, 94

Reconstruction of Confederate states 17–19

Representation of the Natives Act 125

Reservation of Separate Amenities Act 169

Reunited National Party, *see* National Party

Rivonia Trial 228–31
  international response 231–2

Robben Island 112, 229, 231

Roosevelt, Franklin Delano 24, 26, 27, 28

S

Sabotage Act 218

Second World War
  effects in South Africa 131–2, 145
  in USA 24–5, 26, 28, 55, 84

Security Council Resolution 134: 213

Security Police 218

Segregation
  in South Africa 121, 124–7, 131, 132, 135–6, 140, 144, 147, 169, 174–5, *see also* Apartheid
  in USA 19–20, 24, 27, 28, 31, 55, 61, 105, *see also* 'Jim Crow' laws
  see also individual campaigns and cases in South Africa and the USA

Selma, Alabama
  march from Selma to Montgomery 94–5
  march to courthouse 91–2
  voter registration 90–1
  see also Bloody Sunday

Separate Representation of Voters Act 167–9

Shanty towns 129

Sharpeville massacre 206–9
  government response 217
  impact 209–11, 212–14, 216–17
  inquiry 211, 217
  interpretation 215–16
  police culpability 217

Shebeen protests 181

Shuttlesworth, Fred 60–1

Sigcau, Chief Botha 195

Sisulu, Walter 141, 186, 205

Sit-ins 50–2, 53, 58–9, 64, 66, 84–5, 108, 112

Slavery
  in South Africa 121, 122
  in USA 12–13, 15–17, 20
  see also American Civil War

Smuts, Jan 131, 132, 134, 135, 176
  work on human rights for UN 140

Sobukwe, Robert 173, 203–4, 211

Sobukwe clause 218, *see* Sobukwe, Robert

Sophiatown 125, 159–60, 164–5

South Africa
  1910 Constitution 130, 167, 233

  area of country 121
  as a British dominion 122, 130
  campaigns of bombing and violence 210, 225–7
  cooperation between protest groups 147
  economy 132–4, 210, 235
  election results (1948–64) 137
  emigration 210
  ethnic groups 122–3
  European colonialization 122
  far-right groups 235
  firearms 210
  forced removals 160–5
  gold rush 122
  indigenous inhabitants 121
  legislation against blacks 123, 124–6
  New Zealand rugby team denied entry 214
  policies of repression 218–20
  political parties before Second World War 130–1
  white justification for segregation 128–9
  withdrawal from Commonwealth 214
  youth crime 170
  see also individual groups; Apartheid; Separate Representation of Voters Act

South African Bureau of Racial Affairs (SABRA) 156

South African Communist Party 147, 225, 233

South African Indian Congress (SAIC) 147, 161, 184, 225

South African Native National Congress (SANNC), *see* African National Congress (ANC)

Southern Christian Leadership Conference (SCLC) 48–9
  response to sit-ins 52

State government 14, 32, 33, *see also individual states*

Acknowledgements

Abacus, *Long Walk to Freedom* by Nelson Mandela, 2013. About Education, African History (http://africanhistory.about.com/od/eraindependence/p/wind_of_change3.htm). African National Congress (www.anc.org.za). *African South*, 'The Bus Boycott' by Ruth First, volume 1, number 4, pp. 55–64, 1957. Allen Lane, *Malcolm X, A Life of Reinvention* by Manning Marable, 2011. American Rhetoric (www.americanrhetoric.com/speeches/mlkihaveadream.htm). APB Publishers, *Verwoerd Speaks: Speeches 1948–1966* edited by A.N. Pelzer, 1966. Collins, *Naught for Your Comfort* by Trevor Huddleston, 1987. *Daily News*, 18 May 1954. Facing History and Ourselves (www.facinghistory.org/for-educators/educator-resources/resource-collections/choosing-to-participate/her-own-words-text-only-version). Gilder Lehrman Institute of American History. Hamish Hamilton, *Inside Africa* by John Gunther, 1955. Henry Holt & Co., *An Idea Whose Time Has Come: Two Presidents, Two Parties, and the Battle for the Civil Rights Act of 1964* by Todd S. Purdum, 2014. Hill & Wang, *The Struggle for Black Equality 1954–1992* by Harvard Sitkoff, 1993. Howard University ('*To Fulfill These Rights*', 4 June 1965, www.lbjlibrary.org). Institute of Commonwealth Studies, *Collected Seminar Papers on Societies of South Africa in the 19th and 20th Centuries*, 1971. James Currey, *A History of the ANC* by Francis Meli, 1989. John F. Kennedy Presidential Library and Museum. McGraw-Hill, *From Slavery to Freedom* by John Hope Franklin and Alfred A. Moss Jr, 1994. Methuen, *Black Sash: The Beginning of a Bridge in South Africa* by Kathryn Spink, 1991. New Africa Books, *New Africa History* by N. Frick, S. Janari, G. Weldon, A. Proctor and D. Wray, 2006. New South Books, *Bus Ride to Justice* by Fred Gray, 2013. New York University Press, *In the Shadow of Sharpeville: Apartheid and Criminal Justice* by Peter Parker and Joyce Mokhesi Parker, 1998. Oxford University Press, *Sharpeville: An Apartheid Massacre and its Consequences* by Tom Lodge, 2011. Pearson, *Sweet Land of Liberty? – The African-American Struggle for Civil Rights in the Twentieth Century* by Robert Cook, 1998; *The Civil Rights Movement* by Bruce Dierenfield, 2008. Penguin, *117 Days* by Ruth First, 2009; *Better Day Coming: Blacks and Equality, 1890–2000* by Adam Fairclough, 2002; *Lyndon B. Johnson, Portrait of a President* by Robert Dallek, 2005; *The Autobiography of Malcolm X* by Malcolm X, 1968; *The Eyes on the Prize Civil Rights Reader*, edited by Clayborne Carson and others, 1991; *The Rise of the South African Reich* by Brian Bunting, 1964. Politics Web (www.politicsweb.co.za/politicsweb/view/politicsweb/en/page71619?oid=298016&sn=Detail). Princeton University Press, *Cold War Civil Rights* by Mary L. Dudziak, 2000. Rowan & Littlefield, *Debating the Civil Rights Movement, 1945–1968* by Steven Lawson and Charles Payne, 1998. Sampson, Low, Marston & Co., *South and East African Yearbook and Guide for 1921*, 1921. Scholars Online, part of The Choices Program, Brown University, USA (www.choices.edu). South African History Online (www.sahistory.org.za). South African Railways and Harbours, *Travel In South Africa*, 1937. Taylor & Francis, *Atlas of Changing South Africa* by A.J. Francis, 2002. TeachingAmericanHistory.org (*Letter to Martin Luther King*, http://teachingamericanhistory.org/library/document/letter-to-martin-luther-king/). *The Guardian*, June 1983. The Legacy Project (*Blame Me on History* by Bloke Modisane, first published in 1963, www.legacy-project.org/index.php?page=lit_detail&litID=86). The Love All People Institute and Internet Church of Christ ('Letter from Birmingham City Jail', www.loveallpeople.org/birminghamjail.pdf). *The Times*, 15 April 1961, 17 September 1954, 26 May 1948, 29 May 1948. *Transformations*, 'What's In a Name? Racial Categorisations under Apartheid and their Afterlife' by Deborah Posel, volume 47, pp. 50–74, 2001. University Press of Kentucky, *Becoming King – Martin Luther King Jr. and the Making of a National Leader* by Troy Jackson, 2008. University Press of Mississippi, *Race, Reform and Rebellion* by Manning Marable, 1991. Zed Books, *Side by Side* by Helen Joseph, 1987.